William Hastie, Diodato Lioy

The Philosophy of Right

With Special Reference to the Principles and Development of Law

William Hastie, Diodato Lioy

The Philosophy of Right
With Special Reference to the Principles and Development of Law

ISBN/EAN: 9783744666374

Printed in Europe, USA, Canada, Australia, Japan

Cover: Foto ©Suzi / pixelio.de

More available books at **www.hansebooks.com**

THE
PHILOSOPHY OF RIGHT

WITH SPECIAL REFERENCE TO THE

PRINCIPLES AND DEVELOPMENT OF LAW.

BY

DIODATO LIOY,

PROFESSOR IN THE UNIVERSITY OF NAPLES.

TRANSLATED FROM THE ITALIAN BY

W. HASTIE, M.A., B.D.,

TRANSLATOR OF KANT'S "PHILOSOPHY OF LAW;"
"OUTLINES OF JURISPRUDENCE BY PUCHTA," ETC.; AND
BRUNNER'S "SOURCES OF THE LAW OF ENGLAND."

IN TWO VOLUMES.

VOL. I.

LONDON:
KEGAN PAUL, TRENCH, TRÜBNER, & CO., Lᵗᴰ
1891.

This Translation

IS

REVERENTLY AND GRATEFULLY DEDICATED

TO

The Memory of

JAMES LORIMER, LL.D.,

DR. JUR. BOLOGNA ; HON. MEM. OF UNIVERSITIES OF MOSCOW AND ST. PETERSBURG :
MEMBER OF THE ACADEMY OF JURISPRUDENCE OF MADRID ; ASSOCIATE
OF THE ROYAL ACADEMY OF BELGIUM ;

LATE PROFESSOR OF PUBLIC LAW AND OF THE LAW OF NATURE
AND NATIONS IN THE UNIVERSITY OF EDINBURGH.

————

Cui Pudor, et Justitiæ soror,
Incorrupta Fides, nudaque Veritas
Quando ullum inveniet parem ?

"Nostris septentrionalibus eruditis acumen atque eruditionem non minus apud Italos inveniri, quam apud ipsos; imo vero doctiora et acutior dici ab Italis, quam quæ a frigidiorum orarum incolis expectari queant."— LECLERC *in Letter to Vico.*

"—But what of Italy? Italy is the land on which, since Germany went on the 'war-path,' the mantle of scientific jurisprudence seems to have fallen."—PROFESSOR LORIMER.

TRANSLATOR'S PREFACE.

ITALY has again become the living and fruitful home of the Science of Law. The ancient spirit of the "People of Right" was never dead, however it may have seemed to slumber; and it is now breathing again with all the freshness and fulness of the new time. The Nineteenth Century has not had anything to show more fair than the achievement of Italian independence and the organisation in the new national unity of Italian liberty. For this has been wholly the work of the Spirit of Right in its struggle with political and ecclesiastical despotism, and it has been realised by the strength of essential justice, even in the face of external defeat and disaster. That spirit, thus quickened and deepened in itself, is now flowing in a freer and richer stream through the new national channels, and is beginning to mingle once more with the progressive. destinies of the emancipated peoples. Modern Italy has thus entered anew upon her special birthright, and is vindicating her claim to be not only the inheritor, but the continuator, of the jural spirit of Ancient Rome.

The true glory of Ancient Rome undoubtedly lay in the power of her Legislation. As Rudolph Von Ihering has well observed, Rome has thrice dictated laws to the world and given unity to the peoples. This was seen the first time in the Ancient Roman Empire; the second time in the Mediæval Roman Church; and the third time in the reception by the new European Nations of the old Roman Law. These three outstanding historical facts

will always command the interest of the historian of
civilisation, but the deeper insight into the philosophy of
History will not fail to find in the essentially jural spirit
of the Roman people the inner force that determined the
political and ecclesiastical forms of supremacy, the unify-
ing factor of the whole movement, and the element in it
of chief significance for the modern world. The legislative
mission of Ancient Rome—or, as it has been aptly called,
her "predestination to the cultivation of Right"—has, in
fact, become a commonplace with the philosophical historian and the scientific jurist. It constituted what was
most characteristic in the consciousness of the Roman
people. It formed the habit of their great leaders in
peace and war, and it stimulated the makers of their
colossal Empire. It animated their historians and inspired their poets; and it gave its character to all the
products of Roman thought. Above all, it made their
legislators and orators to be what they were, and authenticated itself in the whole of their civilising work. Hence
it was that the System of Legislation which they created
and embodied in the world proved so exceptionally substantial and lasting, and that the Roman Jurists became,
in their own sphere, what the philosophers and artists
of Greece had been in theirs, sovereign and permanent
masters of the world in the department of Law.[1]

The deeper students of the philosophy of history in the
Nineteenth Century have not estimated the greatness of
the ancient Roman Law less justly than their predecessors, while they have given profounder explanations
of its essence and function. Following in the line of
Vico and Niebuhr, Hegel has grasped and elucidated with
characteristic vigour and originality the essence of the
political and legal development of the Roman People.
He has pointed out how the social condition of the

---

[1] Vico has summed up this point
of view in one expressive phrase:
"Ex hac autem juris tutela omnis
Romani nominis gloria orta est."
De uno universi Juris principio,
clxxiv.

beginnings of the City determined the dominant note of the development. Characterising its founders in the severe terms already formulated by Gibbon as "a band of robbers," Hegel sees in the force and deliberativeness of their association the germ of the Roman System of Government and Right. He has briefly but incisively outlined the prosaic, reflective, and formal character of the Roman world, and he finds its distinctive principle in the universal abstract idea of personality as the basis of right. Gans, Ahrens, and others have followed Hegel's view in its essential points; while Ihering, with all his insight into the spirit of the Roman Law, has only formulated it in a more one-sided and popular way by defining the motive of the Roman universality to be "selfishness," and designating the Roman character generally as "the System of disciplined Egoism." Professor Carle of Turin has rightly objected to this formula that it applies too generally to the peoples to be special to any one of them, and finds the distinctive character of the Roman People to lie rather in their "disciplined Will." Again, Professor Bovio of Naples will have it that what the Roman world specially exemplifies is the distinctive rise of "Naturalism" in history, and that it thus formed the transition in the gradual evolution of society from the Hellenic civism to the Germanic individualism.[1]

These and kindred views cannot be followed in the interest of their detail here, nor can they even be discussed generally, but they help us to understand and appreciate both the significance and the limitations of the Roman Law and Jurisprudence. The civic life of Ancient Rome was consciously founded upon a community of will, which was established, maintained, and extended by force, as the source of all individual and social right; and from the outset the idea of liberty was

[1] Hegel, *Werke*, ix. p. 289; Gibbon, ch. xlix.; Ihering, *Geist des römischen Rechts*, Bd. i. § 20; Carle, *Vita del diritto*, p. 170; Bovio, *Sommario della Stória del diritto in Italia*, Cap. Settimo.

identified with privileged participation in this sovereign power. While the common supreme will was thus accentuated in the Roman State as the source of right in distinction from the theocratic legislations of the Oriental peoples, or the arbitrary wills of their individual despots, it also obtained more coherence, purity, and substantiality than it had ever acquired among the mobile and versatile populations of Greece from its being continually determined in detail by deliberative discussion and enactment through carefully devised legislative organs kept in living relation with all the social movement and development of the people. These social and political conditions of Ancient Rome not only emphasised the supremacy of the human will over nature, but made manifest its creative function in the formation and maintenance of human society as a living world capable of being sustained and perpetuated by its own strength and laws. The necessities of the Roman Citizen and the practical bent impressed by them upon him thus gave special reality to the civil forms of will, and in their realisation he found that satisfaction which the Oriental peoples had found in the symbolical forms of religion and the Greeks in the beautiful forms of art. But these forms were entirely conventional, empirical, and conditional in their origin at Rome; and the will to which they gave expression had its subsistence only in the civil community, so that every relation and form of right was grounded upon it. Hence the abstract and external positivism of the Roman system of right, which was never truly universal in its essence or applications, and the relativity and contingency of all its particular rights. The individual had a jural capacity and personality only in so far as he happened to have his life lifted up into the sphere of the civil will, and the highest purpose of that life was the aggrandisement of the State and enjoyment of the utilities it brought with it. The public utilitarianism was only the general form of the particular self-interest of the individual citizens. The extension of the original *jus civile* by the *jus gentium* did not change its character, and the *jus naturale* was only an alien philosophical infusion introduced by Cicero and the Jurists into their expression of the system from the schools of Greece, and especially from the Stoics.[1] Thus slavery was accepted and justified as au institution of the *jus gentium ;* and the extension of the citizenship was only granted on the ground of expediency and not of right. The Constitution of Caracalla, which ultimately extended the right of citizenship to all the freemen of the Empire, was motived by a selfish consideration; and it only loaded the recipients of it with a heavier taxation without giving them any effective participation in the central government. The ancient system of Roman Law, founded as it was upon a convention of force and maintained by a disciplined self-interest, never essentially realised throughout its indefinite range the inherent rights of humanity or the spiritual essence of liberty. With all its acute and minute determinations of the external conditions of ownership and the manifold forms of contract and obligation, it never recognised the rational will as the essential basis of personality nor unfolded the free relationships of the family life. Although it presents the highest development of the Aryan conception of Right in the ancient world, it still retains the naturalistic basis of the ancient life even in its "constant and perpetual will." The more it became separated from the vital customs and usages of the early times, and was unfolded as a logical system through its unrivalled technical development,[2] the more formal and

---

[1] The late Professor Muirhead has excelled all his predecessors in the clearness and accuracy with which he has traced the development of the Roman Law through its stages of the *Jus civile, Jus gentium,* and *Jus naturale* in his *Historical Introduction to the Private Law of Rome,* 1886.

[2] Leibniz compares the work of the Roman Jurisconsults with that of the Mathematicians : "Dixi sæpius, post scripta geometrarum nihil extare, quod vi ac subtilitate cum Romanorum Jureconsultorum scriptis comparari possit."

mechanical did it become, and the more clearly did the
necessity of an equitable tempering of its inherent limitations appear. The more widely, too, it was spread with
the extension of the Empire, the more it obliterated the
distinctive nationalities under the sway of its own uniformity, and the more rigidly it was administered by
the trained officials, the more did it lose its relation
to the moral elements of the social life and to the
higher ends of the individual. It thus formed no real
barrier to the social corruption of the Empire, which
it could neither humanise nor organise nor save, notwithstanding all the external adaptation of the political
mechanism. When the original strength of the common will from which it had sprung was dissolved by
the very luxury and indulgence which it had protected and fostered, the Roman Law lost its spring
and spontaneity. The evolving power of the mere civil
will was exhausted, and the Jurists could only do the
formal work of analysing, classifying, and summaris-
ing the masses of inherited details in the Romano-
Byzantine Codes, without opening up deeper fountains
of Right. The succession and form of the government
became always more subject to chance and caprice.
The provincial municipalities, fainter reflexes of Rome
itself, became ever more isolated and enfeebled; and the
hungry demoralised mob at Rome became always more
callous and degenerate. Without representative government and with a senile Senate, the military despots
naturally reverted to mere brute force, which wore itself
out in selfish and lawless conflicts; and the Empire at
last lay divided and paralysed in itself, with its essential
life worn out, an easy prey to the barbarians who were
pointed from all its frontiers along its highways to Rome.
Rome had thus to bear the penalty of an immoral dominion which had trampled down liberty in the name of
liberty, subordinated every interest of society to itself,

and trusted to the unsubstantiality of an external civilisation supported only by formal law.[1]

The Roman Law could not save the Empire, but rather precipitated its fate by the aggressive and outward ambition which it stimulated; yet it remained as a perpetual possession to the world, and in the Middle Ages, whatever power and vitality it had, entered into the seething and formless chaos out of which the new peoples were to arise. In those ages not merely of historical but of essential mediation, when, amid confusion and violence, the modern world was spiritually begotten by Christianity upon the virgin life of the Germanic race, the Roman Law became the schoolmaster of the young peoples, and trained and disciplined their wild spirits into the forms of a new social order. The "Germanists" have lamented the subjection of the young Germanic world to the old Roman Law, and the English Constitutional Jurists have congratulated their countrymen upon its limited and indirect influence upon England, but it cannot be doubted that its operation was beneficent, progressive, and liberating on the whole. The new Religion which had come to renovate and moralise the inner life soon took on the externality and ambition of the old Empire, and fell into fatal conflict with the new Empire which had arisen in the name of Rome beyond the confines of Italy. When the supreme Pontiffs of Christianity saw the ideal of its crucified Founder in the great Emperors holding the stirrups of the greater Popes, the old Roman Law became the educator and protector of humanity amid this outrage of Religion, which was worse than the old Paganism. And no less did it help to withstand Feudal oppression and the violence of undisciplined

---

[1] Much has been written during the past three centuries on the character and value of the ancient Roman Law which cannot be referred to here. It is interesting, however, to note that the keen strife between the "Germanists" and the "Romanists" has again broken out in Germany in connection with the project of a German Civil Code and the publication in 1887, after fourteen years' labour, of the results of the Imperial Commission on the subject. An extensive juristic literature is gathering around the subject.

individuality. The cultivation of the Roman Law revived and shed new intellectual glory on Italy, and the Spirit of Right lived again in the free and flourishing Municipalities and Communes.[1] Italy, the battle-ground of the forces contending for the mastery of the world, the goal and prey of every conqueror, the mingling point of all the great currents of human life, although oppressed, dismembered, alienated, still remained true to herself in her intellectual love and reverence for the beneficence and majesty of Law. Amid the interminable and chaotic strife of Guelfs and Ghibellines, the two greatest thinkers of their time arose again in Italy to advocate the ideals of human right. Thomas Aquinas, the greatest of the Christian Philosophers, and Dante, the greatest of the Christian Poets, unfolded the ideals of the Church and the Empire respectively as the conditions of the salvation of society. The thought of both of them was shaped and moulded, although to counter issues, by the ancient Spirit of Right in a deepened Christian form, and they laid the foundations of all modern political science. But neither of them solved the problem of the organisation of liberty, although the great poet, haunted by the phantom of the Empire, gave prophetic anticipations of its coming. The Italian genius found its highest political, as well as its highest poetical, expression in Dante.[2]

The Middle Ages struggling through the dualism of the

[1] Savigny is still the great authority on the History of the Roman Law in the Middle Ages. The best work on the Communes is by Karl Hegel, son of the philosopher.

[2] The views of St. Thomas Aquinas are expounded in the *De regimine principum*, of which L. i.–ii. c. 4 are generally recognised as his, the remainder being attributed to his disciple, Tolomei di Lucca. Dante's *De Monarchia* was written, according to Boccaccio, in 1310 (best edition: Dantis Alligherii de Monarchia, Libri tres MSSorum

ope emendati per C. Witte; Halis, Sax., 1863-71). The *Summa* and the *Divina Commedia* also adumbrate the political doctrines of their authors. Professor Frohschammer of Munich has published an excellent work on the Philosophy of Thomas Aquinas; a good summary of his ethical doctrine is given by Dr. Luthardt in his "History of Christian Ethics," vol. i. (T. & T. Clark). There is a thoughtful article on the "Theology and Ethics of Dante," by Professor Edward Caird, in the *Contemporary Review*, June 1890.

Church and the Empire, Feudalism and Municipalism, Cæsarism and Nationality, authority and independence, faith and reason, the ideal and the real, passed through all the pain of the collision, differentiation and commingling of the elements of liberty. While the free impetuosity of the German race emancipated it as with a bound, the practical ineffectiveness of the Renaissance and the suppression of the spirit of the Reformation prolonged the struggle for three centuries in Italy. The hectic flush of Italian Art only bloomed over political decay. The seventeenth century saw the deepest degradation of Italian life and character; and even the great outburst of popular liberty in the French Revolution found but a feeble echo in the land of the Tribunes.[1] This slow and uncertain passing from mediæval twilight to the clear modern day was the period of the Political Writers who followed in the footsteps of Dante and Petrarca in the search for a principle of social organisation, and whose most characteristic expression was given through the gifted but ill-fated Florentine Secretary.[2] Macchiavelli, with what Macaulay not inaptly calls his "cool, judicious, scientific atrocity," marks at once the despair and the futility of this abstract political speculation. Subordinating all thought and action to the hunger of an unsatisfied patriotism, and scorning equally the bastard theocracy and the broken spirit of the people, the student of Livy and observer of the Italian Courts sought to substitute for Dante's dream of a restored empire an artificial and intellectual policy of intrigue and dissimulation as the only available means left for reaching a real

[1] M. de Sismondi's great *Histoire des Républiques Italiennes du Moyen Age* (in 16 vols., 1809–19) is still the most complete and readable work on its subject. It is more interesting than ever to compare its almost despairing conclusion with the rapid progress now being made. Mr. Symmonds has written admirably on the Italian Renaissance, and has given an excellent sketch of Italian History in the *Encyclopædia Britannica*.

[2] Ferrari has given a vigorous and eloquent account of these writers in his *Corso sugli scrittori politici Italiani*, 1863. In an Appendix he gives a chronological list of 1200 Political Writers, mostly Italian, who wrote from 1222 to 1789.

nationality. Macchiavelli in entire sincerity exhibits the complete divorce of politics from morality and the culmination of the old Roman severance of political administration from the essential ends of individual life. The futility of this externalism in the political speculation of the time is equally seen in the fantastic communism of Campanella and the Utopian school. The Italian Political Writers have the merit of having created modern political science, but Government being regarded by them one-sidedly and negatively by itself, Jurisprudence was almost lost sight of in this pursuit of the *ignis fatuus* of a mere political form. The spirit of the time thus came to lose its hold on any concrete principle of right, and the inevitable consequence was the moral corruption and degradation of the people.[1]

The new spirit which has renovated Italy in the Nineteenth Century owes its vitality and strength to the appropriation of a truer conception of human personality and of the ends of human life in the organism of civil society. It was scientifically kindled in the beginning of the Eighteenth Century by Vico, the greatest of the modern Italian thinkers, the founder of the Philosophy of History, and with it of the true Philosophy of Law. Professor Flint has suggestively characterised Vico's " *Scienza Nuova,* one of the profoundest, greatest of books," as " the philosophical complement to Dante's *Divina Commedia.*"[2] We might even go further, and find in Vico the philosophical complement to the spirit of Ancient Rome, as well as to that of

---

[1] The merits and services of the Italian, Alberico Gentile (1551–1611), Professor of Civil Law at Oxford, as the chief precursor of Grotius in founding the Science of International Law, have been well recognised by Professor Holland in his inaugural lecture, "Albericus Gentilis" (1874), and in the edition of his *De jure belli, Libri tres,* 1877.

[2] *The Philosophy of History in Europe,* vol. i. 287. Professor Flint's *Vico* in Blackwood's Philosophical Classics (1884) contains a valuable Chapter on " Vico as a Theorist on Law." This admirable monograph has been received with the greatest approbation in Italy, and has heightened the expectation and impatience with which the learned author's treatment of the Philosophy of History in Italy is awaited.

Mediæval Italy.[1] Vico first clearly enunciated the old Roman principle that it is the spirit of man which makes "the World of the Nations," and according to the faith of the Middle Ages, that this world is regulated by the laws of an indwelling Providence. Vico discovered and promulgated the reality of immanent law in the whole social life of man, and verified it by profounder study of ancient, and especially Roman history. Society thus came to be regarded as a sphere of organised and progressive movement, and the political organisation as subordinated to a divine-human purpose. The essential freedom of man must be realised in the social organism, and his absolute, natural rights become gradually recognised and guaranteed with the advance of civil liberty. Man comes from God, and he returns to God with his nature liberated and enriched by social participation in the directing Justice which is the one principle and the one end of universal right. Jurisprudence exhibits this fundamental truth by the aid of Philosophy and History, and it has its practical embodiment and realisation in law. "Vico's entire philosophy arose from a study of law." He did for Jurisprudence what Galilei and the Italian scientists had done for Physics; he gave it a solid and permanent foundation on the inherent laws of Human Nature and initiated their empirical verification by inductive examination of the facts of history. He thus became the chief teacher and guide in the sphere of Jurisprudence and Ethics of all the leading thinkers of Italy since his time, and his conceptions have given solidity and definiteness to the aspirations

---

[1] Gioberti describes Vico as "a man who appeared to resume in himself the speculative genius of which his contemporaries were deprived; a man raised, it seems, by Providence to save the honour of Italy from entire shipwreck; the man of the vastest and most potent genius Italy has seen since Dante and Michael Angelo." The Italian thinkers never weary in their praise of Vico, and many works have been written on his system. For the "Vico Literature" see Flint's *Vico*, at p. 230; to the works on Vico's Philosophy of Law, mentioned at p. 165, may be added C. Cucca's *Del diritto secondo la mente del Vico* (vol. i. 1879), in which (as in the present work) "a fusion of the views of Vico with those of Gioberti is attempted" (Werner).

for liberty and reform. The remarkable development of philosophical thought in Italy during the Nineteenth Century has proceeded from Vico, as that of France did from Descartes, that of England from Bacon, and that of Germany from Kant.[1] Even the more practical patriotic workers for the emancipation of Italy have been dominated and guided by Vico's ideas. The new spirit of freedom has brought with it not only great activity in the scientific cultivation of Jurisprudence, but corresponding progress in the emancipatory work of practical legislation. Right and Politics have thus been united in a deeper ethical synthesis embracing and regulating the harmonious ends of the social life. In no country has this been more conspicuously the case of late than in Italy; and in reviewing the contemporary relations Professor Lorimer did not exaggerate when he said: "Italy is the land on which since Germany went on the 'war-path' the mantle of scientific jurisprudence seems to have fallen. In no country in Europe is the relation of theory to practice at this moment more intimate, the character of jurisprudence as a branch of the science of nature better understood, or the haphazard 'leap-in-the-dark' legislation on which we pride ourselves more at a discount than in Italy."[2]

And so, as we said at the outset, Italy has again become the living and fruitful home of the Science of Law. The historical antecedents and conditions referred to make the fact intelligible, and it is authenticated by the remarkable

---

[1] A good sketch of the History of Modern Italian Philosophy is given by Dr. V. Botta in the English Edition of Ueberweg's History of Philosophy (vol. ii. 461–516). Mr. Thomas Davidson has done great service by his excellent translation and exposition of "The Philosophical System of Antonio Rosmini-Serbati," London, 1882. Rosmini's *New Essay on the Origin of Ideas* (3 vols., London, 1883-4) and his *Ruling Principle of Method* (Boston, 1887) have also been translated. Nowhere have the principles of the Scottish School of Philosophy been better appreciated than in Italy; and the long neglect of the systems of Rosmini, Galuppi, Gioberti, and Mamiani by the representatives of that school has been as discreditable to them as it has been unfortunate for its history.

[2] *Studies National and International*, p. 103, 1890.

juristic literature which the industry of the recent Italian Jurists has produced in all the departments of positive law, civil, commercial and penal.[1] But it is in the highest department of all, the one which crowns and unifies and completes all the others, that we meet with the most characteristic and original products of the juridical genius of the modern Italians. The Philosophy of Law has been nowhere cultivated with more earnestness, assiduity, and success, during the present century, than in Italy. True to their traditions, every one of the leading Italian thinkers has given his best thought and endeavour to the elucidation of the fundamental problems of Right. Emancipated by their legislation from the mechanical formalism of the old Roman Law, and by the new patriotic spirit from the false dominion of a hybrid ecclesiasticism, they have striven to find a deeper and truer foundation for the reform and reorganisation of the national life. This juristic movement, while presenting a rich variety and independence in detail, has been conspicuously characterised by a faithful regard to the development of history, a keen scrutiny of human reason, and a sober acceptance of established limitations. It has thus been at once historical, speculative, and positive in its method; and progressive, elevating, and regulative in its results. While every school of contemporary European thought has had its representatives, and while the most prominent of them have not

---

[1] That abundant and ever-growing literature cannot be even indicated here. It is not confined to the Italian Codes and their special subjects, but ranges over all the departments and problems of Law. The interest of English Students of Law is now being directed to the important work of the Italians in Criminology, in which they have led the thought of Europe since Beccaria. Among the most valuable recent works on this subject are those of Lombroso (*L'uomo delinquente in rapporto all' anthropologia,* etc., 4th ed. 1890), Garofalo (*Criminologia,* 2nd ed. 1890), Marro (*Caratteri dei delinquenti,* 1887), and Luchini (*Critica della pena e svolgimento di alcuni principii intorno al diritto di punire,* 1869). Great attention is given by the Italian Jurists to the Historical and Comparative Study of Law. The Italian Juridical Reviews are numerous, and give evidence of great scientific activity. The "Rivista Italiana per le Scienze Giuridiche," published at Rome, may be mentioned; it gives the titles and contents of the other Reviews.

escaped the penalty of their one-sided devotion, the Italian
Jurists have been remarkable on the whole for their catho-
licity, breadth, and comprehensiveness.   In this respect it
is no exaggeration to say that they have largely combined
the speculative ideality of the Germans with the practical
reality of the English in a special activity that has been
equally faithful to the demands of science and the requirements of life.[1]   This ideal realism, this dialectical
synthesis, this plastic integration, based upon quick
perception and comparison of relations, seems to be the
characteristic note of the modern Italian genius, and it
has fruitfully authenticated itself in the Philosophy of
Law.   The Italian Jurists have worked out with con-
spicuous fidelity and success the scientific conception of
Jurisprudence embodied by Vico in his admirable definition: "Jurisprudentia universa tribus ex partibus coales-
cit, philosophia, historia, et quadam propria arte juris ad
facta accomodandi."   In doing so they have not only
given remarkable proof of the tenacity and versatility of
the Italian genius, but have largely enriched the juridical
thought and capability of Europe.[2]

It is more than time that the English Students of Law
were giving attention to this realised and advancing
work of the Italian School.   The reasons for its long
neglect have been too many, and are too obvious to
be dwelt on.   The immediate interest of positive law
and the dominant utilitarianism have checked, and even
suppressed, the higher capabilities of English thought
in investigating the fundamental problems of jurisprudence.[3]   But the need of a true Science of Right is

---

[1] The characteristics of the modern Italian *ingenium* in relation to
juridical and social studies have
been delineated with admirable insight and discrimination by Professor Carle, op. cit. Lib. v. c. iv. § 2.
See also Dr. Werner's *Die Itali-
enische Philosophie des neunzehnten
Jahrhunderts*, Bd. v. p. 346; and
Gioberti, *Introduzione*, I. c. iii.

[2] The Bibliography appended to
this work gives a clear, concise, and
useful survey of the literature referred to.   See also the historical
sketch in the Prolegomena.
[3] The Translator has already dealt
with this subject in the Prefaces to
his Translations of Kant's *Philosophy
of Law*, and the *Outlines of Jurisprudence* by Puchta and others.

always becoming more apparent in England amid the increasing political confusion, social unrest, and indefinite thinking of the time. The best-qualified jurists acknowledge it; and our two chief masters—Sir Henry Sumner Maine and Professor Lorimer—have been taken from the field of labour. It is a time when earnest students may well look abroad for light and leading. The supremacy of Germany in the sphere of juridical, as of general philosophical, speculation has been deservedly won, but its ideal products, supremely valuable in potentiality as they are, have never satisfied the practical tendency of the English mind. Nor have the French Jurists of this century, with all their clear and logical faculty, been able to originate anything like an independent or fruitful philosophical jurisprudence.[1] In these circumstances, it may be allowed to point the English Student of Law to the living development of jurisprudence in Italy, in the belief that he will find himself readily at home in its method of dealing with juristic problems, and that he cannot but be enriched and strengthened by any appropriation of its results.[2]

It is from this point of view that the present work has been translated into English. The fact of its having been already translated into German, French, and Spanish, and that it has reached the third edition in Italian, is a guarantee of its interest and value.[3] It is well fitted to be not only

---

[1] Of this too abundant evidence has been furnished by the Preface to the French Translation of the present work. It contains a great deal of interesting information regarding the present state of juridical study in France and other countries.

[2] It does not appear that anything has been done in the way of translating any of the works of the Italian jurists into English for more than a century, or indeed since the translation of Beccaria's tractate, *Dei delitti e delle pene* (1764), a new edition of which was published at Glasgow in 1770, entitled, *An Essay on Crimes and Punishments*, by the Marquis Beccaria of Milan. With a commentary by M. de Voltaire. It is imperfect, and made apparently from the French version.

[3] The German and French Translations are excellent, and have been referred to in order to secure accuracy in the English rendering. The Spanish translation has not yet come to hand. Important additions and modifications have been made on the last edition of the original work by the Author for the English Translation, which has been made with his sanction and kind co-operation.

an attractive and comprehensive Introduction to the Science of Jurisprudence generally, but also a Special Introduction to the Juridical Philosophy of contemporary Italy. Among a large and ever-increasing number of works on the subject, it bears conspicuously the characteristic stamp and form of the new Italian School. Founding upon Vico and Gioberti, the most distinctively Italian thinkers of the Eighteenth and Nineteenth Centuries, it exhibits their principles and spirit in their largest scope and widest applications.[1] Free from all religious narrowness or national prejudice, while yet earnestly religious and intensely national, it bears aloft the highest spiritual interests of humanity, and steers a firm course—with a touch of scorn—through all the eccentric and downward tendencies of the time. Showing much of the spontaneous and easy power of the Italian artist, it exhibits also the practicality of the old Roman understanding and the cosmopolitan adaptiveness of the new Italian character. The metaphysical foundation of the system is only laid

---

[1] Gioberti (1800-1852), "the patriot-philosopher of Italy," may well be regarded as the most distinctively Christian thinker of the Nineteenth Century. His philosophical standpoint is indicated by the Author of this work in the Prolegomena, with the earnestness and enthusiasm of a disciple. Gioberti has not the wonderful metaphysical subtlety and elaboration of Rosmini (1797-1855), but he is more immediate, more impassioned, more Italic. Rosmini has unfolded a Philosophy of Right in the utmost detail of division and definition, while Gioberti has only laid the metaphysical and ethical basis of principles which he gave his whole soul to bringing directly to bear upon the religious and political renovation of Italy. The publication of his eloquent and patriotic work, *Il primato morale e civile degli Italiani*, in 1843, gave a great impetus to the Neo-Guelfic party, and had "an immense success."

His *Rinnovamento*, published in 1851, continued the work on clearer and more practical political lines. Prof. A. Bartoli has said of Gioberti's *Gesuita moderno* (5 vols., 1846), that "it will live as the most tremendous indictment ever written against the Jesuits." Gioberti's *Essay on the Beautiful, or Elements of Æsthetic Philosophy*, has been translated into English by Ed. Thomas (2nd ed., London, 1860 —an indifferent translation, the French translation being much better). "In the United States of America, Gioberti found a devoted interpreter in Dr. O. A. Brownson, whose able exposition of the doctrine contained in the ideal formula was published in 1864, in the Review bearing his name" (see *Ueberweg*, vol. ii. 497-504). Gioberti's *Teoria del Sopranaturale* (1838) and his *Protologia* (1856) entitle him to comparison as a metaphysical theologian with Scotus and Hegel.

bare that it may be proved to be safe to build upon, as the basis of the whole structure. It will be found animated throughout by the magnificent thought so grandly expressed by Hooker, that "of Law there can be no less acknowledged than that her seat is the bosom of God, her voice the harmony of the world." The industry of the historical student appears everywhere in the work, side by side with the keen watchfulness of the practical politician. The Author has himself hinted that the matter of the First Volume might have been condensed, but the enlarging ideal of the time, no less than the conception of the great jurists, pleads his justification. In England especially there is no more necessary teaching required at present than that which would awaken the sense of the largeness of the domain of Right, and guide to a just appreciation of its several spheres. The exposition of political doctrine and of existing forms of the State in the Second Volume should be found interesting both to the politician and the jurist, disclosing as it does the harmony and unity of their tasks. The Italian standpoint of the work makes it, so far as it goes, a contribution to Comparative Politics and Law, and an easy and reliable guide to the political organisation of the new Italian Kingdom. It may be admitted that greater depth might have been exhibited in the treatment of fundamental principles, that the historical expositions might have been carried into further detail, that the analysis and filiation of the jural conceptions might have been sharper and more distinct, but the method, proportion, and presentment of the work is all the more adapted for the want in view, and hardly more could have been accomplished within its limits. No better introductory synopsis of the system could be given than that of the highly competent German translator, Dr. Matteo di Martino, who summarises it as follows :—

The Author of the following work has exhibited the character of the Italian Philosophy in the criticism of the Systems con-

tained in his Prolegomena; and upon that Philosophy he builds
his system of Ethics and Jurisprudence. Morals and Law
pursue one and the same End, the realisation of the Good, but
with different means. Everything is to be regarded as good
which is in harmony with the nature of the universe, and consequently also with human nature. The Good differentiates
itself into singular Ends, for the attainment of which certain
conditions are requisite which guarantee Right. Justice is
the norm for human actions, in so far as these are regarded as
external. Law is the ideality of Right which contains the
criterion for the Just in its application to human relationships.
What then are the cardinal relationships for which Law is
called to provide the most favourable conditions possible?
Ahrens had accentuated Religion, Science, Education, Art, in
its two main branches as beautiful and useful Art, Commerce,
Morality, and Justice. Our Author includes Education under
Justice, and in the First Part of the work he surveys the
Objects of Right, which have ever been, and always must be,
the conditions for the harmonious development of these car-
dinal relationships.

In order to attain this end, Man may be active as a separate
individual or in fellowship with others. In the Second Part
of the work treating of the Subjects of Right, the Author
examines the divers stages of this fellowship or association,
and works out positions different from those of both Ahrens
and Mohl. The former had presented the Individual, the
Family, the Commune, the State, the Confederation of States,
and Humanity; and the latter added the Race and various
permanent Associations, such as the Church. Our Author
adds the Province, but leaves out the Race and the other
Associations.

On the basis of the doctrine of Vico, according to which
Man is an intuitive and free being, the Author begins with
Certainty and ends with Truth. He lays chief importance on
history. The Understanding produces truth, the Will fact.
Ideas and facts proceed from one and the same point; and consequently a necessary harmony must reign between them in
their great outlines. Hence the Author first carefully investigates the origin of the Jural Institutions, and then proceeds to
expound the theory of them. The chief value of the work

lies in its comparison of the Legal Institutions established among the different Nations, the Italian Legislation being constantly referred to as the basis of this comparison.

The Table of Contents has been enlarged in this English edition, and the Summaries and Bibliography left out by the German and French translators, have been also rendered in order to give it the completeness of the original and to facilitate its appropriation. The work may thus be left to speak for itself in detail, in the hope that it may be received with such interest as may justify the attempt to reproduce some of the profounder and weightier productions of the Italian Schools. It cannot, at least, fail to give the student some insight into the vital and organic conceptions, and a clearer and truer sense of the manifold interest both for science and for practice, of the contemporary philosophy of law. And it will achieve its purpose if it helps to stimulate greater devotion to this department of science in the large and comprehensive spirit of the precept which Vico addressed to his young contemporaries, and which may well be prefixed as a motto to the following pages: " *Integram sapientiam excolite, naturam universam perficite.*"

W. H.

Edinburgh, *December* 1890.

AUTHOR'S PREFACE

TO THE THIRD EDITION.

———•———

THIS book had a university origin; but the successive
enlargements of it have adapted it for the use of all cultivated readers. And, indeed, is it possible under a free
government for any one to ignore with impunity the
historical and rational origin of the principal juridical
institutions? The ruling classes are no longer capable
of guiding the community when they cease to have
arguments with which to meet every new paradox. The
poet Heine was wont to say that the troubled end of the
Eighteenth Century would yet seem an idyl in comparison
with that of the Nineteenth Century. We should therefore have the courage to keep in view certain problems
which, if badly solved, may yet lead to the abyss.

What are we? Whence do we come? Whither are
we going? All possible social and political organisation
depends on the answers given to these three questions. If
we are not only sensitive, but reasonable and free, beings,
and come from a Creator with whom we are destined to be
reunited without being confounded with Him, and have
to render Him an account of our actions, then our life
ought to be regulated in a certain way. But if we are
only sentient beings, if we have sprung by natural selec-

tion from the monkey, then we must be subject in everything and by everything to the struggle for existence,
and nothing will remain of us but an empty name. In
order to answer adequately the questions thus indicated,
we have examined human nature under the guidance of
tradition, existing systems, and direct observation; and
everywhere and always we have recognised in it a divine
germ. Everywhere and in all times, we have perceived
humanity in search of the good, with a more or less enlightened conscience; and we have found juridical institutions directed towards the attainment of it.

The philosophers, reconstructing mentally the work of
the people, have put man into relation with the universal
order, distinguishing him when he conformed himself to
it from a disinterested internal motive, and when he acted
with the view of obtaining a certain utility. They have
thus separated morality from right, and specified the good
in reference to essential ends, and they have determined
the mode of obtaining it objectively and subjectively.

It has seemed to us most useful to arrange the juridical material in this order, because the whole human
development can thus be taken in at a single glance,
without ever losing sight of the point of departure and
the goal. In the First Part of our work, dealing with
the Objects of Right, we have been followed by the celebrated jurist Ihering, although with a different meaning.
In Ihering's view ends dominate in the sphere of right;
they are, however, not regarded as adapting themselves
according to an inherent gradation to the needs of the time,
but they have to be kept in check by a complex of forces
which he calls the social mechanism. In the Second
Part of the work, in which we deal with the Subjects of
Right, we are still without companions.

Meanwhile certain fundamental objections have been taken to the point of view here advocated. These have been elegantly summed up in a lecture by Professor Prins of the University of Brussels,[1] and in the inaugural discourse of Professor Nani of the University of Turin.[2]

The former puts his objections thus. For nearly two centuries Natural Right has been considered as a science ; and the theories of a state of nature, of the social contract, and of pure reason, have been both discussed and rejected as sources of right. If Pufendorf, the first occupant of a chair devoted to this subject, were to return to life, he would not find many disciples, but he would find not a few opponents who dispute the basis of his system. Professor Prins then concludes in favour of the Historical School. As he puts it, at first right is an instinct ; justice, religion, and power are found mixed up ; there are no legal rules nor jurisconsults ; right is born from the bosom of the people like the heroic songs. It is sacred as their faith, and is transmitted as tradition. In the same assembly the gods are worshipped, rhapsodies are listened to, and judgment is pronounced. . . . But suddenly the picture becomes enlarged ; justice, power, and faith are separated ; there is not yet a written law ; but there are precedents, and there are judges to make use of them, and now it is no longer instinct but reason which guides them. Customary right appears ; a body of positive rules is formed ; magistrates arise to apply these rules, and they create jurisprudence. . . . Lastly, after a rich vegetation, the dry branches of the juridical growth are cut off in order to render the trunk more vigorous, and legal right becomes a written science, while juris-

---

[1] *La philosophie du droit et l'école historique.* Bruxelles, 1882.
[2] *Vecchi e nuovi problemi del diritto.* Torino, 1886.

consults develop its technical element. . . . The duty of the jurist is simple; he has to cultivate the living legal right, to search for truth in the juridical sources or in the national organisms, without the interests of humanity becoming in any way compromised, because the national organic right thus takes the place of universal right, and the majestic laws of advancing humanity that of the rules of pure reason.

Nani, on the other hand, attacks not only Natural Right, but also the Historical School: the former because it proclaims the omnipotence of the individual, and relegates jurisprudence to the field of abstract speculation; and the latter because if it has been able to indicate the source from which right arises, it has erred in believing it simply to be a product of the consciousness of the people, like language, customs, and the political constitution. Accordingly he seems to associate himself with the learned Professor Dahn, holding the view that the Philosophy of Right is founded on the comparative science of the peoples, on their psychology, or on ethnology and anthropology in the widest sense of the term.

The want felt by the two illustrious professors is to reconnect the fact with the idea, or to reconcile philology with philosophy. Prins accepts the fundamental problem as formulated by Rousseau, namely, how to find a form of association which shall defend and protect with the whole of the common power the person and goods of every associate, while respecting the liberty of each. But he finds the solution of it in assigning the function in question to the collective whole of society when it makes use of its natural organisms, and not in entrusting that power to one or more persons who are called representatives of the general will.

Nani, after having indicated his adhesion to Dahn, confines himself to considering how philosophy penetrates into juridical science under the sociological form ; and he exclaims : " The end of the century will perhaps see it seated anew in the position which not many years ago it believed that it had abandoned for ever."

What the two illustrious professors desiderate, has been in existence for a long time, even from the year 1720, when Giambattista Vico published his golden treatise *De uno universi juris principio et fine uno.* In it he says : " Quae vis veri, seu ratio humana *virtus* est *quantum cum cupiditate* pugnat, eadem est *Justitia quantum utilitates* dirigit et exaequat, quae est unum universi Juris Principium unusque Finis. Utilitates autem quae cupiditatem cient, corpore constant : communis corporum mensura seu regula est *commensus* vulgo dicta *proportio*, quam Mathesis pro nostro argumento demonstrat duplicem, *arithmeticam* seu *simplicem,* et *geometricam* seu *comparatam.* . . . *At quod est aequum dum mctiris, idem est justum quum eligis:* quod in rebus cognitionis et in rebus actionis, modo utraeque sint pro natura sua demonstratae, unum sit genus assensionis. Igitur uti aequum cognitionis demonstratum, ubi id recta matheseos methodo confectum sit ; ita justum actionis, ubi animus sit perturbationibus defoecatuŝ, nec ullo pravo gentis more corruptus, . . . justum, inquam, ei est planissime demonstratum." In another place Vico says more concisely : " *Honestas* is the cause of right ; *utilitas* is its occasion ; and *metaphysica* is the mother of jurisprudence, the *societas veri* being an essential element of the *societas aequi,* and reciprocally." So in the world of the nations the useful is found already connected with the *aequum.* From the examination which every one makes of what he believes useful, arises what is justly due to each; that is, there arises the idea of human justice. But this idea already exists virtually and intuitively, and it is only certain necessities which lead to its being explicated and taking a reflective and scientific form. In this way the Neapolitan thinker foreshadowed the synthesis of History and the Philosophy of Right. We need not here follow the distinguished author in his description of primitive right and the transition from the *jus privatae violentiae* to the *jus civile*. Montesquieu, the worthy continuator of Vico, before plunging into historical researches, declares: "Particular intelligent beings may have laws of their own making, but they have some like- wise which they never made. Before there were intel- ligent beings, they were possible; they had therefore possible relations, and consequently possible laws. Before laws were made, there were relations of possible justice" (*Esprit des lois,* Liv. I. ch. i.).

According to the hypothesis of Kant and Laplace, let us assume, on the contrary, that a nebulous mass became separated from the sun and was consolidated while turn- ing around itself. Gradually this incandescent globe cooled down and brought forth the vegetables which nourished the animals that sprang forth spontaneously. Man was distinguished among his congeners by a more developed instinct, and formed a species of society at first mute, then gesticulating; and finally he found articulate speech from which the primitive civilisation took its origin. Long ages flowed past during the transitions from the horde to the tribe, from the tribe to the city, and from the city to the State. But at last the great Oriental empires arose; then Greece, Rome, Christianity, and the modern nations: all by natural selection and by the law of heredity. The physical world is represented according to this theory as differing in nothing from the moral world; both are subject to the laws of life. Morality is the resultant of two impulses, egoism and altruism. The former arises from the necessity of nutrition implanted in the organic substance in order that it may exist as an individual, and the latter from the necessity of loving in order that it may exist as a species. The notion of justice is a mental equation transported into the domain of action and of morality. It retains some of the rigour of its origin and a certain impartiality which distinguish it. Accordingly there is no longer final causality, nor any will freely exercised in order to attain it. The voluntary activity which is in us takes origin from the excitation of the muscles, and is transferred from the internal domain to the external domain. All phenomena are considered as directed by a will; all events as directed by a Providence; and finally the whole visible and invisible universe as crowned by a Supreme Will. This method of explanation we regard as mere illusion.

We do not ask an act of faith from our readers, but only that they examine with equal attention internal facts and external facts in order to discover their laws. They will find in their mind the ideas of substance, of a creative and regulative cause that is perfect and infinite, as well as the ideas of the good and just which experience cannot give. External reality corresponds to these ideas, and this not by chance. Man feels himself free and responsible, and works in consequence. He differs from the animals by his power of discernment (*discrimen* or *discernimen*, from *discerno*), which is the crown of reason (*ratio*, from *reor*, to think, *logos* meaning thought and speech). Morality, which in the animal is arrested at sympathy, rises in man to duty; and as the moral law is

not realised spontaneously as a whole, there arises the
necessity of coercion in that part of it which it is incumbent on society to see as far as possible actualised. The
animals cannot be subjects of right because they have not
an end to attain. The animals adumbrate man. In the
plants and animals, and even in inorganic nature, there
are found dispersed the properties, including the perfec-
tions and the imperfections, of our being. Wherefore the
ancients, and especially the Stoics, sought in the irrational
beings, and particularly in the brutes and in infants, the
impress of the law of nature, calling them mirrors of
nature. Plutarch wrote on the nature of the animals,
and defended their cause, which had been already patronised
by Democritus. That ancient philosopher said : " We
have already been disciples of the animals in great things,
of the spider in weaving and sewing, of the swallow in
building, and of the sweet swan and nightingale in singing." Speech is congenital to man, and civilisation is his
work, being found by spontaneous reason, and perfected
by reflective reason. As the immortal author of the *New
Science* wrote, the profound wisdom of the philosophers
succeeds the vulgar wisdom, the true process of the human
mind consisting in verifying by analysis the primitive
synthesis, and in thinking by means of reflection what is
learned by intuition.

In this Third Edition of our work, we have taken full
account of the observations of the Italian, German, and
French press when the two previous Italian editions and
the German and French translations appeared, but without
introducing any variation into the order or distribution
of the contents. Although to some the First Part has
appeared a little long, we have deemed it right to preserve it as it is in conformity with the traditions of our

greatest jurists, who have defined the subject in the well-known words: *Jurisprudentia est divinarum atque human-arum rerum notitia, justi atque injusti scientia.* We have carefully followed all the improvements which have been effected in the sphere of legislation at home and abroad, and have kept in view the circumstances of time and place affecting them in criticising the juridical institutions.

Thereby our science, without ceasing to be the link of connection between Philosophy and Right, will be seen to acquire a practical value in enlightening public opinion and paving the way for the work of the Legislator.

THE AUTHOR.

CONTENTS.

PART FIRST.

THE OBJECTS OF RIGHT.

I. RELIGION.

PHILOSOPHY OF RIGHT.

PROLEGOMENA.

WHEN we cast our eyes upon the universe we see ourselves surrounded by phenomena which we naturally desire to know. How is this knowledge attained? Plato says that Science is not learned, as some believe, by introducing it into the mind as sight is given to one born blind; but every one has in himself the faculty of understanding, a sort of organ destined for the attainment of knowledge, when it is applied to the contemplation of what exists. Hence it is necessary to seek for the absolute behind the relative, and to search under facts for the divine or human ideas which produce them.

The ancients regarded things under a double aspect, as we see from the theories of Plato and Aristotle: the former directing all his attention to the ideal, and the latter to the real. Christianity adopted the point of view that had been taken by Plato; but, as it understood human nature better, it subordinated the real to the ideal without annihilating it. Nevertheless such were the obstacles thrown in its way by the barbarism which supervened, that Christianity could then only scatter the germs which it remained for future ages to develop.

The modern period began with a certain disgust at the moral sciences. The hatred of scholasticism led to the abandonment of the rational method, and Galileo, considerably before Bacon, asserted that " the meanings of the

       A

things of nature are to be sought in the works of nature, that the life of nature is always operating, and that it stands before our eyes real and unchangeable in all its facts." Attention, however, did not remain long absorbed in external nature, and the moral sciences did not want illustrious cultivators such as Machiavelli and Grotius. But these sciences continued to advance without connection with each other and in opposite ways, from their being made to consist wholly of the results of observation, or wholly of reasoning. Bossuet took up the theme of St. Augustine's *De civitate Dei* and produced his magnificent *Discourse on Universal History.* Antonius Serra had already explored the laws of the formation of wealth, one of the principal outgoings òf human activity. Vico, taking up again the work of Bossuet, finds the laws of history by analysing man in his individual and social relations; and the moral sciences may be said to have been then really established. Singular destiny that Italy, when involved in such misfortunes, should thus have produced the two great investigators of the moral world!

Thus far practice and speculation independently pursued each its own way; but as the relations among the peoples extended, the influences which ideas had exercised upon facts by means of external revolutions, came to be better appreciated. The human mind was stirred at the close of the Middle Ages, and after the reformation of religion it turned itself to political reform. Among the ancients liberty was synonymous with sovereignty; and as the sovereign was the State, the value of the individual disappeared. Neither the *Republic* and *Laws* of Plato, nor the *Politics* of Aristotle, nor the *Republic* of Cicero, offer us any other ideal. The Germans preserved the spirit of individual liberty; they felt the need and the passion of individuality. After the invasion of the barbarians, the sovereignty became incarnated in property from which were derived independence and power. This power assumed the form of feudalism; but after the struggles of centuries, it fell on the Continent, over-thrown by the Commons and by Monarchy. In England, on the contrary, the Barons united with the Commons in order to resist the royal power; and then was founded that mixed government which has become an object of imitation to all Europe. But how were these Commons to take part in the parliaments or the great national councils? As all the citizens, or even all the muncipal magistrates, could not attend these national councils, it was necessary to depute some of them to represent the entire community, as was the practice in the case of the knights of the shires and of the clergy. If this idea, which seems so simple, had arisen before the irruption of the barbarians, the means would have been found for combining the unity of the Roman Empire with the liberty of the several parts which composed it.

The representative form of government which had sprung up in the Thirteenth Century, and which had been developed by the two revolutions of 1640 and 1688, made England free and happy in the Eighteenth Century. Voltaire and Montesquieu, having visited Great Britain, and having read Locke's treatise on *Civil Government*, understood all the importance of this form of government and described its advantages. Soon thereafter, the English of the New World, the Americans of the north, turned the institutions of the mother country into a republic. Accordingly when the French entered upon the great Revolution of 1789, they had two models before their eyes, the one a monarchy and the other a representative republic. The constitution of 1791 neither founded a monarchy nor a republic, but a government which was without a substantial basis or a probability of duration. This noble nation fell under the influence of those writers who, drawing their inspiration from Rousseau, turned back to the ancient idea which made liberty consist in sovereignty, and right in the will of the nation. Hence they founded equality, and not liberty. The revolutionary anarchy

was succeeded by the Napoleonic despotism, and it was
only after realising the evils of conquest that France
returned to sounder ideas.

Private Right separated itself slowly from Public Right.
We may take for illustration the example of the Roman
Law, which has passed through its whole development and
is best known. At the outset we see all rights absorbed
by the paterfamilias, who was at the same time the priest
and judge. He united around himself his wife, his sons
and their descendants, with his clients and slaves, all of
whom (included under the name of *gens*) were represented
by him as their head. To him belonged the right of the
spear (*jus quiritium*) and the sacrifices (*sacra privata*) ;
and whoever had the spear and the sacrifices also possessed
the land, and the right of taking occupation of the goods
of an enemy. The *gentes,* assembled as *curiae* (from *curis,*
a spear), formed the supreme council of the rising State.
Contracts were rare, and were surrounded with numerous
formalities. The land passed with the spear from father
to son, a necessary and fated succession; and if the father
wished to dispose otherwise, he could not do it without
the consent of the *curiae (calatis comitiis).*

The clients, however, increased in importance ; and,
united with other free men who had come from the conquered cities, they formed the *plebs.* Legal right then
began to divest itself of many formalities. Along with
the *dominium quiritarium* there was admitted the *dominium bonitarium ;* and to contracts *stricti juris* were
added contracts *bonae fidei.* The increase of the strangers
contributed to temper the rigours of the ancient law; and
by means of *aequitas* and the *fictio juris,* there came to be
established by the praetor a *jus gentium, quasi jure quo
omnes gentes utuntur.* Philosophy made its beneficent
influence felt, and Cicero went so far as to declare: "Non
erit alia lex Romae, alia Athenis, sed omnes gentes una lex
continebit."

To Nero is ascribed the institution of a magistrate who

had to receive the complaints of the slaves against the
excesses of their masters. Alexander Severus reduced the
power of fathers over their sons to that of simple correction. The latter had already begun to possess goods of
their own, with the recognition of the *peculium castrense
et quasi castrense.*

As to succession, the praetor had sought by various
expedients to substitute the natural family for the civil
family, or to put *cognatio* in the place of *agnatio;* and he
was followed in this line by Marcus Aurelius, Commodus,
Constantine, Valentinian, and lastly by Justinian, who
crowned this effort by his celebrated Novella 118.

Penal right or criminal law appeared at Rome, as in
the case of all other peoples, as a means of giving reparation for injury received.[1] The idea of penalty was not
slow to spring up with the special laws which punished
offences against the community as crimes. These offences
were judged in the *judicia populi*, presided over by
the king, then in the *comitia*, which elected a *quaestio*
or commission to examine whether the accusation was
founded in fact, and to punish the criminal. Such
commissions were not afterwards appointed for every
single crime, but for a given period and for the delicts
which might be committed, until they became permanent
tribunals, with certain rules for judgment and for the
punishments which were to be inflicted. The imperial
despotism abolished the *quaestiones*, as they called to mind
the commissions by whom they had been elected; and it
assigned an ample jurisdiction to the senate, in which the
emperors voted like ordinary senators. By degrees the
function of punishing crimes passed over to magistrates
directly named by the emperors, and the prerogatives of
the senate were usurped by the private imperial council,
which had become a sort of supreme court of appeal. In
criminal matters, the Digest does not yield to any code as

---

[1] We allude here to criminal law because it is generally treated as
belonging to public law.

regards the variety of the crimes it indicates and the severity of its punishments.

The Roman Law did not perish with the fall of the Empire. It remained as the law of the conquered population, and a part of it also passed into the barbarian compilations of the Franks, the Burgundians, and the Visigoths.

The Glossators introduced the Roman Law into the universities, and increased its authority in the courts. Most of the statutes of the Italian municipalities merely formulated its contents. Alciatus, who was called to teach in France, awoke in that country a love for the Roman Law. Cujacius commented upon it, no longer seeking merely for the meaning of single phrases, but exploring its spirit and expounding its relations with antiquity. The Dutch School continued to study it philologically. Dumoulin and Argentré, on the other hand, applied the Roman method to the national law; and Domat and Pothier, who were powerful generalisers, immediately exercised an influence upon all minds. In Germany, Thomasius, a philosophical jurist, sought to apply to jurisprudence the reform which Descartes had tried to carry out in the other branches of knowledge. Breaking away from all the ideas in vogue, Thomasius wished to make a clean sweep of these by withdrawing jurisprudence from the influences of history and of theology. Vico soon thereafter turned back from this tendency by restoring to history its legitimate influence, but illuminating it with the torch of metaphysics. Nevertheless, about the middle of the last century, legislation was made up of elements taken from the Roman Law, the Canon Law, feudal books, and an endless number of particular edicts and customs. The criminal law was distinguished by the application of torture, the inhumanity of its punishments, the arbitrary application of penalties, and the confusion of all the degrees of the imputability of crime.

These various efforts could not remain without effect on

legislation; and the French Revolution, which aimed at reforming society from top to bottom, could not let the chaos which we have indicated continue to exist. However, the question of the principle of legislation was not settled by the Code Napoléon. It arose again in Germany in 1814, through the publication of a treatise by Thibaut *On the Necessity of a Code for Germany*, to which Savigny replied in his tract on *The vocation of our age for Legislation and Jurisprudence.* Thibaut desired ·that legislation should be as far as possible perfect in its form and matter, so that the language of the laws should be clear and precise, and that it should respond to the wants of the nation. Savigny did not directly deny the advantage of a codification when it could take place, according to the desire of Bacon, in an age that was marked by the superiority of its science and experience; but he preferred that the legislator should confine himself to removing the obstacles which were opposed to the progress of the institutions which sprang up spontaneously, and that he should represent the function of the praetor at Rome or of the old French parliaments when they decided in the form of regulating enactments (*arrêts de règlement*). The fundamental principle of the School of Thibaut was that the will of the legislator might modify and change institutions at pleasure, whereas Savigny thought that the part of the legislator should be on the whole secondary, seeing that Right maintains itself in all epochs in direct relation with nature and with the character of the people from which it emanates.

The same progress has thus been effected in the development both of Public Right and of Private Right. Theory has been elevated in proportion to the measure in which history has presented a new side of the human relationships. Economic science has contributed not a little to perfect the conception of property, and to show the harmony of all interests. There cannot be a scientific treatment of Right and Law without an examination of the principle on which every moral and juridical edifice rests;

and this investigation will form the object of these Prolegomena or preliminary surveys.   They will be divided into
three parts, namely, 1. Metaphysical Speculation, 2. Ethics
or Moral Philosophy, and 3. Jurisprudence as the Philosophy of Right.   In this way we shall thus far see Right
arising, as Cicero has expressed it, *ex intima philosophia,*
and we shall follow it in its historical development.

I.

METAPHYSICAL SPECULATION.

The object of Philosophy is to present a regular system with regard to the essential conditions of knowledge and the existence of things. The principal difficulty which it encounters, lies in its point of departure, and in its method.

A modern French philosopher, Cousin, has reduced the philosophical systems to Idealism, Sensualism, Scepticism, and Mysticism. And in fact, when we examine the various schools, we find that they have started from one of the points thus indicated in order to give a rational explanation of the real and the knowable. By a system is meant a series of ideas which are connected together and subordinated under a single principle. The history of the earliest times shows us man under the control of religion, making everything depend immediately upon God. But he had no sooner fixed his gaze on the external world and on himself than sensation and ideas captivated his attention. A moment of disconcertment produced Scepticism, and the need of faith gave rise to Mysticism. In the history of philosophy we find the names of other systems, such as Materialism, which is a stage of Sensualism; and Pantheism, which admits the unity of substance but which may be readily reduced to Idealism, if the one substance is conceived as ideal, or to Materialism, if it is conceived as matter. The same may be said of the Positivism now in vogue, which is only a disguised Materialism.

Gioberti, an Italian philosopher, has sought to reduce

9

all the philosophical systems to two great categories, namely, Psychologism and Ontologism. Under the name of Psychologism, he embraces the systems which start from experience or from the *Ego*, in order to arrive at the Absolute; and he says that those systems belong to Ontologism which proceed from the intuition of the absolute idea in order to explain the contingent. ˙ This is rather a question of method than of system; but it is of great importance, since method is essential to every system. If the investigation starts from facts, or from what is sensible, it is better to adopt the analytical method; if it begins from ideas or from what is intelligible, the synthetical method is more appropriate. But when the subject is at once a fact and an idea, or both sensible and intelligible, then the two methods are both involved. As the fundamental problem of philosophy is to find the first principle of what is knowable and of what is real, and since this principle, as we shall afterwards see, cannot be a material fact, the synthetical method is therefore to be preferred.

§ I.

The East is recognised by all as the cradle of civilisation, but a considerable part of it, such as Egypt and Persia, did not advance out of symbolism, or a form of theology. Philosophy began to manifest itself in China and in India.

In China there prevailed from the beginning a belief in spirits which symbolised the various forces of nature, and in the sky (*Tien*) as the origin of all things. In the VI. Century B.C., Confucius extracted a species of practical philosophy from the old sacred books called *King*. Mencius, his disciple, formulated a species of mystical pantheism which savours of the influence of the Hindoo philosophy. Lao-tseu, the rival of Confucius, starts from a void unity, the *tao*, from which all beings take origin; and he seems to have numerous points of affinity with the

Pythagorean and Platonic ideas as they were understood in the School of Alexandria. He combats Confucius, who recommended action, and makes perfection consist in inaction. Fortunately for China the ideas of Confucius prevailed; and its society, which was entirely founded on the family, continued to seek for material well-being by means of activity and labour.

In India philosophy began with the simple interpretation of the Vedas. This gave origin to the Mimansa School, which has left its monument in the Sutras or Aphorisms. Its next stage was the Vedanta, which rose to the interpretation of some of the metaphysical maxims contained in the Vedas, and which had for its founder Vyasa. The Vedanta philosophy, according to Colebrooke, was a refined psychology and metaphysic which advanced even to the denial of the existence of matter. Then arose the Nyaya system of philosophy, whose author was Gautama, and the Vaiseshika system, which was founded by Kanada. "Nyaya" means *reasoning*, and "Vaiseshika" means *distinction of parts*, that is, of the elements of the world; and accordingly the former is a system of dialectics, and the latter a system of physics. We have two Sankhya systems of philosophy: that of Kapila, which was irreligious in its results; and that called *Sankhya Yoga*, the head of which was Palandiadi, and which issued in Mysticism. Sankhya means *logos, ratio;* and the first of the two systems was called from its conclusion Nirdovara "*sine Deo;*" while the second was called Tesovara "*cum Deo.*"

All this philosophical development took place under Brahmanism, that is, the religion of Brahma. The Sanskrit scholar Weber distinguishes three periods in the history of this religion. During the first period the sacred hymns called the Vedas were written; the forces of nature were then worshipped, and the first principle was matter. The second period is called by Weber the phase of dualism; and in it, along with matter, which was considered as a sort of chaos, there was distinguished an ordering cause which had fixed matter (in Sanskrit *stalita*), that is, which had created it. In the third period, the world came to be considered as a simple emanation of God, and even as a species of illusion (*Maya*); and science taught men to liberate themselves from this illusion by means of the contemplative life.

This Brahmanic tendency to repose was pushed even to annihilation (*Nirvana*) by Buddhism, a religion which arose in the VI. Century B.C. It inculcated the duty of divesting oneself of existence by meditation and mortification. The common basis of Brahmanism and of Buddhism was the belief in the metempsychosis, but with the difference that the former promised a better existence, and the latter aspired after total annihilation. The most accurate investigations of Buddhism have discovered the complete atheism which is contained in this religious system.[1]

§ 2.

There is no doubt that Greece received its religious doctrines from the East, but that its philosophical development was indigenous.

Sensualism and Idealism show themselves clearly in the Ionic School, and in the Italic School of Pythagoras. Thales had constructed nature wholly and entirely out of the principle of water. Anaximenes, and later Diogenes of Apollonia, believed that this first element was found in air, a more refined principle. Heraclitus found it in the Fire which animates and destroys everything, and which

[1] Bournouf carefully notes that this doctrine appears in the third part of the Canon (the *Atidarma*), and not in the first (the *sutras* or aphorisms) nor in the second (*vinaia* or ethics), which together bore the name of *Dharma* or laws. He also observes that the whole of this part of the Canon is designated by the ancient authors as " not revealed by Buddha." On this Max Müller founds his contention that Buddha attached no other meaning to the word *nirvana* than *repose* or *place of immortality*. Buddha says: all that is created must disappear, must be decomposed; but it is not so with the not made, the not created, the *nirvana*. The successors of Buddha gave to this word the significance of *annihilation*.

generates the movement and variety through which everything passes, and into which everything is transformed.

Anaximander, Anaxagoras, and Archelaus of Miletus, started from an original material principle, ἄπειρον, from which, by means of chemical and mechanical combinations, everything arises, and to which everything returns. Anaxagoras recognised a superior principle, νοῦς, which moves the world without being separated from it. This mechanical explanation was completed by the Atomistic School of Leucippus and Democritus, which suppressed the moving intelligence. According to this School, the principles of things are the *plenum* and the *vacuum*. The *plenum* consists in atoms which are infinite in number and endowed with perpetual motion, and which by their aggregations compose beings. The soul is composed of subtle atoms, and sensation is the only source of our cognitions, bodies giving off atomistic emanations which penetrate into the brain and produce images of things.

The Pythagorean or Italic School, instead of keeping to phenomena, took to examining their relations. It is essentially mathematical, astronomical, and at the same time idealistic. Unity is the principle of all things: ἕν ἀρχή παντῶν. Contraries are the elements of every existence, but everything returns to harmony. Things are composed of perfection and of imperfection. The perfect number is the decad, which is God. The soul is the harmony of the body; it is not the result of the organism, but an emanation of the universal soul. It survives the organism and passes from body into body by metempsychosis.

The Eleatic School stands in the same relation to the Pythagorean School as the Atomistic School stands to the School of Iona; it was an exaggeration and a supplement of it. Pythagoras had signalised the harmony which reigns in the world as the manifestation of his principle. Xenophanes showed a predilection for unity; and Parmenides, perhaps without denying variety, ignores it entirely. Finally, Zeno denies variety, and consequently movement and the very existence of the world. To him is attributed the invention of Dialectic, which he applied negatively by striving to reduce the opinions of his adversaries to absurdity. Empedocles takes a step back, finds in nature the centripetal and centrifugal forces, discord and harmony, and celebrates the triumph of love, that is, of God.

The dialectic of Zeno had yet to bring forth its fruits. Protagoras, a sophist, drew from the Ionic sensualism its extreme consequences, and maintained that human consciousness only consists of the perception of the phenomenal, and that man is the measure of all things. Gorgias did the same by reference to the Italic idealism. Zeno had shown the nullity of sensible appearances by founding upon rational truths; Gorgias endeavoured to reduce the rational truths to simple appearances.

The Sophists had abused reasoning because they had strayed away from reality. Socrates called philosophy back to internal observation, saying that every one can be his own master if he is only led thereto by certain external circumstances, and especially by opportune interrogations. He applied himself to the perfecting of method in order that every one may depend upon himself, and may be able to give an account of the power and forms of reason. This method of Socrates brought forth the Dialectic of Plato and the Analytic of Aristotle. Plato seeks not only for the logical principles of science but for the real principles of things; and he uses Dialectic not only to combat the opinions of his adversaries, but in order to discover the highest principles. Plato discerns in the idea the essence of mundane things, as ideas constitute the intrinsic possibility and reason of these things and act as archetypal causes in the formation of all beings. Ideas have a separate existence and form a part of God. There are two interpretations of this doctrine of Plato. Some hold that ideas are concepts and attributes of God, a view which was held by Plutarch, Alcinous, and some of the Fathers of the Church. Others think that Plato gave to ideas an existence distinct from the world, and that God actualised them in creating them. This opinion has been followed by Aristotle and by the Scholastics, among whom were Albertus Magnus and Thomas Aquinas. Accordingly ideas are beings: τὰ ὄντως ὄντα, eternal and immutable essences that are visible to reason only. They are divine types of all things, and they all spring from the *idea of ideas*, εἶδος εἰδῶν, the supreme idea of unity and of goodness, τὸ ἕν, τὸ ἀγαθόν, which is the principle of physical and intellectual light. "At the extreme confines of the intellectual world," says Plato in the *Republic*, "there is the idea of the good which is perceived with difficulty, and which cannot be perceived without inferring that it is the cause of all that is good and beautiful; that in the visible world it produces the light, and the star from which light springs; and that in the invisible world it produces light and truth." God realised finitely the Idea of the Good in the world which He has produced and which He governs in His goodness and wisdom. The problem of knowledge is resolved in the following manner. Human souls before descending into the earthly life have directly beheld the ideas in the *Logos* or divine Word, and so the ideas are awakened in these souls through simple reminiscence by means of Dialectic.

Aristotle explains the formation of ideas by means of two faculties: Sense and Intellect. The senses have for their object singulars or individual things, and the intellect universals; the senses present the matter of cognitions to the intellect which forms ideas. Are ideas then a product of the human mind? How can the intellect evolve universals out of singulars, since these are diverse from each other? Aristotle replies that ideas are not a product of the human mind, but that the intellect by its abstractive power forms the universals from singulars, extracting from the latter what they have in common, because singulars are universals potentially. The singular or individual thing is not outside of the genus, but is the genus in actuality as it realises itself by becoming individual. We have still to note what Aristotle means by *matter* and by *form*. By matter he does not mean being that is extended, visible, tangible, and divisible, but the simple possibility of becoming something, that is, indeterminate being which becomes real by means of form. But the notions of matter and of form do not suffice to explain the universe; and therefore Aristotle accompanies them with the notions of efficient cause and of final cause. Every object is thus composed of matter and of form, united together by an efficient cause in view of a determinate end. The notion of efficient cause leads Aristotle to the demonstration of the existence of God, the first Cause that moves the world; and the notion of final cause reveals to him the wisdom which has ordered everything and which preserves everything. For it is by a mere inconsequence that he has isolated the world from God and has not recognised the divine providence.

After Plato and Aristotle, philosophy declined. Their systems were succeeded by Epicureanism and Stoicism, and these have this point in common, that they reduce philosophy to moral science. Epicurus reproduced the atomistic doctrine of Democritus, and founded private and social morality on utility. In the Stoical system, reason is the basis of humanity, of nature, and of God Himself, who is not distinct from Nature. Hence the practical rule *par excellence*, is to live according to reason, or, which comes to the same thing, according to nature, *naturam sequere*. This rule is summed up in two precepts: *sustine et abstine*, and it leads by another way to the egoism of Epicurus. The human mind could not stop long at this conclusion, and it fell into the Scepticism of the New Academy, which was developed principally by Arcesilaus, Carneades, Philo of Larissa, who started from idealism, and by Aenesidemus and Sextus Empiricus, who proceeded upon sensualism.

Reason, now weary, turned to the East and sought for

repose in mysticism. The philosophers of the School of Alexandria, Plotinus, Porphyry, Jamblichus, and Proclus, sought union with God by means of ecstacy. But as God was conceived as absolute unity, man could approach Him only by becoming absolute unity. Plato had put forth the idea that man ought to resemble God; the Alexandrians considered that he should be mingled with God, thus destroying all activity and all progress.

To the School of Alexandria the relations of man with God are those of the emanated to the emanating. Plotinus teaches that man has a consciousness of the infinite, but it is through the medium of the contingent Ego, of which he has to divest himself in order to rise to the absolute. God does not produce from need, because He is sufficient to Himself; nor from desire, because He has nothing to desire. He does not generate by necessity, because He is Himself the necessity and the law for other beings. The God of Plotinus therefore generates by His own nature, that is, by something which is superior to liberty and to necessity. He begins to generate the most perfect, and gradually comes to the more imperfect. He therefore generates Intellect, which is His Son, and differs the least of all from Him; then He generates the Soul or Spirit, which also differs little from intellect. These three hypostases, or divine substances, are unequal in the relation of metaphysical anteriority, although they are all three eternal. It is easy to recognise in the first person the God of Plato; in the second the God of Aristotle, and in the third the God of the Stoics. The third person, or the Soul, produces the world, proceeding from things more perfect to those that are more imperfect. These last, however, tend always to perfection, and convert themselves gradually into the more perfect, until they are mingled with the hypostases themselves, which return again into the One.

Porphyry seeks to reconcile Plato with Aristotle, but always in a pantheistic sense. He maintains that the incorporeal rules bodies, and that the soul is found present

everywhere, and can act at any distance. Jamblichus
exaggerates this tendency into a theurgy, and falls into
the grossest superstitions. Proclus tries in vain to reani-
mate the expiring philosophic thought by decomposing
the divine order into so many intermediary beings, because
everything springs from emanation and all returns to it.
What he calls providence can be only regarded as fate.[1]

§ 3.

But a new light had appeared for mankind in Christianity. It began by speaking to the heart and purifying
the morals of men; but it was not slow to make an alliance with philosophy. The cardinal elements of the new
religion are creation and the incarnation, which bring the
creature near to God without confounding it with Him.
"The divine Word is reason, and all the human race participates in it," exclaimed Justin Martyr. "In virtue of
this germinal reason arising from the Word, the ancient
sages were able to teach at times beautiful truths; because
all that the philosophers and legislators have said or found
of good, they owed to a partial intuition or knowledge of
the Word. Socrates, for example, knew Christ in a certain
way, because the Word penetrates into everything with
its influence. This is why the doctrines of Plato are not
contrary to those of Christ, although they are not by any
means the same." Instead of rejecting the philosophical
doctrines, Justin Martyr endeavours to bring them into
agreement, and he manifestly inclines to Pythagoras and
Plato. Clement of Alexandria and Origen continued this
species of eclecticism, but the Church found something
exaggerated in Justin's views and something false in
Origen. Lactantius proclaimed that there was no religion
without philosophy, as there could be no sound philosophy
without religion.

---

[1] See besides the original works *Histoire de l'École d'Alexandrie*, Rit-
Cousin's *Histoire générale de la phi-* ter's *History of Ancient Philosophy*,
losophie*, Ravaisson's *Essai sur la* Zeller's *History of Greek Philosophy*,
métaphysique d'Aristote*, Vacherot's and other Histories.

The Christian Trinity differs from the Alexandrian, for it considers the three divine hypostases as equal and co-eternal. The Son, the Word or Intelligence, cannot be inferior to the Father from whom He proceeds, any more than the Spirit or Love; because otherwise the perfect could generate only the imperfect. The Christian Trinity resembles a circle eternally closed; and the creation of the world takes place in virtue of the divine Love, which is entirely free from any need or desire. This difference produces important moral consequences, because it lays down, as the dominant principle, love to God and love to men from regard to God.

The Christian writers in general are divided into Monks, or solitary ascetics who aimed at the purification of morals, Apologists who combated the doctrines contrary to the new faith, Fathers who accepted the aid of philosophy, and Doctors who made it their principal stay. Over them all towers St. Augustine, who combines in himself the mysticism of the solitaries, the argumentative vigour of the apologists, the authority of the fathers, and the metaphysics of the doctors. St. Augustine perfected the Platonic doctrine with regard to ideas by removing all doubt as to the place of the ideas, since from the uncertainty of the Platonic language it seemed that the λόγος was not consubstantial with God, and that ideas existed in themselves and by themselves. Moreover he destroyed the hypothesis of a pre-mundane life by establishing the view that the human mind perceives the ideas in God by direct, immediate, actual, and continuous intuition. Here are his words: " Probabilius est propterea vere respondere de quibusdam disciplinis etiam imperitos earum, quando bene interrogantur quia praesens est eis quantum id capere possunt, lumen rationis aeternae, ubi haec immutabilia vera conspiciunt" (*Petr. Lib.* I. c. 4). Elsewhere he says: " Sunt ideae principales formae quaedam vel rationes rerum stabiles atque incommutabiles, quae ipsae formatae sunt ac per hoc aeternae, ac semper eodem modo sees

habentes quæ in divina intelligentia continentur." Descending to psychology, Augustine shows that the existence
of the Ego is inseparable from thought, and that the senses
and sensation are a necessary condition of the exercise of
intelligence, and not the matter of all cognitions.

The calamities of the times that followed turned away
the thoughts of men from philosophy. Meanwhile the
reign of Plato was being succeeded by that of Aristotle.
The Alexandrians who had largely taken from Plato, but
at the same time corrupting his original doctrine, turned
round to Aristotle. Porphyry had sought to reconcile
the two systems. Maximus, the teacher of the Emperor
Julian, Proclus, and Damascius, were almost Peripatetics.
The Commentators, Themistius, Syrianus, David the
Armenian, Simplicius, John Philoponus—in a word, the
second generation of the School of Alexandria—had gone
over to the Stagirite, and established him as an authority
which lasted more than ten centuries. Boëthius, by his
translation of Porphyry's *Isagoge*, or Introduction to the
Categories of Aristotle, formed the transition from ancient
to mediæval times. A passage of this work, which puts
the question whether genera and species exist by themselves or only in the intellect, and whether they exist
separate from sensible objects or make a part of these
objects, served as a text for the Scholastic Philosophy.[1]

§ 4

Scholasticism has three distinct epochs. The first epoch
extends from the XI. to the XIII. Century, and in it
philosophy is the *Ancilla theologiae;* the second extends
from the XIII. to the XIV. Century, and in it the two
sciences are rather regarded as allies; and the third extends from the XV. to the first years of the XVI. Century, and in this period their complete separation began.
Scholasticism, in general, may be defined as the alliance

[1] See Ritter's *History of Christian Philosophy.*

of the Christian dogma with the philosophy of Aristotle. This does not mean that Plato was entirely forgotten, but his influence was then less. Plato continued to reign through the medium of Augustine, and thus produced Anselm and Bonaventura. The demonstration *à priori* of the existence of God, which constitutes the most original title of Anselm, was rejected by Scholasticism. Anselm treated this subject twice: first in his *Monologium,* where he expounds the demonstration of Plato, which consists in rising from the more imperfect goods to the Supreme Good, to perfect being, by passing from the contingent to the necessary. In his *Proslogium* he demonstrates the existence of God from the mere idea of God, as has been done again by Descartes; and this forms the most convincing proof of the Theodicy. Before Anselm, the influence of Plato had produced Scotus Erigena, who translated the spurious writings attributed to Dionysius Areopagita, and represented God as the substance of all things. From Scotus and the pseudo-Dionysius sprang the Pantheists, Amaury de Chartres and David of Dinant.

The great problem of the Scholastic Philosophy was based upon the passage of Porphyry we have indicated, and it was brought forward about the end of the XI. Century by the Canon Roscellinus, who said that the genus was a simple abstraction formed by the mind uniting in one common idea what the various individuals have all alike; and thus he created *Nominalism.* From this view he inferred that there is no reality except in the individual ; and thus the unity which forms the basis of the mystery of the Trinity became nominal, only the three individual persons existing. Anselm hastened to combat the new system, by writing a treatise on the mystery of the Trinity. William of Champaux, going to the other extreme, maintained that genera were not mere empty words ; but, on the contrary, that they were the only entities (*res*), and that they were found entire in the individuals (*eadem essentialiter tota simul*), and that the individuals, identical

in their essence, differ only by their accidental elements
(*sola multitudinis accidentium varietate*). This system was
called *Realism*.[1] Then came Abelard, who, although recognising the reality of genera, maintained that they existed
only in the mind, which makes an abstraction from what
the individuals have in common; and thus he created
Conceptualism. He made the boldest applications of these
theories, explaining the Trinity philosophically by reducing the three persons to simple attributes of being, namely,
power, wisdom, and goodness,—which attributes united
together form perfect being. This was the heresy of the
unity of the persons as opposed to that of Roscellinus, who
seemed to maintain three Gods; and hence Abelard was
condemned by the Councils of Soissons and of Sens, and
retired to end his life in a cloister.

The Church sought to guide the philosophical movement
which it was not able to suppress. The institution of the
two orders of St. Dominic and St. Francis gave origin to
two schools, the first of which reckoned among its members
Albertus Magnus and Thomas Aquinas, while the second
claimed Alexander of Hales, Bonaventura, Duns Scotus,
Roger Bacon, and Raymond Lullus. The Middle Ages
had possessed the *Organon* or *Logic* of Aristotle, and it
was enriched by the discovery of his other works, namely,
the *De Anima*, the *Metaphysics*, and the *Natural History*
which came to light in the time of the Crusades. These
treatises had been hitherto known in Europe only in the
expositions of Arabian commentators. The Arabians accepted the Greek encyclopædia of knowledge as it existed
at that time, and they knew Aristotle only through the
medium of the School of Alexandria. This knowledge was
not direct, and it could not be exact. Thus Avicenna and
Averroës interpreted Aristotle in a pantheistic sense, while
Avicebron interpreted him in a materialistic sense. Alber-

---

[1] What was called Realism in the
Middle Ages is now called Idealism,
as the system which makes the principle of all knowledge and of all
reality consist in the idea.

tus Magnus expounded his position in the treatise *De unitate Intellectus*, and the struggle was continued by his disciple, Thomas Aquinas. Thomas Aquinas sets out from the Aristotelian distinction of the passive and active intellect. The soul is a *tabula rasa*, and the images gathered by the senses and the imagination (two faculties which form the passive intellect) are subtle species which are converted into intelligible species by means of the active intellect. Sensation therefore furnishes the matter, but is not sufficient to create knowledge, which requires the concurrence of the action of the intellect. *Intellectiva cognitio fit a sensibili non sicut a materia causae.* The active intellect *facit phantasmata a sensibus accepta intelligibilia;* and thus it perceives unity in particular objects. "Necesse est ad hoc quod intellectus acta intelligat suum objectum proprium, quod convertat se ad phantasmata ut speculetur naturam universalem in particulari existentem." We have therefore only particular ideas, and by abstraction, generalisation, and induction, we rise from the particular to the universal. Thomas does not deny the universal, but he connects the species and genera with their supreme principle, making them concepts of the divine intelligence, the archetypes of creation; and he says expressly that the intelligible light contained in the active intellect is an emission of the divine substance. In this way Thomas Aquinas became a Platonist without knowing it. He admits the proof of the existence of God from the principle of motion; but he corrects Aristotle by adding that God cannot remain external to the universe, since He would not know Himself completely if He did not know the extent of His power and of His will, the one of which is the cause of possible beings, and the other of existing beings. He resolves the problem of individualisation by a triple principle. For sensible objects, it is matter which determines the form; for pure spirits, it is the simplicity of their essence; for the human soul, it is the tendency to unite itself to a determinate body. It would have been much more simple if he had had recourse to the creative act.

Alexander of Hales founded the Franciscan School. He was one of the first to take advantage of the translations of Aristotle made by the Arabians, and he left commentaries on the *Sentences* of Petrus Lombardus, which, after the approval of ten doctors, were recommended by Innocent IV. to all the schools of Christendom. Bonaventura is the most eminent thinker of this school. He unfolds the profoundest reasoning on the idea of God, making this idea the foundation of certainty, on the ground that the Word of God not only gives us the knowledge of primitive truths, but also that of deduced truths, which are connected with the former.

Duns Scotus represents individuals as arising from the union of matter and form. But the determinate cause of this union is placed by him in a particular entity, which his disciples called *Hœcceitas*, which is the principle of individualisation. The universal is contained not only potentially (*posse*) but really (*actu*) in objects; it is not created by intelligence, but is reality itself. He maintains the principle of indifference, and considers moral truths as well as the creation to be dependent only on the will of God.

The efforts of Roger Bacon and of Raymond Lully, may be regarded as a reaction from the excessive realism of Duns Scotus. Roger Bacon cultivated by preference the natural and mathematical sciences, and had a presentiment of the principal discoveries of modern times. He proclaimed the principle that art should imitate nature, and he was the precursor of the discovery of the experimental method. Raymond Lully wished to find formulae by which to attain to universal science in his *Ars Magna*, a sort of alphabet of abstract ideas, and of logical subjects, and attributes, which, divided into certain circles, united or divided by certain lines, were to furnish middle terms for all reasonings.

The open struggle between religion and philosophy begins with William of Occam, who revived and advocated Nominalism. He held that genera could exist only in things, or in God. In things they would be either the whole or the part; but in the first case, there would not be individuals, and in the second case, the part would be a genus. In God they could not exist as an independent essence, but as a simple object of knowledge. After dealing with universals he attacked another celebrated theory, that of sensible or intelligible species, which the philosophy of the time believed to be the intermediaries of ideas. Occam recognised no other intermediary but speech. As regards the mind, he knows it only by its attributes, and is not able to maintain that it is a material or an immaterial being.

Among the most celebrated Nominalists we may mention Buridanus and Pierre d'Ailly. After them there sprang up an indifference which may be regarded as a kind of scepticism, until the movement culminated in thorough mysticism in Gerson and Thomas à Kempis.

Throwing a general glance over the Scholastic Philosophy, we find in it the characteristics both of progress and of barbarism. It is progressive in so far as it indirectly revives the ancient systems, seeking to reconcile them with Christianity. It is barbarous in so far as it seeks certainty in the external forms of reasoning; and so much so that it may be correctly said that its form stifles its matter, and its reason is oppressed by the syllogism. For example, the question of Universals had presented itself to the philosophers of antiquity, and had been resolved according to the different schools, but the problem of individualisation had not entered into the mind of any of them. The Middle Ages not only distinguished the particular from the general, but, following Aristotle, the leading minds of the time were long occupied in distinguishing the form from the matter in the particular. Thus they wished to find out by virtue of what principle the particular separated itself from the universal, and if it drew its origin from form or from matter. Hence they devised hypotheses, as we have seen in the case of Thomas Aquinas, instead of simply having recourse to the creative act. Other schools denied the universals, saying they were empty words or mere concepts of our mind, thus ignoring the immutable order which the particular beings manifest, and which is reflected in nature under the double form of classes and laws, and in our mind by those general ideas whose eternal exemplar exists in the divine intellect. But the principles of reason, through the medium of the philosophical ideas of antiquity, were to break through the hard shell which surrounded them; and this work was reserved for the Renaissance.[1]

§ 5.

The XVI. Century was a revolutionary century; it differs from the XVIII. Century only in that it was not conscious of the fact. The Council of Florence, which aimed at the reconciliation of the Greek Church with the Latin Church, had given occasion in the preceding century for many Greeks coming to Italy, and they spoke of the treasures of antiquity which they still possessed intact. The taking of Constantinople increased the number of the Greeks who settled in Italy, and they brought precious manuscripts with them. But such a circumstance, entirely material as it was, does not suffice to explain the great movement of ideas which was furthered, but not created, by the arrival of the Greeks.

This movement was really occasioned by that restlessness of mind which was striving absolutely to break the fetters which held it enchained. War was declared on Scholasticism, as well as on many of the traditions of the

---

[1] See Haureau, *Histoire de la philosophie scolastique;* Rousselot, *Études sur la philosophie du moyen âge;* Cousin, *Fragments de philo-* *sophie scolastique;* Jourdain, *La philosophie de Saint Thomas d'Aquin;* and other works.

past; and under the guise of antiquity the most extravagant ideas were expounded. The principal sources from which thinkers drew were the two great schools of Greece, those of Aristotle and Plato. But these two great authors now showed themselves under a new aspect. We have already said that the Middle Ages for a long time had known only the *Organon* of Aristotle, and that his other works were only indirectly known through the medium of the Arabians who had principally drawn from the School of Alexandria, which had sought to attenuate the differences that divided Aristotle from Plato. But hardly had the power been acquired to read all the writings of Aristotle which survived in the original, as well as the Commentaries of Simplicius and Alexander Aphrodisiensis, than a more truthful idea was obtained of the philosophy of the Stagirite. No system has given rise to so many controversies as that of Aristotle, which in the present day is still held by some to be materialistic and by others to be idealistic. On the one side it is shown how he unites thought with the body, and that he believes digestion and thinking spring from the same cause; from which it follows that man, when he loses the organic life, loses memory and consciousness, and is therefore incapable of immortality. It is added that he holds matter to be co-eternal with God; and that he maintains that God did not create the world, but remains absolutely alien to it. On the other side it is alleged that Aristotle certainly recognises an invisible principle, simple and one; that this principle is thought, and that it governs the body; and, moreover, that the principal idea of his philosophy and of his theodicy is that of final cause, as he recognises in nature an ascending scale of beings. Above man and nature he puts a Being who owes his movement to his own power, an absolute and immaterial intelligence, an immovable mover of the universe. All this is contrary to materialism. The second interpretation had predominated in the Middle Ages, and the first prevailed during the Renaissance. Two great

Peripatetic Schools arose in the University of Padua, the centre of the movement. The one which followed the Commentator Alexander the Aphrodisian included Pomponatius, Cremonini, Zabarella, and Vanini, while the other which followed Averroës included Achillini, Cesalpino, and Zimara, and they regarded Aristotle as an enemy of orthodoxy.

Plato, on the contrary, had been well interpreted by the first Fathers of the Church, and by Augustine and Anselm. And now he was revived as transformed by the Neo-Platonic School of Alexandria, and he was therefore represented as antagonistic to Christianity. It would be erroneous to confound the God of the Dialectic of Plato with the absolute Unity which is without determinations, and therefore without thought, without action, and without life. This is the Dialectic of the School of Elea, as it was resuscitated by the Alexandrians in conjunction with the method of Plato. The Platonic Dialectic is not a simple logical process, but an experimental and rational method which sets out from the living reality, and on the wings of reminiscence rises to the Ideas, that is to say, to the absolute types of existence and to the principle of all the ideas, which is the Good. Certainly Plato has not well defined the relations of man to God, because he did not know the principle of creation which was brought into philosophy by Christianity; and on this point we see the Platonic doctrine of ideas improved by Augustine, and we shall see that it is completed by Gioberti. Hence the Renaissance resuscitated a false Plato; and thus it was that Gemistus Pletho confounded Plato with Zoroaster. Marsilius Ficinus, the founder of the Platonic Academy of Florence, oscillated between Plato and Plotinus, and believed in good faith that he could reconcile them. Pico della Mirandola applied mystical theories to the cosmogony of Moses. Patricius accumulated a thousand extravagances under the names of Plato and Hermes. Bessarion and the Cardinal of Cusa, wishing to defend Plato, confused his doctrines with those of Aristotle and Plotinus.

Nevertheless in Cusanus there are found the germs of the infiuitesimal theory, and there is much that is peculiar in his doctrines.

The most original author of this period was Giordano Bruno. To the logic of Aristotle he opposed a new logic after the outlines of Raymond Lully; to the astronomy of Ptolemy he opposed that of Copernicus and of Pythagoras; to the physics of Aristotle, with its finite world and its incorruptible heaven, he opposed the idea of an infinite world, subject to an eternal evolution; to the Christian religion, the religion of grace and of the spirit, he opposed a religion of nature without a cultus, without an altar, and without a God. Bruno did not create a well-connected system, but he transmitted to Descartes the notion of methodic doubt and evidence as the criterion of truth; to Spinoza the idea of an immanent God; to Leibniz the germ of the theory of monads and of optimism; to Schelling the famous expressions *natura naturante* and *natura naturata;* and, lastly, to Hegel the conception that a secret logic presides over the order of the universe, that whoever attains to a comprehension of the first elements of thought and the necessary laws of the various combinations of ideas, renders himself master of everything, and that God is the absolute coincidence, the supreme harmony of contraries, the *indifferentia oppositorum.* It may be added that in the material and physical sciences he caught glimpses of the centre of gravity of the planets, of the orbits of the comets, and of the irregularity in the sphericity of the earth; and he perhaps also gave the first idea of vortices. Thus it will be seen how well Bruno deserved the title which he gave to himself of *Excubitor.*

Telesio and Campanella, other two Italians, were also precursors of the modern epoch. Bernardino Telesio published a work entitled *De natura juxta propria principia,* in which he proclaimed that it is necessary to start from real, not abstract beings, *entia realia non abstracta,* and he combated the physics of Aristotle. Campanella trans-

ferred to psychology the axiom which Telesio had applied
to physics, and formed a system which resembles the
sensualism of Condillac. He says that human knowledge
naturally begins from real things, and therefore that sensation is knowledge. Nothing, then, should be presupposed
as certain and known; and consequently we ought to
doubt everything, even our own existence. Hence Cousin
has well said that "when we read the life and the works
of Telesio and of Campanella, we feel that Bacon and
Descartes are not far off." [1]

The Renaissance had its sceptics and its mystics, like
every other period in the history of philosophy. Of the
former we may mention Sanchez, Montaigne, and Char-
ron. Among the latter the first position is taken by the
Cardinal Nicolas of Cusa, who, although a Neo-Platonist
in the strongest sense of the term, is reckoned among the
mystics on account of his book *De Docta Ignorantia*, the
chief argument of which is that finite being cannot embrace
the infinite. Then come Reuchlin, who mixes up Platonic,
Pythagorean, and Cabalistic ideas; Agrippa, who openly
teaches magic; Paracelsus and Cardan, who busy themselves with alchemy and astronomy in order to discover
an occult philosophy; Van Helmont, who reproduces
Paracelsus; and Fludd, who seeks to reconcile him with
the book of Genesis interpreted allegorically. Finally,
Jacob Böhme in 1612 published his *Aurora*, in which he
seeks to demonstrate the impossibility of attaining to truth
without a heavenly inspiration, the identity of the human
soul with God, the difference between them being only in
form ; and he gives a symbolical exposition of Christianity.

Thus the philosophy of the Renaissance, under manifest
imitation of the systems of antiquity, already gives us a
feeling of the new life. [2]

[1] Victor Cousin, *Histoire générale
de la philosophie, Leçon onzième,*
12me edition. Paris, 1884.
[2] See Buhle, *Histoire de la philo-*
sophie moderne jusqu' à Kant. Paris,
1861. Burckhardt, *Die Cultur der
Renaissance in Italien.* Stuttgart,
1878.

§ 6.

The modern philosophy takes its beginning from Bacon and Descartes, because the method of these two philosophers brought about new inquiries. But in order to be just, it must be admitted that these two philosophers did nothing but formulate what the philosophy of the Renaissance had so far anticipated. And in fact, if their principal merit consists in having overthrown the authority of Aristotle, and in having completely separated philosophy from religion, how is it possible to leave out of account what had been done by the Renaissance? In general, we may say that the Sixteenth Century discovers, the Seventeenth Century reorders, the Eighteenth Century destroys, and the Nineteenth Century tries to rebuild.

Bacon transplanted into England the spirit of reform which had been awakened in Italy by Telesio and Campanella, and which had been applied by Galileo. The method of Bacon is observation, or more exactly, it is experience, because he would have nature dissected and anatomised. Induction is the logical process by which we advance from the particular to the general, from phenomena to their laws; and it is warmly recommended by Bacon. We may quote the following words of the *Instauratio Magna* to show that Bacon did not exclude reason, although he gave the preference to experience: "I believe that I have wedded the empirical method and the rational method, the divorce of which is fatal to science and to humanity."

Hobbes, Gassendi, and Locke are connected with the School of Bacon, inasmuch as it may be asserted that these three writers carried the spirit of Bacon into the various departments of philosophy: Hobbes carrying it into politics, Gassendi into learning, and Locke into metaphysics. The philosophical principles of Hobbes are extremely simple, as he only admits bodies: *Subjectum philosophiae est corpus omne.* The phenomena of intelligence are corporeal, being produced by the impressions of bodies. Sensation presents us with objects; man adds or subtracts by means of reasoning, but he has no certainty with regard to what the senses present to him. Liberty is only the determination of appetite, and the state of nature is a state of war, man being the enemy of man, while laws and justice are the creation of the social contract.

Gassendi was a scholar after the manner of the preceding century, and his whole life was spent in renewing the philosophy of Epicurus and in combating Descartes.

Locke was led to devote himself to philosophical inquiry by a question which was raised in a private conversation, and which remained unsolved. He thought that the difficulty involved arose from making use of ideas that were not well defined; and enlarging this observation, he said that as we make use of the mind in philosophy, it is therefore necessary to study it. He assigns two sources to human knowledge: sensation and reflection. Reflection is applied to the operations of the mind, and it makes us know what they are, that is to say, as sensation presents them to us. Locke closes the XVII. Century, and before taking up his successors we must take a step backwards in order to examine the doctrine of Descartes.

The method of Descartes embraces four rules : 1. To trust only to evidence; 2. To divide objects as much as possible (which Bacon called dissecting and anatomising nature); 3. To make many enumerations, even as extensive and varied as may be possible; 4. To reconstitute a system with the parts already divided and examined. Everything is reduced to employing analysis and synthesis in order to attain to evidence. Applying this method, he seeks to demonstrate existence by means of thought with his famous *Cogito ergo sum*, without considering that thought is a phenomenon, and that it does not advance from the sphere of simple perceptions. What is the character of thought? It is to be invisible, intangible, imponderable, unextended, simple. Now, as we may conclude from the attribute to the subject, and as thought is an attribute of the Ego, the simplicity of the one is the simplicity of the other; and in this manner he demonstrates the spirituality of the mind. He admits innate ideas, not in the sense attributed to them by Hobbes and by Locke: that is to say, not as present to our mind from the first day of its existence, but as existing in germ in all intelligences and awakened in certain circumstances. Descartes may be considered as the father of that system which has since been called *subjectivism* or psychologism.

Reflecting on his own thought, Descartes rises to the idea of God; for although thought is imperfect and finite, he nevertheless discovers in it the idea of the perfect and infinite, appropriating the celebrated demonstration of Anselm. He therefore attributes to God a liberty of indifference, holding that He is not subject to any law, not even to that of the good. No being in any moment possesses in himself the reason of its own existence, nor are mathematical and moral truths in any way independent of God, who can change them at any moment. The world being imperfect has its origin from the perfect, that is to say, it has been created by God. Every truth and every existence accordingly depends on the will of God. Man finds the nature of truth and of goodness established and determinated by God. The criterion of certainty which is found, as we have already said, in evidence, can only be subjective. There exists another objective criterion of truth which serves as the basis of all, and Descartes finds it in the divine veracity. According to Descartes, the only reason which we have for believing that our thought is conformable to things, and that the internal evidence corresponds to the external reality, is the idea of an absolute principle which produces both the laws of thought and the laws of being, and which, as eternally willing the truth and eternally manifesting it with the creation, is eternally truthful.

Hence in his definition of "substance," which he repre-

sents as a "thing which exists *per se*," he has in view only
the divine substance, as neither the human soul nor matter
exists of or through itself. The fundamental attributes
of substance are defined to be "extension" and "thought,"
and he denies matter every kind of force. He denies also
the possibility of a mutual action between the two substances, the divine and the created, which he has separated
by an abyss. The soul cannot excite any movement in
the mechanism of things, but can only change a pre-exis-
tent motion. God has arranged the things that are out of
us in such a way that they present themselves to our
senses at a given moment, and He knows that our free-
will will determine itself in a certain manner according to
the occasion. Here we have the germ of the "Occasional
Causes" of Malebranche, and of the "Pre-established Harmony" of Leibniz.

Malebranche sought to establish more completely the
harmony between thought and reality by identifying the
intelligible with the real, and by demonstrating that internal truth is but a reflex of the absolute truth. He says
that "*nothing*" is neither intelligible nor visible; whence
it follows that all that is seen clearly, directly, and immediately, necessarily exists. Malebranche returns to
Plato, maintaining that we do not see things in themselves,
but in their ideas or eternal possibilities. Passing from
idea to idea, from possibility to possibility, we reach a
Being which cannot be conceived as simply possible, since
it does not arise from any superior being. We cannot
conceive God, he says, as simply possible; nothing can
contain Him or represent Him; and if He is thought, it
is a sign that He exists. In other words, God is possible
and intelligible through Himself; and other things are
only intelligible through God. We think of things only
in their intelligibility, or in their idea; and hence we
think them in God, while we think God in Himself,
although we do not perceive Him in any higher idea, as
He is the Idea of ideas, the Being that is absolutely in-

telligible and absolutely real. When we think of God, He is present without any medium to our thought; and when we see or perceive things, we see them in God as in an eternal light. Hence this system has been called that of *ideal vision*, as maintaining " the vision of all things in God." As all activity is attributed to the absolute being, bodies cannot act on us, nor we upon bodies; and they are only the occasion or " occasional causes" of our impressions, of which God alone is the efficient cause. Our own will itself is only an occasion of the movement of our organs which God alone moves, since we are only thinking machines; and God Himself is only an eternal geometrician and an artist. Hence it has been well said by a recent French writer that " Malebranche is Spinoza arrested halfway by faith, or an illogical and unconscious Spinoza." [1]

Spinoza was a Jew, and as such he knew the philosophy of the Cabbala and the philosophy which his fellow-countrymen had derived from the Arabs. That philosophy denied the attributes of God in order to escape from Anthropomorphism, while it makes of man an abstraction, and considers the world as eternal and infinite. It is easy to recognise in it the Oriental pantheism that had sprung from a false interpretation of Aristotle, and which spread over the coasts of Asia and Africa and then into the schools of Spain. It disturbed the University of Paris in the XII. Century through the writings of Amaury de Chartres and of David de Dinant, and it exercised the University of Padua in the XVI. Century in connection with the works of numerous Peripatetics. The most illustrious representative of this philosophy among the Arabs was Averroës. It was represented among the Hebrews by Maimonides, whereas Avicebron remained unaffected by the Arabian influence, and rather represents the orthodox national philosophy with a shade of Neo-Platonism.

The system of Spinoza may be summed up as follows.

---

[1] Fouillée, *Études sur l'histoire de la philosophie.* Paris, 1875.

Substance is what exists of itself and through itself, and which needs nothing in order to exist. This is the definition of Descartes. It follows that it is *sui causa,* that is, it cannot be produced by any cause; and it is eternal and infinite, and therefore unique, as two infinite substances cannot be admitted. This one sole substance is God. God alone is free, because He exists only by the necessity of His own nature, and determines Himself to act of and through Himself. The attributes of God are spirit and matter, as Descartes had found thought and extension to be the attributes of substance. God, considered as free and determining cause, is called *natura naturans,* and all that springs from the divine essence is called *natura naturata,* terms already used by Bruno. Thought, will, desire are modes which belong to the *natura naturata,* since God has neither thought in act nor will properly so called. There are no final causes, as God could not produce things differently from those which He has produced, nor could He set before Himself any end. Man is a being who exists only *in actu ;* the body is a mode of extension, and the soul is the collection of affections which emanate from the body and produce ideas, from the most confused to the most clear, which is that of God.

Leibniz found philosophy divided into two camps. Sensualism was represented by Locke ; and idealism, inaugurated by Descartes, came to a melancholy issue in Spinoza and in Malebranche. Leibniz aimed at a reconciliation of the systems. He began by combating Locke, and to the axiom *nihil est in intellectu quod prius non fuerit in sensu* he added *nisi intellectus ipse,* thereby saving intelligence and necessary and universal ideas. He then attacked the theory of Descartes, which assigned extension to matter as its essential attribute, whereas according to him it is force which constitutes the essence of every material substance. He reduces the universe to a complex of forces, which he calls "monads." These monads, hierarchically arranged and created at a single time, are effulgences of the Deity, placed between the creation which has taken place by the goodness of God and annihilation which the goodness of God prevents. They contain an infinite multitude of obscure perceptions which make them, as it were, a representative mirror of the universe; and the development of intelligence consists in rendering these perceptions clear and distinct. But how are these monads moved, and in what relation do they stand to each other? God, the great Monad, has arranged everything in accordance with a *pre-established harmony.* This hypothesis ruins the whole system, for it reduces man to a spiritual automaton almost in the same way and degree as Descartes, Spinoza, and Malebranche had done. In this way God is the author of reality and of the knowledge of the external world, but in a fashion that is entirely mechanical. Leibniz believed that he had saved everything, and that he had harmonised the sensible world with the intelligible world; whereas he remained in the sensible world alone, that is, in the sphere of internal fact or of the internal phenomenon of the representative power of the monad.

In Italy, Vico combated the philosophy of Descartes, and recalled thinkers to Ontology. He sought to connect his ideas with those of the ancient philosophers, Pythagoras and the Italic Zeno, whom he confounds with Zeno the Stoic. Pythagoras saw in numbers, which resolve themselves into unity, the principles of things; and Zeno admitted a substance incapable of division which exists equally under all things. Vico called this substance the metaphysical point; because, just as the mathematical point (which is a pure abstraction) gives origin to a world of numbers and of figures, so the metaphysical point is . the radical virtue of bodies, and has the power of extension and of motion, although remaining undivided under all magnitudes and extensions, and it explains to us the whole of creation. It is therefore an indivisible power of extension; and although unextended, it is capable of extension, and it serves as a mean between beings and

God, by whom it is called forth. The metaphysical points of Vico are accordingly the created essences of things. They are their substance, and to them properly belongs the *virtus extensionis et motus* by means of which individual things are produced; and they are created essences which are dispositions of God the Creator, in whom they are purest activity (actus purissimus).

Passing to the theory of knowledge, Vico begins by distinguishing *intelligere* from *cogitare*. *Intelligere* is *scire per causas*, and is the *proprium* of God; *cogitare* is collecting the elements of truth that are in things, and it is the proprium of human minds. He adds that truth *ad intra* is convertible with that which is generated, and truth *ad extra* is convertible with fact, which means that the divine origin of ideas happens by means of generation, and their human origin by means of creation. The elements of all divine and human knowledge are three, namely, knowing, willing, and having power to act, the sole principle of which is the mind whose eye is reason illuminated by God. God possesses infinite knowledge, will, and power; man has finite knowledge, will, and power, which tends to the infinite. Man has necessary knowledge, but free will and power. He begins with the *certain* and ends with the *true;* that is to say, he first believes and works, and then he reflects and judges. The intellect produces the idea; the will, the fact; and as they thus set out from a common centre, there ought to be a necessary harmony between them. These principles have been very happily applied by Vico to morals, law, and history.

Scepticism was represented in the XVII. Century by . Huet, Bishop of Avranches, Hirnham, Glanville, Pascal, and Bayle. The scepticism of the first two is comparatively slight, but Glanville examines and confutes dogmatism with reference to the idea of cause, and opens the way to Hume. Pascal is sceptical with regard to reason, but he is tormented by a great need of faith. Bayle is the ideal of the learned sceptics. He attacked everything with great fertility of argument; and he was the precursor of Voltaire.

Mysticism is manifested under its metaphysical and moral form in Poiret, who takes as its basis the impotence of reason and the corruption of the will. Hence arises the necessity of receiving everything from God as truth by means of faith and revelation, and virtue by means of grace. Gale and Henry More make truth wholly consist in revelation. Pordage reproduces Böhme; and Swedenborg develops mysticism under all its aspects, metaphysical, moral, naturalistic, and allegorical.

§ 7.

We have now reached the XVIII. Century, which has left so great an impression in history as the demolisher of the past. Luther believed that he had restricted free inquiry or individual criticism in the religious sphere. Descartes applied it to philosophy, but he took care to remove all suspicion of dealing with the political order of the States. "These great bodies," he said, "are too difficult to raise again when they are overthrown, and their fall would be ruinous; and therefore I could not approve of those restless minds that are always thinking of reforms. My design has never been extended beyond the reform of my own thought, as I wished to build on a foundation that was my own exclusive property." In contrast to this the XVIII. Century wished to overthrow everything in order to reconstruct it all again, including religion, society, and government.

Empiricism could not be arrested by the hypotheses of Leibniz. In England, Collins, a disciple of Locke, denied the liberty of man. Dodwell advanced a demonstration of the materiality of the soul, founding upon an observation of Locke that it is not impossible for matter to think. Mandeville, finding in Locke the theory of the useful as the sole basis of virtue, concluded that there was no essential

distinction between virtue and vice. Hartley and Erasmus
Darwin connected the intellectual man with the physical
man, and identified matter and mind. Godwin and Bentham are the political writers of this school.

In France, Condillac was the father of sensualism. In
his " Essay on the Origin of Human Cognitions " (*Essai sur
l'origine de connaissances humaines*), he follows in the footsteps of Locke, distinguishing in man two series of ideas :
those that come from sensation, and those that take
origin from the mind turning upon its own operations;
although he grants it a certain amount of activity, which
he afterwards denied it in his " Treatise on Sensations "
(*Traité de Sensations*). The soul is at the outset a *tabula
rasa*, and all ideas come from experience. This is the
common principle of Locke and of Condillac. But in the
formation of the ideas which come to impress themselves
on this *tabula rasa*, one calls forth activity and another
suppresses it. Condillac supposes a statue to be organised
internally as we are, and not to have received any ideas ;
and he represents it as opening successively to the various
impressions of which each of the senses of this statue is
susceptible. He begins with smell, which of all the senses
is the least extended, and has the smallest part in the
cognitions of our mind. He repeats successively the same
test in the case of the other senses. After having examined the ideas furnished by each of them, he analyses
those that result from the united action of several senses ;
and thus setting out from a simple sensation of smell, he
raises his statue by degrees to the state of being rational
and intelligent, so that not only he describes the faculties
and the ideas which spring from them, but he explains also
their genesis by analysis of the sensations. He distinguishes two species of faculties : the intellectual, which he
reduces to the understanding, and the affective, which he
reduces to the will. He concludes to this effect: that,
while Locke distinguishes two sources of our ideas, the
senses and reflection, it would logically be more exact to

assign them to one source only, since reflection is in its principle only sensation itself, or the channel by which ideas come to us from the senses.

After Condillac, sensualism became predominant in France, through the advocacy of Diderot, D'Alembert, and the other writers of the *Encyclopédie.* It fell into a pure materialism with Helvetius, D'Holbach, and La Mettrie. Cabanis did in France what Hartley and Darwin did in England. We may mention as exceptions Voltaire, Rousseau, and Saint Martin. Voltaire by reason, and Rousseau by sentiment, rose to a first cause, while Saint Martin reproduced the mystical theories of Böhme.

In Italy Genovesi retained some of the doctrines of the preceding century and of Leibniz, but the philosophy of Locke, and then the system of Condillac, ultimately prevailed in the Italian peninsula, notwithstanding the honourable exceptions of Sigismondo Gerdil and Ermene-gildo Pini in upper Italy, Thomasso Rossi at Naples, and Vincenzo Miceli in Sicily.

In Germany, the Sensualistic School was represented by Feder, Tittel, Basedow, and Tiedeman; but, before the century closed, there arose the grand philosophical system of Kant.

.The reaction began in Scotland, where Hume, starting from Locke and Berkeley, landed in absolute scepticism. Locke had reduced the notions of cause and of substance to simple individual relations of things to each other, or to simple associations of ideas. Berkeley advocates the view that we perceive only ideas or images, which succeed each other without any relation to external objects. Hume inferred from this that causes and effects are in conjunc-tion and not in connection with each other, thus destroying all legitimate belief both in the external world and the internal world.

Reid revolted against the hypothesis of representative ideas, and vindicated the doctrine of immediate objective perception. He and Dugald Stewart wished to found philosophy on observation, and admitted *à priori* truths as fundamental laws of the human intellect. A great step was taken by these philosophers of the Scottish School against sensualism and scepticism. Reid held the doctrine of immediate perception, or an objective and affirmative idea of body in the concrete; but he did not equally recognise the perception of the generic and absolutely concrete, and the objectivity of the judgment which accompanies the perception of these various elements and connects them together. Instead of establishing the position, as he ought to have done, that the judgment belongs to the perceived object, and that the true and first judger is the same object (the absolute idea) which presents itself with all its parts to the subject, he wished to derive the judicative act from the latter, and by this hypothesis he took away all value from the perception. And in fact, how can the perception be immediate and the idea truly objective, if the percipient does not receive the judgment from that on which the reality and the organism of the ideal object depends, and if the judgment belongs to the subject which perceives, and not to the thing perceived? Kant, with great acuteness, saw that, on the one hand, the contingent concrete thing cannot be thought without the generic idea; and that, on the other hand, the subjectivity of the judgment cannot be harmonised with the objectivity of the idea and the immediate nature of the perception. But instead of conjoining the general idea and the concrete absolute with perception, and objectifying the judgment, he subjectified the idea, denied perception the power of embracing the contingent concrete object, and reduced all cognition to the generic element alone, which, when the concrete object was withdrawn from it, could have no other than a subjective value.

Kant was "roused from his dogmatic slumber" by the scepticism of Hume, and in order to combat it, he was not satisfied with merely maintaining *à priori* truths like Reid. He made a profounder analysis of the human intellect, and found two species of cognitions: the first rational, synthetical, à *priori*, general, and necessary; the other analytical, à *posteriori*, and contingent. The former cognitions constitute the fundamental laws of our intellect, and it possesses them anteriorly to all experience. In fact, synthetical judgments are those which enlarge our cognitions by showing us something which is not contained in their subject, whereas analytical judgments do nothing more than show us better the agreement of the predicate with the subject. Kant distinguishes in knowledge its matter and its form. He calls the matter of cognition phenomena, and what unites the diversity of the phenomena in certain relations, he calls their form. In other words, matter is the diversity, and form is the unity in cognition. He distinguishes the forms of the sensibility (which are time and space), the categories of the understanding (which are those of quantity, quality, relation, and modality), and the ideas of the reason, that is, the ideas of the Ego, of the world, and of God, which transcend or go beyond experience.

We see then how knowledge is formed according to Kant. We have intuitions or representations of objects which are furnished to us by experience. To what are these intuitions due? To our capacity for receiving impressions, or, in a word, to our *receptivity*. But it is necessary to co-ordinate such intuitions, that is to say, to reduce them to unity. How, then, can this function be fulfilled? The activity as such must be an activity of thought, with the spontaneity which is proper to it, and which constitutes the understanding. The intuitions, accordingly, are the matter of cognition; they are rendered homogeneous by a common bond, which is that of space and time, without which they would not be possible. In order that a synthesis may be valid, it is necessary that it should have acquired the character of necessity, which the understanding alone can give to it by means of the categories. Reason struggles to pass beyond the limits of space and

time, because it is in accordance with its nature to seek
totality or absolute unity by synthesis of the cognitions, in
order to attain to an absolute principle. Not finding this
in the sensible objects, reason throws herself into metaphysical speculations, and forthwith abandons the field of
experience, gives way to illusions, and falls into continual
contradictions. From this point of view Kant draws out
his antinomies, that is to say, he demonstrates the *pros*
and *cons* in the ideas which form the object of reason.
He infers that reason is *regulative* not constitutive, or in
other words, that it necessarily adopts metaphysical ideas
only in order to discover the systematic unity of the sensible world on account of its being impossible for us to
know things in themselves, or *noumena;* and hence we
ought to stop at simple phenomena.

Fichte held that since we know nothing but what is
produced by our thought, there exists nothing but the
Ego, which must be conceived as absolute, and which, in
virtue of its unlimited energy, begins to determine itself
and posits the non-Ego. Accordingly the external world
is to Fichte the same as what matter was to Plato, that
is, it is a non-being; and it becomes real only in the proportion in which it is converted into idea, that is, in so
far as it is thought by the Ego. Kant confines himself to
neither affirming nor denying the existence of external
things ; Fichte maintained that they are that part of the Ego
which it has not yet realised, and that, if in this continuous
action it does not succeed in overcoming all resistance, this
arises from the fact that its virtuality is infinite, for its
ideal activity is as infinite as its nature. God is to Fichte
an Ideal of all intelligence and reality, which the Ego
strives to realise without ever being able to attain to it.[1]

We have thus seen how the XVIII. Century began
with the purest sensualism and ended in an absolute
subjectivism.

[1] See Wilm, *Histoire de la philosophie allemande depuis Kant jusq' à
Hegel.* Paris, 1849.

§ 8.

The first works of Schelling bear the date of the last years of the XVIII. Century, while the last works of Fichte saw the light in the first years of the XIX. Century; and thus the two schools joined hands. As it is of importance for us to know somewhat more fully the philosophical doctrines of our century, we shall devote a paragraph to each of the nations which have been most occupied with philosophy. And we shall begin with Germany.

Schelling thought that the Ego was able to produce the sphere of the practical life, but that it could not generate physical nature. The non-Ego of Fichte appeared to Schelling, not a negation or limitation, but an affirmation, a positive thing really as much as the Ego. There are then, said Schelling, two positive realities : the one internal and ideal, the other external and real ; the sphere of the mind and that of nature. As to the forces which animate and rule this double world, may they not be relative to each other and correspondent ? May not the principles of nature be found in the human mind as laws of consciousness and of reason, and may they not verify themselves equally in the external world under the form of physical laws ? Both spheres are lost in a common infinite, and this infinite in which the two are absorbed and from which they both descend is the Absolute, which serves as a foundation to spirit and to nature, whose primitive unity is unfolded in two distinct worlds : in that which is developed with consciousness, and in that which is produced without consciousness. The universe is therefore the identical expression of the divine thought, and human reason is the identical expression of the divine intelligence, and consequently of the universe. The ideal world is accordingly the end and the cause of the sensible world ; the sensible world is the image and manifestation of it ;

and philosophy is the science of it, or its reproduction in the mind.

Hegel set out from the system of Schelling, which he applied himself to determine better and to complete by a rigorous method, making a profound application of it to all the sciences. The absolute idealism aspires to omniscience, to the science of God, which according to Schelling we possess by means of the intellectual intuition, and according to Hegel by the immanent dialectic, or the movement of thought. The universe is the product of the evolution of the conception, notion, or absolute Idea. This absolute Idea of Hegel is the eternal notion or conception (*Der ewige Begriff*), the Idea of ideas of Schelling, or the absolute ideality. The world, says Hegel, is a flower which proceeds eternally from a single germ; this flower is the divine absolute idea produced from the movement of thought. First it is the logical idea or the totality of the categories of thought; then by its own activity, without receiving any impulse or the least matter from the external, it becomes nature and spirit, universe and universal cognition, physical and moral world. Nature, man, history are only different periods or moments in the development of this idea. In the first moment, it is solely in potentiality, in an absolute and indeterminate unity; and so we have Logic, that is, the laws of thought. In the second moment, it goes out of itself and manifests itself in various particular existences; and so we have Nature. And finally, the Idea returns into itself and is by itself, that is, acquires consciousness in man; and we have philosophy properly so called.

Jacobi takes an attitude of opposition to the system of Kant, maintaining that the principle of all knowledge and of all activity is faith, or the revelation which manifests itself in the human mind under the form of feeling, and which is the basis of all certainty and of all science. Jacobi, however, does not confine himself to recognising the part of spontaneity and intuition in knowledge, but he also assigns much to feeling and sentiment. From this there arises a confusion, especially in his moral system, where the law of duty, so admirably described by Kant in his *Critique of the Practical Reason,* is reduced to a sort of vague instinct, to a desire of happiness.

Fichte, in the last years of his life, sought to modify his doctrine by distinguishing science from faith, but without showing the link which unites them. His philosophy exercised a great influence, especially in literature. The humoristic school of Jean Paul Richter developed the principal of irony in art, and Solger, and Friedrich Schlegel, hold by this subjective idealism; and from it also sprang the effort of the Ego to escape from itself and the aspiration of the soul towards the infinite and the absolute which generated the mysticism of Novalis.

Schelling, without ever abandoning the principle of his method, which was intellectual intuition, substituted for his subtle and often fastidious deductions a mystical contemplation, a species of inspiration that was the fertile source of most beautiful suggestions. Among those of his disciples who attributed great importance to living nature are to be reckoned Oken, Steffens, Goerres, and Baader.

The system of Krause closely approaches that of Schelling. He divides the universe into two spheres which penetrate each other, that of nature and that of reason, above both of which there exists the Supreme Being. It is a variation of the system of identity, but Krause, like Schelling, has not left a regular and complete exposition of his philosophy.

The opposition of the two worlds is found again in Herbart, the disciple first of Kant and then of Fichte. He endeavoured to open up a new way applying mathematics to philosophy, and subjecting the phenomena of the moral order to the Calculus. Setting out from the hypothesis that ideas are forces, he reduces the intellectual life to a sort of dynamism. Nevertheless he develops his principle with much ingenuity, and his works abound in many just observations. "The successors of Kant," says Herbart, "imagined an *absolute knowledge* by the aid of which the dogmas of the existence of God and of the immortality of the soul were to be put beyond doubt, but on the contrary it has rendered them more uncertain than ever." Schelling and Hegel, in fact, pretended to unite realism and idealism by proving the identity of being and thought, of ideas and things, but they reached only an absolute idealism. Herbart regards experience as the first source of knowledge, and limits the extension of real knowledge to what is furnished to us by observation rectified and completed by thought. Every generation transmits to that which follows it its thoughts better certified, no less than its language its inventions, institutions, and arts. Hence there result phenomena which the individual psychical mechanism could not produce by itself. In each of us the whole of the past lives again. Reason is thus reduced to a psychological fact; and liberty, like reason, is acquired. A man becomes rational only by the action of old ideas upon the new; he is not free unless he has formed for himself a character by means of the union of predominating ideas, and this only comes about by chance, or by a sort of intellectual mechanism.

It remains for us to indicate the vicissitudes of the German philosophy since the death of Hegel in 1832. His school soon came to be divided into a right, a centre, and a left (1840). Michelet was one of the disciples who maintained the doctrine of the master in its purity, and along with him we may mention Rosenkranz, Hotho, Gabler, and Marheineke. It was not long, however, till Michelet seemed to have been seized by a kind of vertigo in his book on the solution of the social problem, and in his conversations with Victor Cousin. Rosenkranz remained faithful; and in his "System of Science," and in his "Reform of the Hegelian Philosophy," he sought to prove that atheism was not in the mind of the great philosopher, who believed in the personality of God,—that primitive being without consciousness and without will, that infinite substance which requires to manifest itself in its contrary in order to attain to cognition of itself, that germ of God which will flower and bear its fruit only on the completed theatre of the universe ;—these, he says, are simple figures used in order to make the old truths of spiritualism penetrate into the mind of the reader ! ! ! Who could enumerate the eccentricities and the sophisms of the young Hegelian School ? Strauss, combining together all the partial negations accumulated by the German theologians from Lessing, undertook to demonstrate that Christ was the work of the thought of all; and Bruno Bauer maintained that the Gospels were not the work of the evangelists, and were therefore an imposture. Feuerbach translated the Hegelian ideas into popular language, showing that man worships his own shadow, *homo homini deus;* and Max Stirner reached the last consequence in proclaiming egoism, *homo sibi deus.* In our days, the same Strauss, in his last book, *The Old Faith and the New,* prostrates himself before the God-universe, while the progress of the natural sciences has led Moleschotte and Büchner to a sort of physiological materialism founded upon positive ideas.

But all the German philosophy did not culminate in materialism. There was one philosopher unknown for many years, Schopenhauer, who published in 1819 a work under the title " Die Welt als Wille und Vorstellung " (*The World as Will and Idea*), which made no noise at the time, because Germany was then entirely taken up with the system of Hegel. On the fall of this system after 1848, the work of Schopenhauer was reprinted, and he then came into great repute. In this work he tries to explain everything by the " will " taken in the general sense of force. In itself the will is one and identical, the plurality of phenomena being only an appearance produced by the apparition of the intellect, a secondary and derivative faculty. Intelligence acts so that the will from being unconscious becomes conscious, and passes from existence *in se* to existence *per se.* He shows that the will is at bottom nothing but desire, and therefore that it is need and consequently pain; and he finds no other ideal in life than the negation of life by delivering ourselves from it, by means of science and asceticism.

The leading disciple of Schopenhauer is Von Hartmann, who explains and completes the doctrine of the master. He says that the first principle, the Unconscious, is not merely will, but at the same time is objective idea, which he regards as inseparable from the will and co-ordinated with it as a metaphysical principle of equal value. To the unconscious will corresponds the unconscious idea. The will can manifest itself even without the brain, the ganglia or nerve centres sufficing for it, as in animals of imperfect organisation. Instinct springs from a will which acts rationally, without having a consciousness of its acting.

The filiation of the system of Schopenhauer is manifest. After Descartes, Kant had believed the Ego to be the originator of all cognition; Fichte had raised it to an absolute principle; and finally, Hegel recognised all reality in the Idea, the immanent dialectic of which, in the world and in history, he described; but he forgot that the Idea alone remained absolutely unfruitful, having need of a will to realise itself. Schopenhauer raised the unconscious will to a supreme principle without noticing that the will has need of an object, of an end, of an Idea. Consciousness, then, does not result from the action of organised matter upon the unconscious mind, but reveals itself in it as its occasion.

Let us see now how this philosophy resolves the great metaphysical problems. Matter in relation to the intelligence is a non-being; in relation to the will, it is a fact, that is to say, it is reduced to force according to Schopenhauer. Hartmann corrects him by saying: Matter is will and idea. For both of them the real individuality resides only in the atomic forces, and we are mere physical coincidences. God is the All-One; and as at the same time he is will and idea, a logical succession reigns in the universe, and thus neither the disciple nor the master deny final causes. For man, happiness consists in unconscious sleep. The earth is in the afternoon or post-meridian hours of its planetary course, and is approaching the twilight of its evening.

Yet all Germany was not seized by this vertigo. Adolph Trendelenburg, for example, in his *Logical Investigations*, explains the order of the universe by the ideas of Plato and the actuality of Aristotle. He recognises final causes, and expounds their realisation in right and morality.

§ 9.

Italy at first followed the sensualism of the XVIII. Century. According to Gian Domenico Romagnosi, reason is a sort of superior sense, the logical sense; and the ideal of life does not transcend experience and happiness. The philosophy of Melchiorre Gioia differed little from that of Romagnosi. But as the Italian speculative thought began to acquire its autonomy, it reacted against sensualism, Kantianism, and pantheism. Pasquale Galuppi, following the Scottish School, admitted an immediate perception of the concrete. Analysing this perception, he clearly explains the spontaneous and natural synthesis of the Ego with the non-Ego (the *me* and the *extra me*), so that, according to his view, there is found in the commonest fact of consciousness the double sentiment of the subject feeling and of the thing felt. At the end of the second book of his *Critical Essay on Cognition*, he says—"I have destroyed with invincible arguments the system of representative ideas, and with Reid I have put our mind into direct relation with objects; but this relation, which in the system of Reid is arbitrary, is essential in mine. I have furnished a remedy for the defects of the philosophy of experience on this important point; and I have established that the direct relation of the sensible perception necessarily supposes the reality of the object, and that sensible perception is the intuition of the object."

In his theory of cognition, Galuppi has not been so happy, since he retains the general idea as the product of an operation which is called generalisation, and which is preceded by abstraction and attention. In order to separate himself from the School of Locke, he admits in the human mind the idea of relations of identity and of diversity, which he calls *ideal* relations, and those of cause and of substance, which he calls *real* relations. Real relations have their foundation in direct feeling and in the perception of reality, internal and external; whereas ideal relations depend essentially on the ideal synthesis which forms them and on the synthetic unity of our thoughts. In order to restore to thought all its independence, Galuppi was led to combat the synthetic judgments *à priori* of Kant, and to reduce them to analytic judgments, because the former present themselves as mysterious data of which reason is ignorant, while the latter are the result of the decomposition of thought.

In moral science, Galuppi re-established the true relations between happiness and virtue, by recognising duty as the supreme law of life, and happiness as an end whose realisation is subordinated to justice.

In the view of the Neapolitan philosopher, reason, if not a derivation of sense, was regarded as a subjective abstract thing devoid of necessary and absolute value. Antonio Rosmini endeavoured to repair this grave defect. By a subtle analysis he reduced all ideas to that of possible being, for which he recognised an objective and absolute value, and which he constituted a unique and universal form of truth. For this end he establishes the view that experience gives the matter of cognition, and being gives its form; and he distinguishes two species of perceptions, the sensitive and the intellective. Sensitive perception is sensation with its relation to the sensible term. Intellective perception comprehends: 1. Sensitive perception ; 2. The affirmation of actual existence; 3. The idea of being. He calls the body a co-subject of the mind, and affirms that the relation between being and its modes can only be manifested by feeling; and he goes on finally to maintain that we cannot know the divine reality except negatively, because, in order to know it positively, it would be necessary to feel it and to perceive it. However, neither sensation, nor feeling, nor reflection (in the sense of Locke) contains the idea of being. Our mind has the consciousness of seeing it and not of producing it, as the eye contemplates the stars of the firmament without believing itself to be their creator. The idea of being is intelligible by itself, and renders all other ideas intelligible. It manifests itself under the three forms of identity, reality, and morality; in other words, of the ideal, the real, and their relation. Nevertheless it is merely a logical and universal possibility, which contains all ideas with the interminable series of genera and species and their perfect types; and it comes forth in the approximation which takes place in intellective perception between sensation and intelligible truth. This ideal being is also the initial being, that is to say, it is something divine or of God. It is objective and intelligible, eternal and necessary, but it is not the absolute. It is infinite as idea, but it is not all the infinite.

What, according to Rosmini, is the passage from the ideal to the real? All the essences united compose the model or exemplar of the world, but they are not the Word of God, nor can they be identified with the absolute perception of being, the unity and simplicity of which suffer neither division nor limitation. The creation is the work of the creative liberty of God, who, from loving being, is driven by love to create it in so far as it is relative and finite. Creation takes place by a sort of divine abstraction, by that operation through which the intelligence of God determines in itself the relatively primordial idea from which spring all the objects of our knowledge and the types of things. The existence of God is proved by a sort of integration of being, which is at first indeterminate and is then completed under the real and moral form; for in reasoning on the infinite, which appears to us under the ideal form, we very soon perceive that there can only be a single infinite, as that which unites reality to ideality and therefore attains perfection.

The passage to morals was easy to Rosmini by his establishing the proposition that the idea of a perfect essence is a good, because it includes all that can be attributed to a being of a given class according to its nature, that is, according to the end of its movement and of its tendencies; so that when a being approaches the fulness of its essence and of its perfection, it obeys at the same time an ideal necessity, and becomes what it was to be by conforming itself to its own good and to good in general.[1] *Possible being* is the relation of the absolute reality to our knowledge and to created things. Now a relation cannot be known without knowing its terms. But Rosmini would not admit that the absolute reality is immediately known. To him the ideal remained disjoined from the real. Accordingly this possible being remained, as it were, suspended in the air; and it offered a side to attack from two opposite quarters. The partisans of the philosophy of experience attacked it on the one hand, reproaching Rosmini for having intruded into the primitive cognition of the real, the abstract, and the possible, in that operation of the mind which he calls intellective perception; whereas Reid had shown that the reality of the thing perceived was immediately felt and known, because it was at the same time sensible and intelligible, and that judgment and affirmation are subsequent acts

---

[1] See Ferri, *Essai sur l'histoire de la philosophie en Italie au XIX. Siècle.* Paris 1869.

destined to analyse what was confusedly contained in the primary perception.

Vincenzo Gioberti, on the other hand, has shown that rational knowledge cannot depend on the intuition of a possible Being, but rather on the relation of the intelligence to an infinite reality, an inseparable condition of all thought and of all existence. He has established by the solidest arguments the impossibility of separating the ideal from the real, by making relative being with its double aspect, ontological and idealogical, enter into the rational intuition of the synthetic judgment *à priori: "Being creates existence."* He maintains that all judgments resolve themselves into ideas, and that all ideas include judgments which are all synthetic *à priori* and *à posteriori*, since all express the common relation of ideas to the impenetrable term of the infinite or finite essence. The only exception is the judgment: *Being is*, which is analytical, because by it the absolute idea is posited and is affirmed before our thought. Intuition accordingly includes the primitive synthesis, or in other words, the intelligible data and their relations. Reflection decomposes this synthesis in order to reconstruct it, and to express it in language. Language is necessary to reproduce in thought what is contained in the intuition, which being unlimited and infinite cannot fall under the finite power of reflection except by means of sensible signs. These are produced by the creative act itself, which, giving existence to the intuition, at the same time manifests the intelligibility of being. Accordingly the signs correspond exactly to the ideas. Such signs compose language, which is internal and external, natural and artificial. Internal and natural language declares sentiments and modifications of the mind of which external signs and artificial language are thus the expression. Not only is language the instrument and organ of what is rationally intelligible, but of whatever transcends it. Gioberti distinguished in the mind the supra-intelligible element which was not adequately observed before by the philosophers. He analysed it minutely. He considered it as the product of a special faculty which he called supra-intelligence; he showed its connections with the products of the other faculties; and he marked off what corresponds to it in the order of reality, that is, the supra-natural, reserving himself for a profounder study of it, and intending to make of it a separate science in later works under the designation of the *philosophy of the supra-intelligible or of the supra-natural.* When Gioberti began to print his works he had already in his mind a system of philosophy well outlined and organically put together. But as it was eminently different from the philosophy in vogue, he proposed to make the understanding of it easier by means of an *Introduction to the Study of Philosophy.* In this introduction he aims at showing that the being primarily intuited was real, not shut up in itself but creative, and hence that the order of knowledge proceeded identically with the order of things. He distinguished psychological reflection from ontological reflection, and the latter from intuition; but he did not enter on discussion of the intimate nature of intuition, nor as to whether the intuition of finite reality was in everything identical with the intuition of the infinite reality. He laid down the substantial difference between intelligence as a faculty apprehensive of the absolute Intelligible, and sensibility which apprehends the contingent; but he did not inquire as to whether what is sensible was in its essence a relative intelligible. He indicated and promised to speak of it afterwards in detail whenever he should have expounded the new and recondite part of his doctrine which is found in his posthumous works, where is explained the being of immanent thought, and its distinction from successive thought.

To the double state of thought he makes the double state of nature correspond; and this is not wonderful, since spirit and nature constitute the existent, which in so far as it is created by Being ought to resemble it. Now being is one and infinite, and the existent ought to be in like manner one, except that its unity being finite has to include multiplicity, and therefore must be a manifold unity or a manifold one. Similarly the existent must be a relative intelligibility, a potential infinity which corresponds to the absolute unity; which analogy between the existent and being, or between the copy and the original, is designated by the term *methexis*,[1] which means properly participation. The sensible, which Gioberti calls *mimesis*,[2] will gradually become intelligible. Mysteries are to be cleared up by the way of analogy, and the cosmos will be succeeded by the palingenesis. In nature as in mind, under all the forms of being and of cognition, there is hidden and there moves a force which opposes contraries to each other, puts them into harmony in a third term, and draws from them incessantly new oppositions and new harmonies. The propositions which compose the interminable *sorites of beings*, spring from the categories: fundamental ideas produced by the infinite thought in its marriage with spirit and with the things which it engenders. The categories are the most general ideas; the ideas are in God, and form in Him only one single Idea which differentiates itself and passes from the absolute to the relative by means of the creative activity. The categories are divided conformably to the terms of the primitive formula to which they are related; for they are divine and incommunicable (Being), mathematical and mediating (Creation), cosmic and communicable (Existence).

In other passages Gioberti developed his doctrine in a sense more favourable to Platonism and Christianity, combining together the methexis and creation, and substituting partial unity for the absolute identity of Hegel, without breaking the unity of the universe; for the idea and its eternal causality are the supreme condition of all the ideal relations and of the substantial unity of the world. According to Gioberti, the identity of contraries is

---

[1] Μέθεξις.   [2] Μίμησις.

verified in an absolute manner only in God, and their
distinct division and apparition begins really only with
the creative act. In the view of Hegel the dialectic is the
unity of the absolute negation and affirmation, which is
the total transformation of the contradictory terms. To
Gioberti, on the contrary, being and existence compose a
primary proposition whose terms are irreducible, that is,
are not convertible; and their ontological dependence has
place by means of the creation, that is, by means of a
causality which is imperfectly intelligible so far as we participate in it. According to Gioberti, dialectic is not barely
formal, but real and objective; it is not a pure art but a
science: the science of opposites and of their harmony.
It is developed in the world and in the human mind, not
in God. The divine dialectic is subjective and apparent;
it is not in the object which is one and immanent, but in
the subject which apprehends it, seeing that the opposites
do not harmonise but are identified, their opposition not
being real and effective. He represents it to himself as
the movement of finite thought which realises itself in
time and space, and is parallel to the life of the world.
Hegel was wrong, according to Gioberti, in substituting
contradictories for contraries, and in transporting them
from Existence to Being. The possibility of transforming
the cosmological categories into each other may, it is true,
have for a foundation the unity of the cosmical substance,
that is, the one and finite reality which is intermediate
between individuality and generality, and from which
dialectic, aided by experience, draws the various forms of
beings; but this metamorphosis stops at the finite. For if
the chain of the categories is prolonged further, this arises
from its traversing the creative act and sinking in the
mysterious bosom of the absolute unity, which takes
away from this transformation any pantheistic significance.
Accordingly, Gioberti neither admits the unity of contradictories, which he regards with Plato and Aristotle as
the destruction of reality and of science, nor the identity

of contraries, between which he only admits harmony, as Pythagoras taught.

Thus Gioberti in his second period, in spite of appearances to the contrary, due to the imperfection in which he left his posthumous works, has done nothing but perfect his doctrine by rising from successive thought to immanent thought, and establishing the dialectic.

Gioberti deduces the science of the good from his ideal formula as follows. The human good is a conformity of the human will with the divine will, as the true is the accordance of the human intellect with that of the Creator; whence it follows that our two principal faculties, reason and free will, derive their value from their participation in the excellence of the divine nature.[1]

Mamiani takes a position intermediate between Rosmini and Gioberti. He adopts what is truest and most certain in their systems to compose a third of greater strength and solidity. It hinges on the principle of identity, which in his view is concrete not abstract, and is wholly one with the absolute reality in a direct and most immediate relation with thought. According to Mamiani, intuition apprehends real, not possible being; and every necessary truth already contains the real and the substantial. He is opposed to Kantianism, which he combats in all its forms. While he maintains that being is concrete and real, not possible and abstract, according to the view of Rosmini, he, however, does not agree with Gioberti in holding that intuition also apprehends the creative act. It

[1] Among the most learned interpreters of Gioberti we mention Professors Pietro Luciani and Vincenzo Di Giovanni. Luciani, in his work on *Gioberti and the New Italian Philosophy* (3 vols., Naples, 1868–1872), combats Hegelianism, and shows the intimate agreement between the first and last works of Gioberti. He maintains that this philosopher, like the great masters of antiquity, had besides his exoteric doctrine an acroamatic doctrine which was gradually unfolded. Di Giovanni, alarmed at the bold thoughts contained in the posthumous works of Gioberti, keeps closely to those published in his lifetime; and in his various works on the History of Philosophy (printed at Palermo) he finds a precedent for the philosophy of creation in the works of Monsignor d'Acquisto, his fellow-countryman.

does not appear to him that the principle of cause is contained in the immediate and common intuition of being itself, but is a cognition posterior and reflex inasmuch as it demands a clear consciousness of our passivity, and is born from the need of combining in a single judgment the object and the subject together with their connection. Creation, then, he regards as necessary, not free, caring little whether this is repugnant or not, and may even lead logically to pantheism ; and all the more that he has placed the principle of identity in the unique and absolute judging of the real and knowable. Ideas are representations which the Absolute makes of Himself, unveiling them to such intellects as are sufficient for it. They are all real, all objective in the absolute reality and objectivity of the being which sustains them, but they are not themselves the divine paradigms and the archetypal and efficient causes of things, although their representations are faithful and perpetual. In this mediate nature of the ideas, Mamiani finds the qualitative character of the Platonic revival of the modern Italian philosophy. Every one of these ideas furnishes the firm support for particular sciences. Thus on the conception of absolute justice, he founds all his books which treat of right. On the conception of the holy, he founds the theory of religion, and so on. Although all his works abound in subtle analyses, in acute psychological observations, and in rigorous argumentation, yet they are deficient in coherence, and above all they want logical connection. In fact he admits the contingent and the necessary, sensible facts and ideas, but he does not explain scientifically how the one depends on the other, or how they are united to each other. In his view, the conjunction of phenomena with the ideas, and of the ideas with the absolute, constitutes the relation which is reflected from being in science, by means of perception as the ideal representation and intuition of the infinite. He maintains creation, especially in his Cosmology, where he has philosophically co-ordinated the ultimate results of the natural sciences ; and he vindicates progress, which he makes to consist in a *successive increase of being appropriated and co-ordinated to its end.*

There were other thinkers in Italy who sought with much ability to harmonise the doctrines of the Scottish School regarding the perception of the external world, with the innate activity of the mind which is reflected in consciousness. They thus continued the work of Galuppi, as did Augusto Conti. Others tried by a bold scepticism to prepare the way for positivism, as was done by Guiseppe Ferrari.

§ 10.

France began to pass from the sensualism of Condillac with the writings of Laromiguière, who distinguished attention from sensation. Royer Collard brought the Scottish School into honour, and Maine de Biran examined the voluntary and free activity which constitutes personality. Cousin introduced the German philosophy into France, wedding it with the Scottish philosophy. Their union resulted in a system to which he gave the name of "Ecclecticism." He starts from common sense in order to descend into the depths of consciousness, throws a glance over the external world, and then rises to the eternal ideas of the true, the good, and the beautiful. He thus believed that he had adopted whatever truth the various systems contained. In the conclusion which he added to his *General History of Philosophy* a few days before his death, he speaks no longer of "ecclecticism," but of "spiritualism," and exclaims: "Let us then enter without fear upon the uncertain and obscure path that has been opened before us by the French Revolution; let us enter upon it under the auspices of common sense to which the last word in all things belongs; let us attach ourselves to this experienced guide; let us never abandon it; and let us be persuaded that in the crash of the world and among all the ruins of the past it will guide us and will bring us always back to the soul and to God." We see that, notwithstanding certain for-

mulae adopted from Schelling and Hegel, Cousin remained
faithful to the method of Descartes and to psychology.
The impulse given by him to philosophy in France was
beneficial, and it was carried on by his disciples. Thus we
owe to Jouffroy some fine psychological analyses, to Saisset
and Janet learned polemics against pantheism and a more
or less disguised sensualism, with important historical
works by Jules Simon, Vacherot, Ravaisson, and Barthé-
lemy Saint-Hilaire.

We have seen that the scepticism of Hume begot the
subjectivism of Kant. Auguste Comte admits with Hume
that the causes of phenomena are other phenomena which
are their invariable antecedents; and he also admits with
Kant that we can know nothing of things in themselves
or *noumena,* declaring that such knowledge is of no value
to us. According to Comte human opinions in this regard
have not varied by chance. They have obeyed a law which
makes them pass through three successive states. The
first state attributed concrete forms to the absolute cause
of events by a pure fiction of the mind; and this Comte
calls the *theological* state. The second state gave to this
same absolute cause an abstract and purely ideal form;
and this Comte calls the *metaphysical* state. Finally, the
third state renounces investigation of the origin and destination of the universe for the knowledge of the immediate
causes of phenomena, and confines itself to discovering
their effective laws, that is, the relations of succession and
resemblance, their *positive and real state.* The first explanation gradually raised itself to its perfection by substituting the providential action of a single being for the
numerous independent divinities which it had primarily
imagined. The second explanation, which substitutes for
the one divinity a being of reason, follows the same road,
reducing all unities to a single unity, which is nature,
a grand entity regarded as the one source of all phenomena.
Finally, the third explanation, which is that of the positive
state, considering facts as particular cases of more general

facts, is tending to its perfection, which it will probably never reach, but which would consist in being able to represent the various observable phenomena as particular cases of a single general fact, as, for example, the fact of gravitation.

The method of Comte is the scientific method; and he himself says that his positive philosophy has much analogy with that which since Newton has been called in England "natural philosophy." This philosophy emerges from two operations: the determination of general facts by each of the sciences, and the reunion and co-ordination of these facts. It therefore presents the conception of the world which results from the systematic aggregation of the positive sciences; and hence the great importance of the series of the six fundamental sciences: mathematics, astronomy, physics, chemistry, biology, and sociology, which succeed and complete each other in turns. All ideas come from experience; and every experience is proved and verified by perception of the external world.

In the second half of his career, Comte tried to create a religion without a God and without a worship, but directed towards an object at once ideal and real, namely, the human race conceived as a continuous whole which embraces the past, the present, and the future, and has need of our services and of our devotion. Comte found a worthy interpreter and continuator in Littré, who stripped the system of the barbarous language and of the autocratic and hieratical tendencies, which Comte had borrowed from the economist Saint-Simon, and which he carried out to an exaggerated degree in his second period.

§ 11.

Kant had preserved the notion of the absolute in the supra-sensible world above the sphere of experience. He at least retained it as a necessary limit of reason which cannot carry up the chain of the phenomena of beings to the infinite. In Scotland, Sir William Hamilton showed himself more radical, as he reproaches Kant for not having once for all exorcised the phantom of the absolute. Kant, he says, ought to have shown that if the unconditioned has no objective reason, this is because it is not susceptible of a subjective affirmation, since it cannot yield any true cognition from its containing nothing that is conceivable. Notwithstanding this, he admits immediate perceptions with Reid, and the pure forms of thought with Kant.

John Stuart Mill denies both the immediate perceptions of the Scottish School and the *à priori* forms of the German School. He maintains that the belief in the external world is not a primitive fact, but the result of induction derived from experience. The *Ego* is the bond which unites the various sensations, and matter is "a permanent possibility of sensation." Every species of knowledge springs from the association of ideas. Induction is the key of nature; it discovers and proves the general propositions by which we conclude from the individual to the class, and from one time to another. Axioms are only a class, the moŝt universal class, of the inductions drawn from experience; they are generalisations of facts furnished by the senses and by experience. The only useful propositions are those which connect one fact with another so as to enable us to conclude from one particular fact to another particular fact. Mill in his *Inductive Logic* establishes four methods for the experimental discovery of connection: that of "agreement," that of "difference," that of "residues" (which consists in taking from the phenomenon the part which is known to be the effect of certain antecedents in order to see whether the residue of the given phenomenon is the effect of the antecedents that remain); and that of "concomitant variations," which operates not upon two phenomena directly by themselves, but upon their variations.[1]

---

[1] These four methods are found almost literally in Bacon, in his theory of the three Tables of Presence, Absence, and Gradation,

Induction is founded on the law of causality; but as Mill admits only phenomena or combinations of phenomena which follow each other in an invariable and unconditional manner, the relativity of knowledge follows from this position. Mill is distinguished from Comte by the greater importance assigned by him to psychology, which Comte had denied a place among the fundamental sciences in order to make it dependent on biology.

Alexander Bain deepens the furrow traced out by Mill, showing by a greater range of observations that all the phenomena of the mind spring from the association of ideas. Bain treats psychology as a continuation of physiology, and studies all its phenomena under the physical and mental aspects. In contrast to other psychologists who are advocates of association, he gives much prominence to the activity and spontaneity of the mind. Sensation, memory, and association are passive facts which may serve to explain our dreams, our phantasies, and our fortuitous thoughts. Bain shows that the brain does not simply obey impulsion, but that it is self-acting; that the nervous influence is not transmitted by it to the motor-nerves automatically, nor without rule and cause, but is produced by the organic stimulus of nutrition. He seeks the germ of the will in the spontaneous activity which resides in the nerve centres. Excitation produces movements, changes of posture, and in consequence sensations. There is thus established in the yet empty mind a connection between certain sensations and certain corporeal movements; and whenever afterwards sensation may be excited by some external cause, the mind will know that a movement will take place at some point. In

which contains the essential conditions of all positive investigation. Bacon founds his method on the theory that the only way of discovery in the sciences consists in ascertaining certainly all the important circumstances which accompany a phenomenon, then in suppressing successively all these circumstances until we come to that circumstance which, when suppressed, suppresses the phenomenon itself, and, finally, in making that circumstance which is presumed to be the cause, vary, in order to note the concomitant variations of the effect.

a word, consciousness verifies effort, but does not constitute it. Effort is produced by the organic state of the nerves and muscles. The moral laws which prevail in almost all societies, if not in all, are founded in part on utility and in part on sentiment. The individual conscience is an internal imitation of the external Government, and is formed and developed by education.

Herbert Spencer does not stop at psychology, which, like Mill and Bain, he regards as a continuation of physiology, but he seeks to enter the field of metaphysics. He admits with Comte the exact correspondence of perceptions with sensations, and holds that we have two classes of states of consciousness : the internal state which is called the subject, and the external state which is called the object. Ideas are formed on the model which is furnished to us by things, through a constant repetition of the same associations during an incalculable number of generations. The forms or laws of thought are absolute uniformities which the world engenders in us : the most comprehensive kinds of a vague experience lasting through an immense period, during which the correspondences of groups of states of consciousness with groups of the states of the world are formed, and during which the relations of succession and of co-existence are gradually fixed, so as to serve as a rule to individual experience. The indissolubility of an association of states of consciousness, is what regulates thought and constitutes necessary propositions. The infinite variety of phenomena depends on the metamorphoses of force, and all movements obey the laws of evolution, that is, equivalence, rhythm, and cohesion, which are corollaries of the principle of the persistence of force. Matter and motion are manifestations of force variously conditioned. The concentration of matter implies the dissipation of motion; and reciprocally the absorption of motion implies the diffusion of matter. Hence arises a consecutive integration and disintegration of evolution and dissolution. If we are obliged to conceive an immense series of evolutions, past and future, we cannot attribute any limit to the visible creations. These are manifestations of force which may be regarded as the conditioned effect of an unconditioned cause, as a relative reality which presupposes an absolute reality; our thought conceiving an unknown force co-relative to the known force. In this transformed realism we see the phenomenon and the noumenon in their primordial relation, and we are obliged to regard them both as real. Thus the absolute which Hamilton chased out by the door, is brought in by Spencer through the window.[1]

The purely naturalistic school has furnished a considerable part of the arguments of the philosophers just referred to. Towards the end of the last century, Lamark tried to explain the creation of organic nature without the intervention of final causes. The ancient Epicureans had tried to show how the fertile and moist earth produced by spontaneous virtue every species of living beings, and how atoms by combining with each other according to the laws of weight and deviation (*clinamen*) had here formed men and there animals and fishes, on the ground that at times they had seen many incomplete bodies emerge from putrid mud. This view is expounded by Lucretius in his *De rerum natura.* Such a system was no longer able from its simplicity to satisfy the modern mind. Accordingly Lamark had recourse to various principles and agents, and chiefly to the action of the environment (*milieu*), of use or exercise, and of want, which gradually transformed the monad into humanity. Facts, however, show that the action of the environment (that is, air, water, meteorological variations, and education) is effective only to change the skin and the accessory characters of animals; and Lamark himself admits that it is insufficient to produce the organic forms and their adaptations. He therefore invokes the vital force, which is excited by want and strengthened by exercise. If the

---

[1] See Ribot, *La psychologie anglaise contemporaine.* Paris, 1881.

environment is changed by terrestrial and telluric revolutions, a change in the organism will be necessary in order to adapt it to the new conditions of existence. But this last change will be produced by an internal force, that is, by the vital force. The use of the organs will then complete what the vital force had hardly begun. Facts, however, have abundantly demonstrated that exercise may strengthen organs, but cannot create them.

Charles Darwin saw that it was necessary to have recourse to other principles in order to explain the transformation of species. He was struck by the method of crossing used by English agriculturists in order to improve the breed of cattle, swine, sheep, and horses, and which consists in selecting individuals possessing in the greatest degree the qualities which are in demand, such as the slimmest for swiftness, and the largest for the production of fatness, &c. Why should nature not have reached spontaneously what man obtains by his art, transmitting by way of heredity in the course of ages certain individual qualities that were due to mere chance? Such perfecting by transmission is what Darwin calls "Natural Selection." This principle is at work in the "Struggle for Life," that struggle which animals carry on for subsistence, and from which the strongest survive; and the good results are perpetuated by means of heredity and "adaptation" to the various conditions in which animals and plants are called to live. Thus Darwin explains the origin of species from some ten primordial types created by the Creator. Every type may perfect itself accidentally and its varieties will not deteriorate, because they are well armed, although in diverse modes, for the struggle for life. Those types, on the contrary, which have not acquired any advantage, perish. According to this law the primitive type disappears when the varieties by acquiring advantages become diversified, and the trace of their common origin is lost. So it is not true that man is descended from the monkey, for if it were so, as he is immensely superior to the monkey, he would have conquered it in the struggle for life, and therefore would have absorbed and destroyed it. Rather are man and the monkey descended from the same type, which has been lost, and of which they are divergent divisions. In a word, according to this hypothesis, the monkeys are not our ancestors, but our cousins-german. Generalising this example, it is not necessary to hold that the vertebrates have been molluscs, nor that the mammalia have been fishes or insects, but that the four branches may have been four rays parted from a primitive centre, which by removing from each other have become infinitely varied.

Darwin has found followers everywhere, especially in Germany. They generally hold that all organic beings have sprung from one primordial form, that is, from the cell or ovular vesicle. The plants and animals, even the most perfectly organised, are only an agglomeration more or less complicated of this first elementary organic form, the cell. Haeckel adds that the cell is not the last term, but that it is necessary to seek it among those forms recently discovered which are not yet cells, and which consist simply in small animated vesicles, or in almost formless mucosity. The cell has already too complicated a conformation, and cannot be considered as the primordial form, which would rather be a fleshy bit of matter (sarcode) to which the name *plasma* would be more applicable. What distinguishes the animal from the plants is *contractility*. There were beings intermediate between the animal and plants, which are called *protisti*. Then there arose structureless organisms, which nourished themselves by absorption and reproduced themselves by scission. These were only little masses of contractile albumen capable of nutrition and reproduction; and in their case all the functions, instead of being performed, as in the case of the superior animals, by means of special organs, proceeded directly from the unformed matter. On account of their simplicity, Haeckel calls them *moneres*, from the Greek μονήρης (single). The transition to the cell is effected by a condensation of the central point, which becomes the nucleus in the plastic mass of the *monere;* then there appears a viscous substance, and finally the membrane which encloses this nucleus.

But how were these *moneres* produced? In the ocean which surrounded the earth when yet hardly cooled, there were brought forth, says Haeckel, great quantities of *moneres* of the same kind; and the diverse conditions of life to which they had to adapt themselves, produced modifications on their homogeneous albuminous mass. It still remains to be known what was the origin of the organised compounds of the globules of albumen from which the primordial cells were formed. In the present day, chemistry extracts organic compounds from inorganic materials, such as alcohol, grape-sugar, oxalic acid, formic acid, fat bodies, and even albumen and fibrin, which are not crystallisable, but only coagulable. This has been called "spontaneous generation" (*generatio aequivoca* or *heterogenea*). It was indicated by Lucretius of old when he said: "Living worms are seen to emerge from the mud when the earth, saturated by the rain, comes to a state of putrefaction. The elements, set in motion and brought together in new conditions of existence, give origin to animals." This doctrine had still followers in the 16th and 17th Centuries. Van Helmont describes the means of bringing forth mice; and others taught the art of producing frogs and eels. An experiment of Redi destroyed these illusions by demonstrating that the worms which are found in putrefying flesh, are the larvæ of the eggs of flies, and that by enclosing the flesh in a very thin veil these worms are not brought forth. The microscope has furnished to the predecessors and successors of Darwin other arguments for spontaneous generation, but the latest experiments of Pasteur are decisive against it. He proves that the air contains millions of corpuscles organised like germs, and they decrease in proportion as we rise in the atmosphere. He shows that when we remove these organised corpuscles which are supposed to be germs, we no longer obtain the production of infusoria.[1]

The impossibility of spontaneous generation having been proved, the system of Darwin is reduced to an investigation of the question, whether the Creator created a few types or all the existing species ? The first objection to this system arises from its improper assimilation of artificial selection with natural selection. The difference of these two things is evident, because the first is intelligent and produced by man, who knows what he wishes, while the second is represented as the work of blind nature, that is, of chance. It may be added that experience has shown that in the case of artificial selection, animals are as a rule no sooner left to themselves than they return to their primitive type. A second objection not less grave arises from an absolute absence of intermediate types. There have been found in the pyramids of Egypt, and in excavations elsewhere, animals that existed more than three thousand years ago exactly similar to the actually existing species. Moreover, it is also the case that, even in the geological strata which go back to thousands of thousands of years, while there are found extinct species, at the same time there are also found almost all the species still existing, and that these do not differ in the least part from those which we still have before our eyes.

§ 12.

It is now time to gather together these scattered ideas, and to show the progress of philosophy in its fundamental systems of Sensualism, Idealism, Scepticism, and Mysticism.

We have said that if Greece received its religious traditions from the East, its philosophical development was indigenous.[2] The first philosophers of the Ionic School

---

[1] See Janet, *Le materialisme contemporain.* Paris, 1864.
[2] § 2.

sought for the primary elements without explaining change. Heraclitus presents himself as the philosopher of the becoming, and he is the precursor of Democritus and Leucippus. On the other hand, Anaxagoras held that all was confused, and that a mind intervened and ordered all, without, however, distinguishing it from material nature. Plato, after having defined matter as a being extremely difficult to understand, an eternal bond that is not clear to the senses yet perceptible, says that the supreme orderer took this mass which was agitated by an unbounded and unregulated motion, and from the disorder made order spring. According to Aristotle, indeterminate matter at the highest degree of abstraction is without attributes. If it always tends to form, to actuality, it is because it has in itself a principle of potency, of force. In the view of Aristotle, force is the principle of form which is substantial.

Christianity was not favourable to matter, which it represented as a dark inert substance, fixed and absolutely passive; in a word, as an obstacle to the spiritual and noble nature of man. Accordingly the Christian system embraced the opinion of Aristotle, which represents form as a necessary attribute of matter, as an external principle.

The Renaissance reacted against Aristotle, and materialism became predominant. Bruno himself seems to follow the principle of Lucretius. "There are no determinate limits to the universe; a real limit is not intelligible; God, the world, and matter, are but one sole and same thing; and the universe is an infinite being animated in all its parts. The human mind is a fraction of the divine mind." Matter is to Bruno the mother of all that has life; it includes in itself all germs and all forms. "What at first was seed becomes herb, ear, bread, chyle, blood, seed, embryo, man, corpse, which becomes earth or stone or some other inert matter, and so on. Nothing seems stable, eternal, and worthy of the name of principle, unless it be matter." There is but little difference between this statement and the language of Huxley, a continuator of Darwin. We open one of his *Lay Sermons,*[1] entitled *On the Physical Basis of Life,* and there we read as follows: "What, truly, can seem to be more obviously different from one another, in faculty, in form, and in substance, than the various kinds of living beings? What community of faculty can there be between the brightly-coloured lichen, which so nearly resembles a mere mineral incrustation of the bare rock on which it grows, and the painter to whom it is instinct with beauty, or the botanist whom it feeds with knowledge? . . . If we regard substance, or material composition, what hidden bond can connect the flower which a girl wears in her hair and the blood which courses through her youthful veins? . . . But I propose to demonstrate to you, that, notwithstanding these apparent difficulties, a threefold unity—namely, a unity of power or faculty, a unity of form, and a unity of substantial composition—does pervade the whole living world." Nutrition, growth, reproduction and contractility are common to all living things; and they are all composed chemically of carbon, hydrogen, oxygen, and nitrogen, which thus united form *protoplasm.* As they live they waste and repair their forces. "Every word uttered by a speaker costs him some physical loss; and, in the strictest sense, he burns that others may have light—so much eloquence, so much of his body resolved into carbonic acid, water, and urea. . . For example, this present lecture, whatever its intellectual worth to you, has a certain physical value to me, which is conceivably expressible by the number of grains of protoplasm and other bodily substance wasted in maintaining my vital processes during its delivery."

Bacon did not deny mind, but intent on formulating the method of induction, he gave it very little attention. Descartes, by his incomplete definition of substance, estab-

---

[1] *Lay Sermons, Addresses, and Reviews,* by Thomas Henry Huxley, LL.D., F.R.S. 2nd ed. Lond., 1871.

lished a dualism. He revived the idea of mechanism in nature, but he required the "shove" of the Creator to set it in motion. The Greek atomism, resuscitated and strengthened by Descartes by aid of the hypothesis of the ether, was adopted by Newton and the modern mechanical school. This school has followed out the discoveries which have calculated the celestial motions; it has investigated the nature of the ether which is moved by the sun; and it reduces force to the product of mass by the velocity. On the other hand, Leibniz made dualism disappear by resuscitating the actuality ($\dot{\epsilon}\nu\epsilon\rho\gamma\epsilon\iota a$) of Aristotle; because if matter tends to form, this is because it has in itself a principle of potency or force. The dynamism of Aristotle was indeterminate, and Leibniz completed it by demonstrating that the type and source of force is the mind. The new dynamical school of the present day has proved the absolute indestructibility of energy, and has demonstrated by numerous examples the fundamental identity of the appetent and elective forces of chemistry and of crystallography with those that psychology reveals.[1]

The atomic school formulated a first theory of knowledge. It considered the soul as composed of atoms very subtle and spherical like those of fire. The soul makes every possible effort to go out of the body, but it is retained by the breath, and death takes place with the suppression of the breath. Sensation is the sole source of our cognitions; for bodies send forth atomistic emanations which penetrate into the brain and excite the images of things. Pythagoras was the first to rise to general relations, making the principles of things consist in numbers. The numbers of Pythagoras are the first germs of the ideas of Plato, the prototypes of things, and of the actuality of Aristotle. The Alexandrians tried to make it more conceivable how the intelligible implies the intelligent and the ideal the mental, by considering the intelligible species as Ideas of God, and thus explaining the theory of Plato under this

[1] See F. Papillon, *La nature et la vie.* Paris, 1874.

aspect. Christianity, with its doctrine of creation *ex nihilo*, furnished St. Augustine with the means of putting man into mental communication with God and the universe, under the divine influence, without in the least confounding the physical substance with the infinite substance. Thomas Aquinas revived Aristotle's theory of actuality, but connected the species and genera with their supreme principle, by making them concepts of the divine intelligence or archetypes of creation; and he expressly maintained that the intelligible light contained in the active intellect is an emission of the divine nature.

Whereas the Middle Ages had abused reasoning, and the Renaissance had sought to conceal its own ideas under the veil of the ancient systems, the modern period turned frankly to external observation with Bacon, and to internal observation with Descartes. From Bacon have proceeded Hobbes, Locke, Condillac, and the contemporary positivists; from Descartes have come Reid, Kant, Galuppi, and all the psychological school. Descartes, considering clear and evident ideas as certain, had formed a criterion of truth which was wholly internal, and which he was obliged to supplement by faith in the divine veracity, a higher principle of harmony between thought and reality. Malebranche felt it necessary to identify immediately what is in thought with what is in being, the intelligible with the real, and to show that internal truth depends on absolute truth. The system of Malebranche lacked a clear criterion as to the creation ; and thus he attributed to God all efficient causation, saying that we see all things in God, who alone acts and modifies us. Malebranche, without knowing it and without wishing it, opened the way to all the pantheists, materialists, and idealists, from Spinoza to Hegel. Leibniz endeavours to reconcile Plato, Democritus, and Aristotle, with Descartes, and the scholastics with the moderns, by extracting from all their systems a *quaedam perennis philosophia.* " The foundation of the truth of contingent and singular things," he says, " lies in

the fact that sensible phenomena are in agreement with
intelligible truths." Let metaphysics therefore compare
things possible with each other and seek for the best, that
is, that which will contain most convenience, simplicity,
and beauty, and thus it will penetrate into the secret of
creation. In order to attain this it will have to make use
of the principles of contradiction and of sufficient reason.
The first will conduct us to the possible, the second to
the real. As ideas are linked together with each other, so
beings are interconnected with each other, since the laws
of thought and of nature are the same. Substance is
essentially active; that is, it is composed of forces or
monads which strive after and comprehend each other
reciprocally, according to the degree of their development.
How is this possible, seeing that monads are independent ?
By means of a harmony *pre-established* by the Creator:
a view which takes from man all true liberty. Gioberti
has perfected philosophy by rightly distinguishing intui-
.tion from reflection, and immanent thought from successive
thought, and by this he puts the objectivity of the idea
beyond all doubt. He has also better explained the nexus
between the subject and the object, between things and
ideas, by his theory of the creative act. This explanation has been always present to the human mind, and has
been more or less clearly enunciated in the systems that
are truly idealistic, such as those of Plato, Aristotle, St.
Augustine, Thomas Aquinas, Leibniz, and Vico. It reduces itself to the principle of contradiction, and to those
of causality and of sufficient reason, resumed in a primary
judgment. Vico had said openly—" The true is the fact,
i.e., what *is*, is what is *done*, and therefore God is the first
truth because He is the first doer ; God does or makes,
that is, creates *ad extra*, and He generates *ad intra.*"
Gioberti has the merit of having definitely formulated
the theory of the creative act, around which the battle of
modern science is being carried on.

Psychology is the substratum of metaphysics, and some

schools have wished to reduce all philosophy to it, as the reader may have remarked in the course of our rapid sketch. Materialism could not but necessarily attribute thought to matter, and define the soul as a subtle matter, or a breath. Cabanis says expressly that thought is a secretion of the brain. Carl Vogt has added for the sake of greater clearness that the brain secretes thought as the liver secretes bile, and as the kidneys secrete urine. Sensualism says the same in terms that are only less crude. Condillac introduces us to the birth of all ideas and of all the faculties of sensation. The English School, which prefers to call itself positive, seeks the germ of our faculties in the reflex action of the universe upon us. Thus Herbert Spencer says that reflex action becomes instinct, and from instinct there spring on the one side the faculties which he calls "cognitive," such as memory and reason, and on the other side the affective faculties, the sentiments and the will. Similarly Bain reduces the laws of intelligence to intellectual molecules which are conjoined and held together by association. All the efforts of this school tend to confound psychology with physiology (which Jouffroy forty years ago had taken so much pains to separate), and to bring human physiology into close connection with animal physiology in order to subject it to the law of evolution.

Plato considers the soul as an active force, and distinguishes in it the rational part and the animal part, which are united together by the θυμός.[1] It is a prisoner in the body, and it rises to knowledge by means of certain notions or ideas proper to reason, which are, as the basis of every thought that resides in us, anterior to all particular perception, and determine our actions. Such ideas are resuscitated in the mind by the perception of things made in their image, and this takes place as by a species of

[1] This word is usually translated by the terms "soul," "courage," "appetite," but it properly indicates the affective faculty which participates in the reason and the senses.

remembrance. Plato distinguishes with sufficient exactness the faculties of knowing, feeling, and willing, and the different kinds of perceptions, sentiments, and determinations.

Aristotle defines the soul to be the first "entelechy" of a natural organised body which potentially contains life. He enumerates five kinds of souls: the nutritive soul, common to animals and plants; the sensitive soul, the cause of sensation; the locomotive soul; the appetitive soul, the source and spring of the will; and lastly, the rational soul. He does not distinguish well the organic part from the rational; and he has thereby given occasion for the most opposite interpretations.

Plotinus explains that the soul is present in the whole of the body and in every part of it. St. Augustine adds that we know the soul directly, and that we know it as immaterial; and therefore that it can be present in every part of the body, and can contain images of the most extended objects. As Augustine perfected Plotinus, so Thomas Aquinas perfected Aristotle. He finds that the nutritive faculty, the sensitive faculty, the locomotive faculty, and the rational faculty belong to the same soul. "Anima enim est primum quo nutrimur et sentimus et movemur secundum locum, et similiter quo primo intelligimus." The identity of the soul in its various operations is demonstrated by the fact that when it employs one with energy the others are suspended. The superior form accordingly comprehends the inferior; that is, the rational soul includes the sensitive and nutritive souls of Aristotle. This opinion was recognised as a dogma by the Council of Vienne in 1311.

Descartes asks, "What am I? I am," he replies, "a thing that thinks, or that doubts, understands, conceives, affirms, denies, wills, does not will, and that imagines and feels." To Descartes the essence of man consists in thought, which, as we have seen above, is one of the modes of substance. Leibniz directs his mind to explaining the notion of substance, and he rises to the idea of force or energy. Active force is not the abstract power of the . scholastics, that is to say, it is not a simple possibility of acting which, in order to be reduced to act, should require an external stimulus. Real force includes action in itself; it is an entelechy, a power intermediate between the simple faculty of acting and the determinated or effected act. This active force is inherent in every substance which cannot remain a single instant inoperative; and this applies to corporeal substance as well as to spiritual substance. The soul is an active force, and as such it knows immediately what it does, and mediately what it feels. Free activity is the necessary condition of immediate perception, or of the knowledge of self (*conscientia, scire cum*) as well as of mediate external apperception conjoined with feeling of the Ego, which is essential to every feeling or idea. The soul does not know itself as a sensible force; it does not know that it lives, feels, and acts. This is the source of the obscure perceptions which Leibniz attributes to the soul in the state of a simple monad or living force. The pre-existence of the obscure perceptions, especially of those which are immediately bound to the functions of the animal life, cannot escape the attentive observer who is able to distinguish the previsive dominion of the spirit from the passivity (*fatum*) of the body.

Descartes had said · "I *think*, therefore I am." Maine de Biran corrected him, saying: "I *will*, therefore I am." Without action thought would not exist, and the true name of thought is will. We only attain gradually to the knowledge of this truth. We have hardly a gleam of it in the sensitive life which is common to the animal and the child; but in the perceptive life, or the life of reflection, we become aware that the motive force makes us perceive objects which become known to us by their resistance and the acting subject as well by a sort of reverberation. To perceive is therefore to move oneself and to act. To have consciousness is also acting; it is willing. Reason itself is only an extension of the will.

We are now able to formulate our conceptions of nature, knowledge, and the soul.

We have seen Leucippus and Democritus teaching from the most ancient times that matter is composed of corpuscles that are indivisible but indestructible, the number of which is infinite as is the greatness of the space in which they are scattered. These corpuscles are solid and endowed with figure and motion. The diversity of their forms determines the diversity of their movements and of their mode of aggregation, and consequently of their figure. The Greek atomism, however, had an enormous lacuna which Descartes has filled up by discovering the ether which serves for the transmission of motion. But, exclaimed Leibniz, everything can be explained mechanically except the mechanism itself. In ancient times this was understood; and Pythagoras, Anaxagoras, and Plato gave the predominance to a spiritual principle. According to Aristotle, matter at its highest degree of abstraction is indeterminate, and tends to form or to actuality. It has in itself a principle of potency, of force, which is a simple, unextended, incorporeal principle. The universe is a vast dynamism, a wise system of co-ordinated forces. Leibniz reproduced the doctrine of Aristotle, denying all immediate action (*influxus physicus*) between the monads, and believing that an ideal connection, or a disposition to the internal modifications which would make them harmonise with each other, was sufficient. Neither Aristotle nor Leibniz wished to exclude substance, which they considered essentially active. Kant, in his *Metaphysical Foundations of Physics*, seems to have wished to construe nature with the simple notion of force. He imagines two elementary forces, attraction and repulsion, which compose the universe. This doctrine is followed by Schelling. It is necessary to come to an understanding as to the meaning of the word " force." In mechanics, force is the cause of motion; in metaphysics it is not only a cause, but it becomes a substance, a species of spiritual atom. Substance and force are indissolubly united so as to compose what we call a being. The basis of corporeal things cannot be extended substance, although there will always remain a residuum irreducible to the notion of force, which it has been sought in vain to absorb into this notion. Substance without force is nothing, just as the concave is nothing without the convex. Leibniz was right in seeking the origin of mechanics and mathematics in metaphysics; but he was wrong in stopping at the notion of force, which is itself a mechanical and mathematical notion, and in not ascending to the actuality of Aristotle which is the inexhaustible source of force.[1]

What philosophers called "the Soul of the World," was an immaterial force mingled with matter, not extending beyond it, and which served as a motor and plastic principle giving it movement and that variety of forms which we admire in the universe. Plato, thinking that pure intelligence or the substance of the eternal ideas could not act directly on matter, imagined a substance intermediate between these two principles. He conceived it as formed of an invariable identical element, like intelligence, and of a variable element like sensible objects. The active substance of Leibniz, the metaphysical point of Vico, and the *methexis* of Gioberti, ought not to be confounded with the soul of the world, which has been set aside as a useless hypothesis, because there is nothing to prevent God from acting directly upon bodies or to hinder the manifold immaterial forces from producing all the phenomena of nature. Here arises the somewhat indiscreet question as to whether God created one substance of a single species which, by transforming itself, has produced all other species; or whether He created all the existing

[1] See Janet, *L'idée de force et la philosophie dynamique.* Revue de Deux Mondes, 1ᵉʳ Mai 1874.

and extinct species, which differ from each other not only in degree but also in essence.

The theory of knowledge may be applied to elucidate the theory of existence. If ideas are the prototypes of things, and if their totality constitutes the essence of God in which our mind perceives them, it follows that specific essences ought to correspond to the specific ideas. The proper form of the intellect is the intelligible species, which abstraction separates from sensation, and which is found in all minds, and is applied to all the objects of the same class. The controversy became burning in the Middle Ages, first in opposition to the Nominalists, who considered the genera and species as *flatus vocis*, and then in opposition to the Averroists, who maintained thought to be impersonal and identical in all men. In our days the controversy has been renewed again with Positivism and Darwinism; and we have no other means of defending knowledge and existence than the Platonic doctrine of ideas as carried to perfection by Gioberti. A singular way this of proving facts by a hypothesis! will be the exclamation of some minute observer of nature, not considering that there are not only physical facts but also mental facts. Men, says Plato, are like prisoners chained in a cave underground, and above them over their shoulders there is an opening through which there penetrates a light, produced by a fire which they cannot see, because they are chained to the walls of the cave in such a way that they can neither move their body nor their head. Before the aperture of their dungeon men pass over a low wall who carry objects, the shadow of which is reflected on the walls of the cave. What do the prisoners think of these shadows? They fancy that they are realities, the only realities which exist; and if the passers by to whom we have referred should speak and their voices were to be repeated by the echo of the cave, the prisoners would naturally believe that the shadows were speaking. If one of these prisoners were to be suddenly led up to the open air, he would begin to distinguish the shadows and then the objects in themselves. This is the history of the soul. It is a prisoner here below, and by meditation it has to release itself from the bonds of the body in order to contemplate the ideas in themselves. By means of the senses we are enabled to understand that all equal things tend to an intelligible equality, below which, however, they always remain. Whence can the idea of this equality come? Certainly not from sensation, but from thought. It is one of the modes of thought, or something substantial. In order to reach it, we must go out of ourselves and turn to an invisible point in which the object touches the subject and forms the unity of the synthesis of thought.

This point, according to Gioberti, is the first intuitive judgment: *Being creates the existent.* But is the intuition which apprehends Being the very same, or at least is it realised in the same way as that which apprehends the existent? In such a case, seeing that in the intuition of the existent the subject and the object are equal and the one acts upon the other, the same ought to happen in the intuition of Being, and this intuition would exist before Being had created. There is therefore another mode of knowing different from and superior to that which we call successive and reflective. It has as its proper object the creating Being, to the exclusion of the existent; whence its immanence is transferred into the act which contemplates it, from which therefore all succession is excluded. This being an immediate synthesis between the infinite and the finite, it ought to have certain special qualities, the most singular of which is that, while the creating Being works in us, we do not work in that Being, although it is the object of our contemplation. Thus it is that the cognition is totally determined by the action of the creative cause, and consequently it is a true infallible revelation. In this primitive and immanent state of cogni-

tion, the activity involved is not distinct nor separated
from thought, but they are one and the same thing.
Hence thought has not for its immediate cause the thinking activity or the existent, but Being, which at a certain
point creates the thinking activity. And on this account
the spirit introduces nothing of its own into the object,
seeing that that object arises at that very point at which
it springs itself into existence, and it cannot unfold any
act of its own before it thinks; and thus its essential
activity is just thought. In this way Being, wholly
stripped of any subjective property, offers itself to our
immanent thought. Consequently it cannot be that the
spirit has cognition of itself in this immanent thought,
although it does yet know itself in a certain way; but this
primitive manner of knowing itself may be compared to
the eye which sees the light and itself in the light, because
light is its essence. It does not know itself in itself as
existent, but in its cause and in the transition of the
creative act. The immanent thought is a pure intuition
of the intelligible; it is a sort of terminus or an effect
which regards the intelligible Being as its principle and its
cause. It is perfect, identical in all men, not susceptible
of progress, necessary, and out of time. It is a perception
of being without judgment, since every judgment implies
an act of attention and consciousness, which cannot have
place in this thought, as it is included in the creative act
of this Being, which as it is alone truly operative, so it
alone truly affirms and gives place to the two objective
judgments : *I am ; I create.* Hence it follows that immanent thought cannot be directly apprehended, although
every act of attention or reflection implies a human judgment, and is related to the succeeding thought. Similarly
this immanent thought does not by itself constitute science,
which involves consciousness. It only furnishes the confused matter or the germ of science; and science is therefore the explication of the material thus furnished by

means of reflection and speech.[1] This mental process may be verified by every attentive observer because it is a fact.

To this double state of thought there corresponds a double state in nature, because the existent as created by Being ought to resemble it. Now Being is one, infinite, and essentially ideal and creative. The existent has a finite unity which does not exclude multiplicity; it has a relative intelligibility, a potential infinity, and a con-creative power, which correspond to the absolute identity, the actual infinity, and the creative power of Being. This analogy between the existent and Being, between the copy and the original, is expressed by the term *methexis*, which properly means participation. The Methexis is the universe viewed as an intelligible unity which combines in its bosom an always increasing number of forces. There are three *methexes :* the initial methexis, the medial methexis, and the final methexis. The medial methexis is differentiated from the first and last, because in it multiplicity prevails over unity, chaos over order, and the sensible over the intelligible. The medial methexis is the passage and transition from the initial methexis to the final methexis. This transition involves the issuing of the diverse from the identical, of the individuals from the species; and as an intermediate factor it binds together power and act, and has the contrary qualities of the two extremes. Hence Gioberti calls it *mimesis*, or imitation. The mimesis is essentially progressive, inasmuch as the initial methexis goes on actualising itself in order to become final, and the more the mimesis approaches the final methexis, the more does the intelligibility and unity of things increase. Everything is thus on the way to

---

[1] This is the highest point of metaphysics. We have adopted in our exposition the words of Professor Luciani in his work, already referred to, on Gioberti and the new Italian Philosophy (*Gioberti e la* *filosofia nuova italiana*, vol. iii.). Luciani has first shown that the *Protologia* of Gioberti constitutes a new science distinct from the *Ontologia* which is subordinate to it.

become thought; the essence of things is thought, because it is the methexis. It is to be noted that what is here spoken of, is created thought and not uncreated thought; for the methexis is not the Idea.

The soul in the methexis occupies a distinct place; but it may be asked: is it a force and is it only a force? If so it would be necessary to hold with Herbart that psychology is a part of mechanics, and that the laws of number and weight are applicable to spirit as well as to matter. But there is in the soul a different element higher than force, and this is mind. Force is attached to the soul, depends on it, and emanates from it, but does not constitute it. In order therefore to have an adequate idea of the soul we must not stop at force, but rise to the activity which is the inexhaustible source of all force. Maine de Biran has given a new development to dynamism, bringing into light the properties of effort and of the will which produces it. The ancient philosophy had left a lacuna in reference to the free will. In the view of Plato the intellect had always the power of making us determine for the good; love, according to him, was a species of fatal desire; and virtue cost hardly any effort. Aristotle approached the truth when he conceived of morality as the proper and personal activity of the agent; but he stops at the supremacy of the intellect, not understanding that man possesses in his free will an infinite and absolute worth which makes him an end and never a means or an instrument. Stoicism retained liberty, regarding it as necessity rightly understood. Christianity put forward charity as the love of our neighbour, and consequently gave prominence to duty, leaving law and right in 'the shade. The first systems of modern times, those of Descartes and Leibniz, did not assign to the will the place that was due to it. Descartes did not exactly distinguish the faculties of the mind, and he confounded the will with the . intellect. Leibniz, not recognising any reciprocal action among his monads, had recourse to the hypothesis of the pre-established harmony. Vico, however, said clearly: "Knowing is necessary; willing is free." Kant afterwards put the will into strong relief, reconstructing in his *Critique of the Practical Reason* what he had demolished in the *Critique of the Pure Reason.* Maine de Biran, studying facts, put the activity of the will out of doubt; and a whole school of young Leibnizians is at present carrying on the war in France against the attacks of the positivists.

Such are our philosophical conclusions, and they determine us for idealism as against sensualism. We have not spoken of scepticism and mysticism, although we reckoned them at the outset among the fundamental systems. In fact, scepticism and mysticism represent two essential sides of our nature. The human spirit has its moments of weakness and of impatience, and then it becomes sceptical or mystical. It is not desirable that it should be otherwise, because a little scepticism or a little mysticism is a useful corrective of a dogmatism which might become presumptuous and impertinent, or of a rationalism which would dry up the soul. Or to speak more exactly, scepticism and mysticism are rather two states of the soul than two doctrines. They are accidents in the history of metaphysics. Thus the remark of Leibniz is verified that the systems are generally true in what they affirm and false in what they deny, so that it is necessary to adopt the better part of their doctrines, but, as he adds, by making at the same time always a step of advance. This is what every new system does, or believes it does; that is to say, it professes to embrace and improve the one which has preceded it. And thus humanity does not turn round in a fatal circle, but accumulates observations and raises itself always higher. It might be difficult, however, for us to prove this by a minute comparison of the metaphysical systems of Plato and Aristotle with those of Leibniz and Gioberti. The two former saw farther because their horizon was unexplored; but the latter two have discerned things more distinctly because they have profited by the observations of all their predecessors.   What is there that is not comprehended in the system of Gioberti?   We have seen how the "methexis" from being initial and then medial becomes final.   If space allowed us we might show how the supernatural is an anticipation of the final methexis, and how the supra-intelligible will diminish without being annihilated.

Having thus found a *quidquid inconcussum,* we may now begin to rear our moral and juridical edifice.

II.

WE feel, think, and will. This being recognised, it remains for us to see how these faculties act in practical life, and whether their activity proceeds in view of a final end. Undoubtedly sense predominates in the first period of life; our life is then instinctive and wholly animal. Reason appears with speech, and then we act no more from impulse, but from calculation. Later on reason shows other relations, such as those referring to order and to the good in itself, and the will does not allow itself to be determined merely by pleasure or by the useful, but feels itself obliged to actualise the good. The moral life, properly so called, appears only in the third period of man's life, the first and the second periods being common to us with the animals. All the fundamental systems of philosophy have not recognised the three periods; for sensualism, scepticism, and partly also mysticism, deny the power of the will to elevate itself to the moral law, as well as the universality of this law. Idealism alone demonstrates the insufficiency of the instinctive and egoistic state to explain all the moral phenomena. We have already shown the close relations of knowing and willing; and it now remains for us to indicate what the principal philosophical systems have gradually unfolded with reference to the doctrine of morals.

Ethics as a moral doctrine seems to spring full armed from the head of Plato, for he sums up Pythagoras, the ancient sages, and especially his master Socrates. No one

has better distinguished than Plato what the absolute
good is; and he identifies it with God, whom we ought to
seek to imitate. The good in everything is order; and
the soul to be happy and wise ought also to be well
ordered. The soul realises the good by means of virtue,
which is composed of four elements : wisdom, courage or
constancy, temperance, and probity or justice. There is
nothing more beautiful than justice; and love leads us
to it. Injustice is an evil and demands a remedy which
consists in punishment and expiation. Punishment, says
Plato, liberates the soul from evil.

Plato, however, in his psychology, does not rightly distinguish the faculty of knowledge from that of will. Evil
is committed only from ignorance. We do not find any
description of that intermediate state in which the soul
does not do the good which it knows and loves, and in
which it prefers the evil which it knows and hates. The
personal activity is thus limited; and this is a point which
Aristotle undertook to correct.

Aristotle, in his Metaphysics, distinguishes between
potentiality and actuality. In his Ethics, he explains that
actuality is identical with the end or purpose; and he
called the aspiration which every being has to pass from
potentiality to actuality, desire. The end of a being can
consist only in the good; and the perfect being will be
that one in which there will be no more potentiality, but
all will be actuality. Man loves action, and virtue consists in attaining actuality. Pleasure springs from action;
it is an adjunct or complement which is superadded to
activity as beauty is to youth. Aristotle, in his theory of
the virtues, distinguishes free will, personal responsibility,
and the influence of habit in the exercise of the virtues.
In these points he excels Plato, who had confounded
virtue with science, and had left the practical conditions
of morality in the shade. He approaches Plato again,
when he gives the predominance to the intellectual
virtues over the moral virtues, and makes the highest

happiness consist in thought, which renders us like the gods.

Epicurus made happiness the end of morality, but he did not regard it as consisting in the actualisation of the good, but rather in the prudent search for pleasure. He reduced all virtue to the avoiding of the greater pain and seeking the better pleasure which is the tranquillity of the soul. "Our wants," says Epicurus, "are of three kinds: natural and necessary, such as hunger and thirst; natural and not necessary, such as the desire of delicate foods; and factitious, such as the craving for spirituous liquors. The wise man combats the last of these, moderates the second, and satisfies the first. What is strictly necessary ought to satisfy the happiness of the wise man; with a bit of barley bread and a cup of water, he may be as happy as Jove."

Zeno the Stoic combated pleasure as unstable and deceitful, and he found happiness in the fulfilment of duty, that is, in the observance of the laws of nature. Man has a place assigned him in the universe by an inexorable destiny, and he cannot desert it except by suicide. By combating his good or bad passions, man may attain to a state of insensibility which Zeno and his followers call happiness.[1]

Christianity regarded morality as a resurrection. The soul, having lost its purity by original sin, the sacrifice of a God was necessary for its redemption. The fundamental precept of the Christian doctrine of morals is this: Love God above everything, and thy neighbour as thyself. The love of God is generally inseparable from the love of our neighbour, which is charity; but the true perfection lies in the contemplative life, in prayer, and in ecstacy. Plato established a sort of natural society between man and God; Christianity proclaimed the absolute dependence of man. St. Augustine starts from the Platonic idea that man by reason perceives the eternal law of all truth and

---

[1] See Denis, *Histoire des theories et des idées morales dans l'antiquité,* 2nd ed. Paris, 1879.

all justice, and actualises it by means of free will. But in the later period of his life, in connection with his controversy with Pelagius, he abandoned this idea, and maintained that the soul after the fall lost the liberty of abstaining from sin, but preserved that of committing it, and that God immediately directs the will to do good, granting or denying this grace according to His pleasure. This is the Augustinian doctrine of election and predestination. The Church modified the Augustinian doctrine by establishing the view that human liberty is not annihilated, but is supported by the divine grace, which is granted to whoever does not reject it.

As Augustine had thus sought to attach the Christian ethics to Plato, Thomas Aquinas endeavoured to connect them with the doctrines of Aristotle. He lays down the position that all beings have an end, and that the final end of man is happiness. But he asks, what is this happiness? It is not the happiness which springs from material goods, which are transitory; nor that of a tranquil soul, as the soul cannot rest in itself, but only in its final end, which is God. He therefore distinguishes an imperfect happiness, which is that of this world here below, from the perfect happiness, which must be exempt from all evil, and which being attainable only in the other life, consists in the contemplation of God face to face. By this distinction, Aquinas departed very far from the views of Aristotle, as Aristotle placed happiness in meditation, or in the philosophical life, and believed that the natural virtues were sufficient. Thomas Aquinas, on the contrary, shows, like Plato, that every created being is imperfect, because it is only in part, and that the supreme good is in God. And he adds as a Christian, that the natural virtues which are derived from the intellect and the will are insufficient to elevate us to the supra-natural order; that intelligence is subordinate to the supra-intelligence which is faith; and that the will is attracted by faith and love. Faith, hope, and charity do not pass above nature, but complete it.

The Renaissance attacked scholasticism; and in a more disguised way it attacked Christianity itself in the name of reason and nature. The Court of Rome was seduced by the splendour of the arts and by eloquence; and paganism seemed to be reviving. A vigorous reaction was not long in manifesting itself; and Luther and Calvin denied all efficacy to human works by resuscitating and exaggerating the Augustinian doctrine. Melanchthon was regarded as almost a heretic when he maintained that we have the liberty to resist grace.

The modern period was opened by Bacon. He divides moral philosophy into two parts: the good in general, which he says has been well treated by the ancients and the scholastics; and the mode of regulating our conduct in life, which deserves to be better cultivated. Bacon denies the superiority of the contemplative life when it does not tend to better the active life. He desiderates that the passions and affections be studied and described, a thing which had been done till then rather by the poets and historians than by the philosophers.

Bacon's wish was soon carried out. In 1649 there appeared a treatise by Descartes on the passions, which he analysed from the physiological and psychological side, and he also considered the method of regulating them. Nevertheless, Cartesianism was not directly favourable to moral philosophy, as Descartes did not recognise the action of second causes, but regarded them as existing only because they are created every moment by God. Malebranche, with a certain originality, distinguishes in things the relations of quantity and perfection, that is to say, he distinguishes the mathematical and the moral truths. The mind uses the mathematical relationships in order to know things and to submit them to calculation; but the relationships of perfection induce and oblige it to prefer and love those things which possess them. Man is therefore driven by his nature not only to know but to love; and he loves what is most perfect, that is,

God, and then things in proportion as by their perfection they approach God. But as God creates in us our ideas, He also creates our acts. Thus our liberty consists in the attention which we accord to the work of God; and virtue consists entirely in spiritual force. Malebranche was the first to divide the science of ethics into three parts, treating respectively of the duties towards God, towards ourselves, and towards other men. Spinoza carried out to its extreme issue the definition of substance given by Descartes, and he found only one substance which develops itself according to secondary laws. How is a doctrine of morals possible in this system ? The good and the evil are merely relative ideas. Virtue is power, and it consists in having adequate ideas, as the soul is passive and enslaved in inadequate and confused ideas. It is necessary therefore to make reason predominate over the passions, and to get near to the supreme intelligence. Leibniz vainly endeavoured to eradicate the germs of pantheism which he discerned in the Cartesian philosophy, by substituting for the view of a continuous creation that of a continuous participation, and for the absolute passivity of the creatures their essential activity ; for he does not explain the physical and moral order otherwise than by an hypothesis, namely, that of a pre-established harmony.

Vico, considering God as the immovable mover of all created things, makes Him also the mover of the human spirit. This movement, however, does not consist in an impulsion or mechanical push, but in its virtuality as communicated to it by creation, a virtuality or power which includes what are called faculties, such as are exhibited in thought and will. And as the mind cannot but think Being, that Being which is the true and the good in itself, so it is never separated therefrom, not even in its errors, as it is not possible that the mind even in its aberrations should think of nothingness, nor that the will, however culpable, should wish it. Thus we lay hold of the false only under the appearances of the true, or we will what is evil under the appearance of the good.

Sensualism, which had shown itself timidly in the Middle Ages and more openly in the Renaissance, came to its full manifestation in modern times with Hobbes. This philosopher distinguishes the cognitive faculties from the affective faculties. Sensation commences with the action on the brain; is communicated to the heart; and there produces joy or pain, love accompanied with desire, or hatred accompanied with aversion. When there is experienced in reference to the same thing, now desire and then aversion, this alternative while it lasts is called deliberation. When in consequence of deliberation one of the two movements conquers the other, it takes the name of will; and when the will produces execution, there is liberty of choice, so that liberty is not independence, but simply the absence of any obstacle to the will.

Locke sought to save the activity of the mind by distinguishing reflection from sensation. But he failed; for in order to escape from the innate ideas of the Cartesians, he made the mind a *tabula rasa,* and reflection served only to elaborate what sensation furnished to it. Deriving everything from sensation, moral good and evil could be nothing else, according to Locke's principle, than the pleasure and pain which accompany an action. Helvetius, Saint-Lambert, Volney, and Bentham were the faithful interpreters of this doctrine.

The Scottish School of philosophy distinguished *à priori* truths from *à posteriori* truths, designating the former by the names of fundamental laws of belief, primitive beliefs, and truths of common sense; and it proceeded to show that these could not come from experience. Hutchison, the first thinker of this school, started from Locke's theory of knowledge, and he sought to endow us with a special sense which could discover moral good in human actions. Adam Smith took a step in advance and derived the good from the moral sentiments, which were all reduced by him to sympathy. It did not cost Price much trouble to demonstrate that the idea of the good can only take its origin in the intuitive reason, and he was followed in this line by Reid and Dugald Stewart. This school rendered great services to moral science by its fine psychological analyses. This is sufficiently shown by referring to the investigations of Reid relating to instinct, the appetites, the desires, and the affections, which he designated by the complex term, principles of action.

We have already seen that Kant in his *Critique of the Pure Reason* became imprisoned in the *Ego;* but he did not suffer this imprisonment long, for he sought to break his fetters in the *Critique of the Practical Reason.* The moral law, he said, is given by pure reason, as a fact of which we have consciousness *à priori*, and it is apodictically certain. In the universal and obligatory character of this law, Kant sees the passage to objective reality; and therefore he does not make it depend on the idea of the good, which according to the first of these Critiques would be a concept of our mind. The existence of this law is attested by the consciousness of all, as well as the freedom which consists in conforming our actions to it. The moral principle is called by Kant the *Categorical Imperative*, and it is thus formulated: "Act so that the maxim of thy action may be capable of being raised by the will to a universal law." Here it seems evident that Kant confounds the will with the reason, maintaining that the will is autonomous, or that it obeys only its own law, that is to say, that law which is conformable to it, and which may be valid for every rational will. Duty consists in conforming our actions to the prescriptions of this law, so that our actions acquire a moral value, not by the end which they put before them, but by the principle which determines them. But of this, consciousness ought evidently to apprise us. Now if we hold with Kant that consciousness is a mode of the sensibility, how can it reveal to us the law of duty? And what else could this law be but the simplest form of the relations of phenomena among themselves ? From the existence of the law of duty, Kant deduces as a postulate the immortality of the soul and the existence of God, who distributes rewards and punishments according to desert.[1]

Fichte carried out the system of Kant to its extremest consequences both in metaphysics and in ethics. The German philosophy, having thus developed the notion of liberty in Kant and Fichte, proceeded in Schelling and Hegel to absorb it in the notion of necessity. It always maintains the idea of freedom in the third moment or phase of the metaphysical evolution, but in such a transcendent sense that it rather denotes the rational unity of the *great whole*, than the individual unity of the human personality. The successors of Hegel have understood this necessity in a wholly material sense, and they have taken for their idea the mechanism of matter and the organism of life, subjecting effects to causes, means to ends, the individual to the State, the weak States to the strong States, and the alleged inferior races to the superior races. We have already spoken of the ethics of Schopenhauer and Hartmann in dealing with their metaphysics. Against these doctrines, Fichte the younger, Wirth, and Ulrici, have combated in the name of liberty and reason, in the "Review of Philosophy and Philosophical Criticism."

France availed herself of the aid of the Scottish and German philosophy in order to combat sensualism. Maine de Biran, in restoring activity to the Ego, by an excess in his reaction, concentrates it entirely in the will, which he confounds with force. Jouffroy puts everything in its proper place. What was the principal thing to Maine de Biran becomes accessory in Jouffroy. The will appears and disappears in the intellect which persists always, both in the voluntary state and in the state of spontaneity. Jouffroy carefully distinguishes the physiological func-

---

[1] See Cousin, *La philosophie de Kant.* 3rd ed. Paris, 1857.

tions from the psychological functions. He recognises three primitive tendencies: the desire of knowing or curiosity, the love of others or sympathy, and the love of power or ambition; and he shows the pleasure and pain which the satisfaction or repression of these tendencies causes us, and the part taken in them by the external world, the reason, and the will. Obstacles serve to develop our liberty and to form our personality; and life has the double merit of making us free, and putting our freedom under the empire of reason. Jouffroy is not satisfied like Kant with deriving duty from liberty, but he has recourse to the principal of finality. What then is our destiny? Every being, says Jouffroy, is predestined by its nature to attain to an end. This end is its good; and the end of man is indicated by his primitive tendencies to know, to act, and to love. These tendencies are blind and disinterested, because they impel us to action before knowing whether it will bring us pleasure or pain. The first development of human activity is instinctive and innocent; but as soon as we have learned that the satisfaction of our tendencies procures us a pleasure and their non-satisfaction a pain, we act no longer from instinct, but from calculation. Reason has now intervened; and it has learned that all our tendencies look to the individual good, but that this good cannot be complete. It makes us aware that it is necessary to sacrifice the lively pleasures of the moment in order to attain to pure and more lasting pleasures in the future. It assigns to actions the principle of interest well understood. Our nature runs after this end, which is indicated to us by reason, and the love of the well-understood interest is superadded to the primitive passions, which always subsist. This new state is called egoism or selfishness, which did not exist in the instinctive state. But this is not the ultimate state of human nature; for reason is not long in coming to understand that as all beings have to attain an end, the individual good is part of the universal good, of the absolute good, or of the good in itself; and that if the good of an individual is opposed to the good of other individuals, we ought to prefer the greatest sum of possible good. Thus the idea of the obligatory good appears to our reason; and our reason rises from the idea of the universal order to the idea of God who has created this order; and our submission to order becomes submission to God. Morality and religion are different expressions of this fact. In the arts, beauty and ugliness are only the expression of order and of disorder. The beautiful is an aspect of the good, and the true is another aspect of it. The beautiful is order expressed; the true is order thought; and the good is order realised. The good in itself appears only when reason shows us the universal order and presents it to us as obligatory. In the two first states, the individual served only himself, at first instinctively, and thereafter with discernment and egoism. In the third state, the individual serves order, and he is now able to raise himself to sacrifice. It is then only that there are manifested the ideas of merit and of demerit, of moral satisfaction and remorse, and of penalty and reward.[1]

This theory of human destiny was invested by Jouffroy in a popular form after the manner of a catechism. Why has man been created? In order to know, love, and serve God in this life, and to enjoy Him eternally in the other life. To know God is to know the order established in the world; to love Him and to serve Him is to conform ourselves to His designs, that is to say, to the universal order so far as our powers go. Accordingly they are mistaken who promise on this earth the harmonious development of our tendencies, because the struggle will not be able to cease till the obstacles in our way have ceased; and our aspirations after science, love, and power cannot be completely satisfied here below, so that our life demands further completion.

It is evident that Jouffroy seeks to give the doctrine

---

[1] *Cours de droit natural*, passim. 3rd ed. Paris, 1858.

of morals an objective basis. He had as his associate in this attempt, Cousin, who lost himself in the subtleties of his theory of the impersonal reason.

It remained for Gioberti to substitute the ontological process for the psychological process in the knowledge of the good, and thus to give us an exact synthesis of the modern principles of ethics in his elegant treatise *Of the Good.* He exhibits the Creator in intercourse with man as will and thought. As will, He manifests Himself in the quality of the obligatory law to which Kant gave the name of the *Imperative.* But the Kantian Imperative is purely abstract and subjective, and accordingly it has little or no efficacy on the human will. The Imperative of Gioberti is founded in a commanding person who is the intuitive concrete of which the imperative is the reflective abstract. Both of these are the volition of God with reference to the liberty of man. This volition prescribes to free spirits the observance of the orders established in the sphere of the cosmical forces. God says to every man: Maintain the order of the creation. The Imperative accordingly is the voice of the Supreme Being who speaks to our conscience and promulgates an absolute and divine command. From this it follows that the imperative includes the notion of right, that is, the idea of a supreme and absolute will having the power to command the creatures. In the primitive order of things, the conception of duty springs and proceeds from the correlative notion of right. The absolute right of God creates the absolute duty of man, who has in relation to his Creator duties without rights. From such absolute duty, which is the effect of that absolute right, then arise the relative duties which bind men among each other, and finally the relative rights which are the necessary correlation of these relative duties.

It remains for us to speak of the positivist and naturalistic schools of Ethics. Positivism began by maintaining that it was vain to attempt to construct science *à priori,* seeing that every metaphysical system, whatever may be its pretensions, has only a logical value, and in the real order expresses but more or less perfectly the science of its time. As an example of this the Ionic School is adduced, as its systems correspond to a first glance cast upon nature, and the Pythagorean School, which transferred to its system the discoveries made by it in geometry, astronomy, and acoustics. It is added that Plato himself, when in his *Timæus* he expounds *à priori* the plan followed by God in the creation, uses the imperfect theories of the astronomy, physics, and physiology of his time. And finally the positivists assert that the universe which Hegel believed that he had constructed solely by means of his transcendental logic, is found conformable at every point to the *à posteriori* cognitions of his time. Positivism was not long in displaying its inconsequences, by making an imperfect use of observation and reducing psychology to a species of cerebral physics, the soul being defined as the complex of the functions of the brain and of the spinal marrow. In making physics the basis of psychology, it follows that anthropology and history will have to become social physics. Positivism is thus confounded with naturalism, and we see an interchange of theories between these two systems.

What then can the moral law be according to positivism? The whole doctrine of morals, says Littré, springs from two impulses: the love of self and benevolence towards others, egoism and altruism. The first of these impulses springs from the necessity of nutrition, which is experienced by the organised substance in order that it may subsist individually; and the second from the necessity of loving, which by means of the sexual union serves to preserve the species.[1] Moral science accordingly will have as its object to deduce from the laws of life and from the conditions of existence, rules of conduct for the attainment of the individual and social well-being. This well-being or

---

[1] Littré, *La philosophie positive.* Paris, 1870.

good consists in pleasure and utility; and it will be produced mechanically, for in us liberty lies only in the
execution and not in the volition, which is determined by
causes independent of us.

For the brutal selfishness of Hobbes, Bentham substituted a moral thermometer by means of which he hoped
that the science of the passions or mental pathology
would be able to measure pleasures both in their intensity
and in their extension. The question of duty was thus
reduced by him to a problem of arithmetic. John Stuart
Mill took up the problem, recurring to the association of
ideas as a view that was dear to the English psychologists,
who put the criterion of the justice or injustice of an
action in its foreseeable consequences. A mental habit
associates with an action an idea of approbation or disap-
probation. The moral sense is an acquired sentiment,
not a primitive faculty. Conscience, being only a series
of instincts and hereditary habits, is subject to the laws
which preside over the formation of the instincts. This
is found in divers degrees in all the divisions of the
animal kingdom; and natural selection develops it in the
higher animals. Darwin claims to have discovered in the
animals a sort of moral instinct which rises to the consciousness of social solidarity, and intelligence being added
to this instinct there arises, according to this celebrated
naturalist, the sentiment of moral obligation and duty.
The law of adaptation to the environment, of which the
law of association is only a consequence, gives to the
moral sense new energy; the instincts contrary to the
conditions of existence created by external circumstances
disappear, and the others form organs. Every instinct,
says Darwin, which is permanently stronger or more
persistent than another, brings forth a sentiment which
we denote by the expression, *must obey.* This is the moral
sanction. The conclusions of Darwin have been adopted
by Bain, and have been somewhat modified by Herbert
Spencer. Spencer holds that just as the intuition of space

possessed by a living individual is the result of the experiences of the individuals that have preceded it, so the experiences of utility accumulated by the whole human race have produced corresponding nervous modifications which by hereditary transmission have produced in us certain faculties of moral intuition, and awakened certain emotions relative to just or unjust conduct, which have not any apparent foundations in the experiences of individual utility. Spencer differs from the other utilitarians not as to the end which has to be attained, but as to the means which have to be followed. Happiness is the ultimate end of morals, and not the proximate end. The object of moral science ought to be to deduce from the laws of life and from the conditions of existence what are the actions which conduce to happiness; and as humanity is only a part of the universe, moral science thus depends in ultimate analysis on cosmology.

This school holds that for us there is no liberty of choice. Hence John Stuart Mill distinguishes three kinds of determinism: the first consists in the invariability of the particular effects even when the particular causes change, and this may be called absolute fatalism; the second finds place when the effects are invariable, because causes do not change, and this may be called a mitigated fatalism; and the third is the complement of the preceding view, and is established when variation of the causes makes the effects also vary. Mill holds to this third species of determinism, and teaches that moral obligation can only be understood in an impersonal sense, that is to say, that something produces in us the thought and the desire of perfecting our own character.

Is free will then an illusion? Positive science only develops the doctrine of necessity; or as the English say, it only recognises *uniform causation*. A. Herzen, in his *Physiology of the Will*, sums up the results of the latest researches in the following terms:—" 1. Spontaneity of actions in living beings does not exist any more than it

exists in any phenomenon of the universe whatever; every
change is the effect of a preceding change, and no effect
can be spontaneous. All the acts of any being whatever
are reactions excited by the influences and impressions
which the being receives from the external universe. It
is an influence when there is no consciousness, and an
impression when there is perception by means of the
organs of the senses. In the absence of motives arising
directly from without, it is impressions which act on the
senses, including ideas, images, and representations—that
is to say, the subjective sensations indirectly excited in
the nerve centres. In either case, there is no activity,
because there are no motives. 2. The will is the consciousness of the determining motive combined with that
of the 'image of the act, or of the series of acts which
have to be executed after the victory of the predominating
motive. In other words, the will is only the perception
of the tendency to act or not to act in some particular
way, in consequence of a particular combination, or of
the resultant of all the causes which provoke the action.
3. Individual liberty or free will is a subjective sensation
arising from what is incalculable and unexpected, conditions which always exist in our actions, and which render
it impossible for us to foresee all the circumstances which
may supervene and influence the final resolution. Hence
the feeling of freedom or of the resolution is simply the
consciousness of the possibility of a change in the tendency
to execute this or that other act in consequence of a modification in the external or internal motives which may arise
and exert an influence upon our action. The illusion of the
spontaneity of an already completed action, persists only
when the agent has not been conscious of the determining
motive, or has ignored it; not having observed it, or having
forgotten it on account of its small importance. The
illusion of the freedom of a future action subsists until
the moment in which the victorious motive makes all its
force felt. As soon as we know what we are going to do,

we know also the reason of it; and accordingly we know the determining motive of our action. But before knowing it there is for us a moment of undecided equilibrium among the different motives; and being ignorant of the final result we form a representation of various possible results. This moment produces in the individual the illusion of freedom as a faculty of free choice or free will. 4. The final determination of the will is the infallible, necessary, and exclusive product of the following three factors : *a.* The individual organisation, or the innate physical or moral constitution, including the dispositions, the desires, the passions, the character, &c. ; *b.* The state of the nervous system at the moment in which it receives the impression which sets it into activity, that is, the moral state of the nerve centres, produced by education in the widest sense of the term; *c.* The sum total of the impressions perceived in the moment of acting, whether they are derived directly from an external source, or are awakened by reflex action or by association in the internal ramification of the nerve centres. 5. Individuality is the positive and real conception which ought to take the place of the metaphysical conception of freedom. The term freedom or liberty, when applied to the individual activity, precisely signifies the absence of obstacles external or internal, physical or moral, which might possibly prevent the individual from acting conformably to the tendencies inherent in his physical or moral constitution, or the conditions in the midst of which he is developed. In other words, the freedom of the individual consists in the capability of being able to react in his own way, and without constraint, according to the volitions or desires awakened in him by the concourse of circumstances. The individual is therefore free to do whatever he wills when the execution of his willing is not impeded; but he is not free *to will what he will*, since his volitions are produced by the conditions above enumerated, which conditions in no way depend on the individual. But just because the organisation is one of the three factors of the volitions to which it gives an individual character, the positive conception of individuality is clearer and much more suitable than the negative conception of freedom."

Free will being denied, the question arises, will it be possible to foresee human actions? To this question Herbert Spencer gives the following in reply :—A free body in space subject to the attraction of another single body, will move in a direction which can be predicted with great precision. But if it is attracted by other two bodies, the displacement can be calculated only approximately, and with still less precision if it is attracted by three bodies. Finally, let us suppose the said body surrounded by various bodies of all sorts of dimensions, situated in all directions and at all distances, its motion will be apparently independent of the influence of each of them; it will move in an indefinite and oscillating line, and it will seem *free*, just as if it determined itself spontaneously. In the same way, in the degree in which the relations of any psychical state are multiplied, the psychical modifications become incalculable and appear independent of all law.

And now, turning our attention from the individual man to collective man, it may be similarly asked, whether we shall be able to foresee anything of the future. Here Littré answers as follows: Sociology is the sixth of the fundamental sciences, and it is therefore subordinated to biology, which depends upon physics and chemistry. The physiological man—that is, man regarded as without any acquired quality material, moral, or intellectual—is transformed into the sociological man, or rather the historical man, by evolution. What takes place by means of natural selection in the animal kingdom, says Littré, is attained in the human kingdom by means of education, which is first instinctive and unconscious, and then determinate and conscious. The sociological evolution is produced by the capacity which the societies have for accumulating cognitions. Tradition, monuments, and writing are, as it were, the organs of this faculty. The societies are stationary when the sum of the cognitions remains the same; they are retrograde if it diminishes, and progressive when it increases. History is therefore a natural phenomenon, and is not subject to chance nor to caprice. It proceeds by the filiation of the social states, or by a process of generating them from each other. It shows us humanity in its various degrees of development, until it becomes mistress of itself, in the stage of the positive sciences. The end of individual life accordingly is to increase and adorn the collective life. The past generations laboured instinctively for this end, and the future generations will strive towards it with a full consciousness of their social mission.

Let us now pause in order to cast a glance over the path we have traversed. Founding on a psychology that is generally received, we saw that there are three faculties in the mind, namely, feeling, thinking, and willing; and to these correspond three states of the soul, the instinctive, the egoistic, and the moral. All the systems, however, do not recognise these three states; sensualism stops at the first two, and idealism alone rises to the moral law. We have reviewed the struggle between sensualism and idealism in the course of the ages, a struggle which has become a livelier conflict in our age owing to the immense progress of the natural sciences. These sciences have, however, brought out clearly the unity of design pervading the various types. "From one pole to the other, and under all the meridians," says Agassiz, "the mammalia, the birds, the reptiles, and the fishes reveal the same plan of structure. This plan denotes abstract cognitions of the most elevated order, and it far surpasses all the generalisations of the human mind. The most laborious investigations have had to be carried on in order that man might be able only to form an idea of it." [1] These types, both

---

[1] *De l'espèce et des classifications._ Paris, 1869.*

animal and vegetable, are likewise most exactly adapted
to every part of the globe, and instead of having recourse
to the vain hypothesis of transformation, this celebrated
naturalist bows before the creative wisdom. In life we
observe not only physico-chemical phenomena, but there
is a sort of vital design for every being and every organ,
and this in such a way that the various phenomena of the
organism taken isolatedly, are subjected to the general
forces of nature; but considered in their succession and
in their totality, they reveal a special connection, and
seem directed by an invisible condition. This invisible
condition is the power of evolution immanent in the egg,
which includes the phenomena of nutrition and generation. Biology is not capable of explaining the moral
phenomena, just as sensation could not give account of
consciousness. The soul makes use of the organs and
comes under their influence. The beasts have a soul, but
they have not an ego on account of the imperfection of
their mental faculties. The animals do not pass beyond
the instinctive, or at most the selfish state; and as they
do not possess the intuition of the true they cannot direct
their will to the realisation of the good. Hence it is that
the animal is born and dies an animal, whereas man is
born an animal and becomes a free person.

In what does freedom properly consist? When cognition
is involuntary the mind acts unconsciously and calls itself
free, because it follows its nature. When cognition is
voluntary and the mind acts after deliberation, it is said
to be free, because it is always possible for it to do the
contrary. This possibility of doing the contrary is denied
by the positivists, because according to their system all
our ideas come to us from sensation and have nothing
absolute in them, and the strongest motive must always
prevail. In the view of the positivists there is no other
way of making man better than by multiplying motives
by means of instruction. That attentive observation which
has discovered intuition and reflection in the sphere of

metaphysics, has also recognised in the moral sphere the possibility of doing the contrary. This is expressed by the Latin poet in the well-known words : Video meliora proboque, Deteriora sequor. This freedom in doing evil makes our good actions meritorious, as it is necessary the more frequently to combat the strongest motive in order to make the most reasonable motive triumph. Nevertheless we are not alone in this struggle, because as we attain ideas in God, we likewise obtain the strength to realise them in action. "Man," says Maine de Biran, " is a being intermediate between God and nature. He touches God with his spirit and nature with his senses. It is possible for him to be immersed in nature by allowing his Ego with his personality and freedom to be absorbed, and by abandoning himself to all the appetites and impulses of the flesh. It is possible for him up to a certain point to be identified with God, by transporting his Ego into God by the exercise of a higher faculty. Hence it follows that the lowest degree of degradation and the highest point of elevation, may be equally connected with two states of the soul in which it loses its personality, according as it is confounded with God or annihilated in the creature." [1]

We observe in society as in the individual the struggle of the passions with reason, and the triumph of reason by means of the free will. The passions, however, in passing from the individual to the social body, lose in strength. They agitate only the surface, leaving the foundation of society, or the ideas on which it is based, almost unmoved. It is not long since it began to be perceived that there is a logic and a progress in the political, religious, civil, and military institutions of the peoples. Pascal was the first to indicate it in an important fragment from which we

---

[1] We have quoted Maine de Biran in order to show that the strongest champion of the will, in his last work, *Nouveaux essais d'anthropologie*, had to admit divine action on the human will. Fichte, likewise, after having exaggerated the power of the Ego, closed his career by adopting a species of mysticism.

may quote the following words : " Man in the first age of his life is in ignorance, but he goes on learning without ceasing as he advances; for he derives advantage not only from his own experience, but also from that of his predecessors, and because he always preserves in his memory the knowledge which he has once acquired, while the knowledge of the ancients is always present to him in the books which they have left. And as he preserves this body of knowledge, he can also easily increase it, so that men are to-day in the state in which those ancient philosophers would have found themselves if they had been able to have lived on till now, and to have added to the knowledge which they had, the further knowledge which their study might have enabled them to acquire through so many ages. Hence it follows that by a peculiar prerogative not only does every man advance from day to day in the sciences, but all men together make continual progress in them as the universe grows older, because the same thing happens in the succession of men as takes place in the different ages of an individual. In this way the whole succession of men during the course of so many ages, ought to be considered as the same one man who subsists always and learns continually." [1]

The ancients attributed all change in society to the passions and to the characters of individuals. The moderns have come gradually to recognise an affiliation between ideas and facts, and they have thus created the philosophy of history. Bossuet, following in the footsteps of St. Augustine, described the part taken by God in events. Vico taught that "the world of the nations is the fruit of the human mind." Herder showed the influence of nature upon man. Thus the moral development takes place in the same manner both in the individual man and in the social man. Virtue is always an effort, a habit of making reason triumph over the senses and follow the dictates of the moral law. Politics does not differ essen-

---

[1] Pascal, *Fragment d'un traité du vide.* Paris, 1663.

tially from ethics, only the peoples are allowed a greater latitude in the fulfilment of their proper duties' as they are not confined within the narrow round of a generation. This may be shown by an example. A courageous man does not hesitate to sacrifice his life to his honour; but a people takes account only of grave offences, and even dissembles them till its armaments are ready and its alliances are concluded. Without denying that the statesman has a greater variety of means, we come to the conclusion that just as in private life virtue is what is supremely useful, so in politics honesty is the best policy.

III.

THE PHILOSOPHY OF RIGHT.

MAN does not always act for a disinterested end, or in view of an absolute good, but most frequently he seeks to obtain what is useful for himself and for others. His actions are then measured by another standard; abstraction is made from the determining motive, and the result is considered. The rule in such actions is no longer absolute goodness but justice; or, as Vico says, it is the good recognised in its equality.

Plato, as we have seen, makes justice one of the four elements of virtue. Justice, he says, makes man a measured whole that is proportional and full of harmony. It has its realisation in the State, which is man on the large scale, and which has to actualise the whole good. It is evident that Plato confounds justice with goodness, and right with morality. Aristotle, on the other hand, lays down a principle of distinction, maintaining the position that justice is virtue in relation to others; that it is the good of others; and that the State should not absorb the whole citizen as Plato wished. Stoicism gave greater prominence to the inner man and endeavoured to emancipate the individual from the State, recognising the unity of the human race and the harmony of all the parts of the universe.

Christianity weakened the feeling of right, as a religion giving the predominance to morality. As Christians we ought to bear injustice, and even to rejoice at it; but we are not bound to this as a matter of right. As Christians we ought to love our persecutors; but in right we may oppose force by force. Without doubt the Christian idea is more sublime than that of right; but the idea of right is indispensable in order to maintain order in society, and to prevent some from abusing the candour and charity of others.[1]

Christianity, however, was not able to dispense with a legal doctrine for the common uses of life. Thomas Aquinas defines justice in almost the same words as Aristotle: "Ordinat hominem in his quae sunt ad alterum." In order that justice may exist, there must be a relation of equality subsisting between the things exchanged; and this relationship or proportion between two objects, the will of the agent not being taken into account (*non considerato qualiter ab agente fiat*) is what is termed right (*jus*). Dante only fills up and completes this definition when he says: "Jus est realis et personalis ad hominem proportio, quae servata hominum servat societatem et corrupta corrumpit."

Controversies concerning the origin of political power were carried on very keenly in the Middle Ages; and it is curious to observe that the supporters of kings maintain their divine origin in order to render kings inviolable, while the supporters of the Church hold that power is of human and popular origin, in order to make the kings dependent on the Pope as the sole representative of God on earth.

Hugo Grotius wishing to circumscribe the rights of war, began by emancipating jurisprudence from theology, and he thus founded the science of natural right. This is how he enters on the subject: "Many authors have undertaken to comment upon and to summarise the civil law, both the laws of the Romans so called by autonomasia, and the particular laws of every nation. Nevertheless the right which has to be observed between different peoples, or towards the rulers of the various States, and

[1] Janet, *Histoire des doctrines morales et politiques.* 3rd ed. Paris, 1886.

which is founded on human nature, established by divine laws, or introduced by customs and by a tacit convention of men, has occupied the attention of few; and no one has examined the subject in all its extent and in a systematic form. However, it is not the less a need of the human race that every one requires to be instructed through a work of this kind." He then investigates the principle of right, and finds it in human sociability, or in the need of maintaining society in a manner conformable to the cognitions of the understanding, that is to say, by abstaining religiously from taking the goods of others, by keeping the word which has been pledged, by repairing any damage that has been done, and by accepting a punishment for every violation of these principles. It is at once evident that Grotius does not regard sociability as a material fact common to men and animals, but as an index of reason. "From this idea there arises another more extended idea to which has been given the name of *Right.* The superiority of man over the other animals consists not only in the feelings of sociability of which we have spoken, but also in the faculty of valuing things that are pleasing or displeasing, whether present or future, and discriminating the useful from the prejudicial. It is recognised that it is conformable to human nature to regulate oneself according to a right and sound judgment, in as far as the weakness of the mind permits it, and not to allow oneself to be intimidated by an impending evil, nor to be seduced by a present pleasure, or to be conquered by an unconsidered impulse. All that is opposed to such judgment is regarded as contrary to natural right or to *the laws of our nature.*"

Samuel Pufendorf, although severely characterised by Leibniz as *vir parum jurisconsultus et minime philosophus,* rendered services to the new science by developing what Grotius had sketched. He distinguishes natural right from moral theology and from the civil laws, explaining natural right as that which is ordered by right reason, civil right as that which is commanded by the legislative power, and moral theology as that which is prescribed by the sacred Scriptures. From these principles two important consequences are derived : the first is that natural right does not extend beyond this life, and the second that it is limited to the regulation of external actions. Christian Thomasius, called by Leibniz " *sylvestris et archipodialis,*" takes a step forward, being the first to draw a sharp distinction between right and morality. He distinguishes the juridical obligations from the moral obligations, calling the first perfect obligations because they may be imposed by force, while the second are imperfect obligations. The juridical obligations, he adds, are only negative, and are determined by the precept, *quod tibi non vis fieri alteri ne feceris;* whereas the moral obligations laid down by the precept of the *honestum et decorum* are positive.

To Leibniz these distinctions appeared not to be exact, and he proceeded again after the manner of the ancients to confound morality and natural right. "The end of natural right," he says, " is the well-being of those who observe it (and accordingly it does not exclude the questions of the immortality of the soul and the future life); its object is everything that has regard to the good of others, and which it is in our power to do (and it thus comprehends the moral actions); and finally, its efficient cause is the light of the divine reason which illuminates our mind." Right is therefore a moral power, as duty is a moral necessity.

Wolf did for Leibniz what Pufendorf and Thomasius had done for Grotius. He explained that we are led to the good at first by appetite and then by pleasure, but that reason alone makes us discern and love the true good by revealing its end and determining its means. The good consists in perfection. He says: " *Actiones bonae tendunt vel ad conservationem perfectionis essentialis vel ad acquirendum accidentalem.*"

Kant, in his *Critique of the Practical Reason*, shows us the human will subjected to the rational law of duty, which he calls the Categorical Imperative. It remained for him therefore to make a scientific enumeration and co-ordination of the duties; and this he did in the *Metaphysic of Morals*. Here he divides the duties into two classes: those which may be the object of an external and positive legislation, and these are the duties of right; and those which are immediately imposed on the will by reason, and these he calls *the duties of virtue*. These two classes of duties are treated in the two parts of the *Metaphysic of Morals*, the one of which is entitled *the Metaphysical Elements of the doctrine of Right*, and the other *the Metaphysical Elements of the doctrine of Virtue*.

Kant lays it down as a general principle that every action which does not hinder the accordance of the liberty of each individual with the liberty of all, is conformable to right. The idea of right, according to Kant, is therefore founded upon that of freedom, which is its condition; and hence the canon: "Act externally, so that thy liberty may be able to co-exist with the liberty of all." The power of coercion springs immediately from the notion of right, since the capability of removing every obstacle to our freedom is an integrant part of our freedom. Right accordingly is the form of the will, and it therefore consists in agreement, whence arise all contracts, not from desire, nor from regard to their end. Right takes no account of good or bad motives, and only looks to injuries.

But we may ask Kant: Why is human freedom not to be impeded, and why is accordance or harmony in it to be sought? He can give no other answer than the rule which is incidentally formulated by him in the *Metaphysic of Morals:* "Act so as to consider humanity both in thy own person and in the person of others as an end, and so as not to use it as a means." Right will thus not be a condition nor the sum of conditions, but subjectively a *facultus agendi* of the moral being anterior and superior to the conditions in which it may be able to manifest itself; and objectively it will be the good in relation to free beings.

In Schelling's "System of Identity," the divine action, fatal and unconscious in nature, becomes free and conscious in the spiritual world, where it is manifested as will. The idea of an organism was transferred from the physical world into the moral world; and the individual considered till then as a whole in himself was viewed in his organic relations with the family and the State from which he cannot sever himself.

In Hegel's view, Right is always liberty realised; but when we reflect that we are only a mode of the Absolute, it is soon understood that liberty is only realised fatally. Hegel says in so many words: "Man is undoubtedly an end to himself, and he ought to be regarded as such; but the individual man has to be regarded as such only by the individual and not by the State, because *the State or the nation is his substance.*"

Krause begins by making an analysis of our faculties, and he finds that by means of reason we rise to the universal. God is the immanent and always active reason of the existence of the universe, with which He does not cease to be united. Creation, according to Krause, is both eternal and temporal: it is eternal in so far as spirit, nature, and humanity, being the form of the eternal attributes of God, are eternally willed by Him; and it is temporal in so far as spirit, nature, and humanity, while developing themselves under the successive law of time and of space, demand the incessant action of God. The will is that operation by means of which the spirit determines its own activity, or realises its eternal essence in time. Freedom is the form of the will, and its object is the good. The absolute law of the good may be briefly expressed thus: "Will and do the good purely and simply, or, be the temporal cause of the good." God does not remain extraneous to the fulfilment of this law, since

He reveals Himself to our mind as the absolute reason of the subject and as the object of our desire. When we accomplish the good unconditionally we are in the domain of morals; when we work for an external end we enter the domain of right.

Ahrens, the distinguished follower of Krause, in his celebrated work on Natural Right, insists on the conditional side of right. He explains that all that exists in the world is, at least under one aspect, finite and conditional. God alone is the Being infinitely absolute and absolutely infinite; He is the Being from whom the world draws its essence and its existence, but who in His absolute and supreme unity is above the world and all that is finite and conditional. The unity of origin attributable to all that exists in the world, establishes among beings relationships of dependence and community by means of which the existence and life of some are more or less determined by the existence and life of others. The relation according to which beings depend on each other and are reciprocally determined in their existence and their development, is called a condition. Conditionality therefore supposes a higher unity; it involves a community and a solidarity in the existence and life of finite beings who, not being able to suffice for themselves, demand the concurrence and assistance of other finite beings. These conditions are of two kinds. Some are established by God and are independent of the human will, and such are the laws of nature; others are dependent on the will, or on the individual and social activity of man, and these last only enter into the domain of right.

The differences between right and morality are determined by Ahrens as follow:—1. Morality considers the motive of an action, right views it in its effects. 2. The precepts of morality are absolute and invariable, or independent of places and times, whereas the conditions imposed by right may vary according to the degree of the culture of the people. 3. Conscience is the sole judge of morality, while right may be recognised externally, whence follows the necessity of an authority which may determine right and compel to its observance. 4. Hence it further follows that all juridical obligations may be enforced by coercion, a circumstance which on the whole is secondary, because the difference between right and morality would subsist, even although men should observe a conduct so perfect as to render any external coercion superfluous. 5. Finally, Ethics, whose object is morality, is a formal and subjective science, whereas Jurisprudence, which deals with right, is an objective science, inasmuch as it has regard to human development.[1]

The chief defect of the moral and juridical doctrine of Ahrens lies in the way in which he understands individuality, which, following his master Krause, he believes to be an eternal divine determination, and which has consequently no proper existence of itself.[2]

The question under consideration has also been examined by Trendelenburg in his work on "Natural Right on the basis of Ethics." Trendelenburg shows the impossibility of separating right from morals, without reducing right to a fact or to a phenomenon. Right is the external sanction, the guarantee of morality, and it would exist even although men should render coercion useless by their perfection. Nevertheless right does not sanction the whole of morality, but only the part necessary for making the individual co-exist in harmony with the whole. The consideration of this point carries Trendelenburg into metaphysics and psychology. "The ultimate problem of metaphysics," he says, " is directed to reconcile the widest contradiction which exists, that, namely, between blind force and conscious thought, and the relation of these two terms can only be conceived in three ways, so that either blind force stands as the original prior to conscious thought and subordinates it to itself as its product; or thought as

---

[1] See Ahrens, *Cours de droit naturel.* 5th ed. Bruxelles, 1860.
[2] Ahrens, *Cours de psychologie.* 2 vols. Paris, 1838.

the original precedes blind force and rules it; or finally, both are really the same, only different in our understanding, and as they are nothing but different expressions of the same being, they do not stand in a causal connection with each other. And hence there can only be three essentially different views of the world: the first is the conception of an acting cause (*causa efficiens*) which gives the physical or mechanical view of the world; the second is the conception of an eternal end (*causa finalis*) which gives the organic or teleological view of the world; and the third is the conception of the indifference of the acting cause and of the end. These three views of the world may be called after their originators, Democritism, Platonism, and Spinozism."

Trendelenburg attaches himself to Platonism as corrected by Christianity, and he finds the ethical principle in that organic conception of the world which is based on the great fact of vitality, and which brings the blind forces into equilibrium and presents thought in nature. What is will in the absolute becomes duty in the relative, and man transforms duty into an ethical value when he wills what he ought, or what God wills. The destination of man is to realise the idea of his nature. All the great objective systems have had as their aim the realisation of man as man. The ethics of Plato are realised in the State, but to Plato the State is man on the large scale, so that the psychological tendencies of man pass over into the State and form a harmonious unity. Here psychology enters into alliance with metaphysics, and shows that man is organised in such a way that by his feeling, thinking, and willing, he fulfils the end of the creation.[1] The individual, in so far as he is an organ of the idea, is the

---

[1] We have been delighted to read in § 33 of the general part of Trendelenburg's work the following statement: "According to the organic conception of the world, the essence of things rests on a creative thought; and consequently the ethical principle may be understood as a way of taking and treating things according to the divine destination." Has the system of Gioberti then penetrated into Germany, or did Trendelenburg arrive at the same results in another way?

instrument of a special purpose which is properly the object of consciousness; and by this correspondence these actions include the true in the strictest sense of the term. The internal ends of morality are the moving forces of right; and the necessity of their conservation and development gives origin as a necessary consequence to the notion of right. Right is defined by Trendelenburg as "the sum of those universal determinations of action by which it comes about that the whole of ethics and its parts are able to be preserved and developed." All right, he adds, in so far as it is right and not injustice, springs from the impulse to preserve a moral existence. This conception of right is the only one that is possible in the ethics of an immanent teleology.

Reduced to these terms, the difference between morality and right is a difference in degree and not of essence. Yet it is a very important difference, as it reduces the power of coercion to *what is absolutely necessary for the harmonious co-existence of the individual with the whole.*

All the systems, however, do not derive right from justice. Thus from the earliest antiquity we see the Sophists maintaining that man ought to seek only for pleasure, as by Callicrates in Plato's *Gorgias.* Carneades maintained that utility is the mother of justice and equity. Epicurus taught that justice is the utility of the greatest number; and that we ought to obey the laws because they shield us by their protection and accordingly secure us a pleasure, and because if we violate them we shall be punished, and we would accordingly have to undergo a pain.

Among the scholastics, John of Salisbury is the only one who can be reckoned among the utilitarians. In his treatise entitled *Polycratus seu de nugis curialium,* he lays it down as a principle that the pursuit of the useful determines all human actions; and he approves the end assigned to human life by Epicurus, although he blames the means adopted by his followers in order to attain it.

At the close of the Middle Ages, the human spirit became impatiently desirous to differentiate right from morals and theology; and it need not be wondered at that in some the distinction almost degenerated into divorce. The great rulers, Louis IX. and Ferdinand of Arragon, furnished the facts; and Machiavelli raised them into a theory. The highest object was success; the end justified the means; and it was reckoned better to anticipate than to await the effects of astuteness and violence. If Machiavelli did not found the new science of politics, he established its method by introducing into it freedom of inquiry, historical and critical analysis, and direct observation.

According to Hobbes man is born with bad propensities, and his natural state is war. In this state, accordingly, there is neither justice nor injustice. Force and cunning are the cardinal virtues. Justice and injustice are qualities neither of the body nor of the spirit, and they do not belong to man as man, but as a citizen. However, if the greatest good of man is his own preservation, and the greatest evil is the fear of death, it follows that the state of nature is insupportable, and that man must seek all the means of going out of it by establishing peace and security, which are to be obtained by natural law. Hobbes distinguishes natural right from natural law, making the former consist in the liberty which each one has to use his force as best pleases him for his own preservation, while the latter consists in the rule which he imposes on himself in order to abstain from all that may turn to his disadvantage. Thus the law serves as a limitation of right; and there is the same difference between them as there is between liberty and obligation.

Spinoza, starting from different principles, arrives at the same consequences as Hobbes by identifying right with might or force. By natural right, says Spinoza, must be understood the natural laws of every individual according to which he is predestined to act. For example, fishes are naturally made to swim, and the larger fishes to eat the smaller, so that in virtue of natural right all fishes swim, and the larger fishes eat the smaller ones. It follows from this that natural right prohibits only what is not desired and what cannot be done. It does not prohibit rivalry, nor hatred, nor wrath, nor cunning, nor, in short, anything that is inspired by passion; nor should this excite astonishment because nature is not subject to the laws of human reason, which look only to utility and to the conservation of man. Reason, however, when duly consulted, teaches us that peace is better than war, and that love is better than hate. Whence it comes that man gives up to society all his power in an absolute manner, and that what remains to him is only a concession made by the State to the individual. In the application of their principles, however, Hobbes enlarges the sphere of the State, while Spinoza restricts it; but this is accounted for by the surroundings in which they lived, the former living in England after the revolution of 1640, and the latter spending his life in peaceful Holland.

Locke finds that there exists a natural law that is obligatory even before the institution of governments. This law is manifested to us by reason, and it is sufficient to interrogate reason in order to learn that all men are equal and independent in relation to each other, no one having a right to interfere with the life, liberty, or safety of his fellows. Men have all the same origin; they are all servants of the Lord; and they are put into the world to fulfil the mission assigned to them. All are endowed with the same faculties; all participate in the gifts of nature; and there cannot be admitted the least distinction among them which would entitle the greatest to oppress the least. Every one is bound to preserve his own existence, and not to abandon his post voluntarily, but he ought at the same time to co-operate in the preservation of others by abstaining from hurting their persons, liberties, and possessions. Governments are instituted in order to guarantee natural law, and they only exist by the general consent. If it is asked whether a state of nature has ever existed, Locke replies that all peoples and independent princes are found in this state of nature, before they have concluded compacts by means of which they enter into a certain political community.

Rousseau modified the juridical doctrine of Locke for the worse, by making right spring from the will instead of from the reason. According to Rousseau contract creates right, whereas according to Locke it declares it. Rousseau vainly seeks to distinguish the general will from the will of all. His consequences are always unfavourable to the individual, and his fundamental maxim is always the one which was applied with so much atrocity by the French Convention: *Salus publica suprema lex esto.*

The influence of Rousseau on the German philosophy is undeniable; it is attested by Hegel himself in his *Lectures on the History of Philosophy.* " Rousseau," he says, "proclaimed that the free will is the essence of man; this principle is the transition to the doctrine of Kant, of which it is the foundation." Schelling and Hegel traced out another path, as we have already seen, in dealing with ethics; and Schopenhauer says expressly: "In the human world, as in the animal world, it is force and not right that reigns. . . Right is only the measure of the power of each individual." Alexander Ecker, in his essay on natural selection as applied to peoples, concludes as follows: " The last war has proved that the history of nations rests equally on natural laws, and is composed of a series of absolute necessities, in which the balance hangs always on the side of progress." Prince Bismarck, in a speech to the German Parliament, formulated the same principle in the words: *Might before right.*[1]

[1] *Gewalt vor Recht.* Bismarck has said that he does not remember pronouncing these words, which are found in the parliamentary reports because he has no time to revise his speeches. In conciseness and cynicism they surpass the words put by Thucydides into the mouth of the Athenians after the taking of Melos, and those spoken by the English ambassador to the Prince of Denmark when his capital had been bombarded during a time of peace.

The successors of Locke in England had not his prudence and circumspection. The most important of them is Bentham, who, with imperturbable logic, says: "Give me pleasure and pain, and I will create for you the whole moral and social world; I will produce not only justice but generosity, the love of country, philanthropy, and all the amiable or sublime virtues in their stability and exaltation." Sir James Mackintosh applied himself to perfect the work of Bentham, endeavouring to show that even remorse and the feeling of justice are derived from utility. James Mill added nothing essentially new. Austin answered certain objections taken to the possibility of moral accountability, and made a profound analysis of the relations of law to ethics. John Stuart Mill, in his treatise on Utilitarianism, gathers up the ideas of his predecessors, and defends them against all objections. He proves that through the principle of solidarity the individual interest is identical with that of the greatest number, and that justice is the chief part of social utility. He defines right as a power which society is interested in according to the individual.

Alexander Bain shows that the rules of justice are eternal and immutable, because they correspond to the most essential conditions of social existence. They have as their object the most important part of utility, namely, security. A permanent violation of these rules would occasion in a short time the destruction of the human race. This is why their fulfilment becomes obligatory, and why those who infringe them ought to be punished. Man is therefore moved by selfishness and by the sympathy which prudence and benevolence engender; but these qualities are not sufficient to regulate his conduct, which is marked out for him by an external authority. Government, authority, law, obligation, punishment, are all comprised in the great institution of society. Morality is not produced by prudence and benevolence, but by external law; and the moral sense is formed by education in conformity with the law, and by the fear of punishment.[1]

Herbert Spencer explains the universal and immutable character of the principal moral rules by the hereditary accumulation of experiences of the useful, and by evolution; and instead of deriving morality from right, as Bain would do, he anticipates a state of equilibrium between the nature of man and the social organisation—a state in which man would have no desire which he could not satisfy without going out of his sphere of action, while society will impose no other limits than those which the individual will freely respect. The progressive extension of the liberty of the citizens and the abrogation of the political institutions, is the ideal of Herbert Spencer. Government, he says, is a function correlative to the immorality of society.[2]

Darwin seeks to fill up the abyss which moral science had hollowed out between man and the beast. He endeavours to show that the moral sense is not the exclusive privilege of man, but the highest manifestation of the tendencies which are common to him with the higher animals, and that the same causes which explain the graduated evolutions of nature from the lowest stages of animality up to the quadrumana, are sufficient to give account of all the steps of progress by which the delicate morality of the civilised peoples has gradually disengaged itself from the primitive brutality of the ancestors of our race by means of natural selection and heredity.[3]

The English School thus returns to its point of departure, to Hobbes, with this difference, that the *Leviathan* no longer represents society merely, but all nature. Science has shown that the being that desires to live must adapt itself to the environment in which it lives, or it will perish. The universe is the environment to which humanity

[1] *Mental and Moral Science.* London, 1868.
[2] See his *First Principles*, London, 1862; and later works.
[3] See *The Descent of Man*, &c. 1862.

adapts itself; and humanity is the environment to which the individual has to adapt himself. And thus both individual morality and public right only express the extreme progressive movements of such adaptation, and put the human species into the alternative, in which all the other species are placed, of perfecting itself or perishing. According to this science, the necessity of nature alone suffices to evolve from the solar heat the mineral forces, and from these the vital forces. And from these, again, arise the human forces, and, finally, society, which when ultimately analysed is nothing but a transformation of the sun: the radiation of light in virtue of the simple and fruitful laws of motion having become the radiation of thought.

Following the lines of Darwin, the languages and customs of the more savage peoples have been studied in order to discover the origin of the juridical ideas. Giraud-Teulon, in his book on *The Origin of the Family*, summing up the results of the inquiries of Bachefen, M'Lennan, and Morgan, endeavours to show that the patriarchal family was preceded by promiscuity. Sir Henry Sumner Maine, in his work on *Ancient Law*, and in his *Lectures on the Early History of Institutions*, shows us the natural origin of all the juridical institutions. Of these works we shall have occasion to speak further on.

Italy has had its Bentham in Gian Domenico Romagnosi, who not only produced useful works in the sphere of legislation, but investigated the origin and progress of civilisation. In his metaphysics, he preferred to accept certain intermediate axioms in order to use them as a means of defence against the transcendental schools. Man is a social being, he said, and hence the science of the heart and of the mind is part of jurisprudence. Civilisation is an art, and it supposes the necessity of employing certain means in order to attain the end of the social well-being. This necessity, which is imposed by the nature of things for the perfectible conservation of the human species, constitutes for Romagnosi the conception of right and duty. The principle of moral education is nothing but the necessity of conforming our actions to the order of the means indispensable for attaining the end of our perfectible conservation; and the foundation of justice is only the expression of a calculation of utility founded on the inevitable order of things. Consequently every positive obligation or bond not legitimated by the hope of a greater well-being is juridically null, while those obligations by which a lesser advantage is sacrificed to a greater are juridically binding. The science of right having to develop its obligatory rules parallel to the ordinances of the art of civilisation, should not be limited to considering abstractly the relationships subsisting among living men, but ought to follow *pari passu* the development of civilisation in the course of centuries; and accordingly it should elevate the whole order of progressive perfection to a rule of rigorous natural right. Civilisation tends to the equalising of goods and powers which this civil justice will alone be able to make us attain.

The doctrine of Romagnosi may be summed up as " a theory of the co-efficient forces of *human interest* expounded in conceptions, axioms, and general mediate precepts (that is, such as are neither too general nor too special), from which there results a grand connection and similarity for the whole system of the individual inner man and of the social inner man, and which tend to their perfectible conservation under the dominion of nature and of reason." The modern positivists have done nothing more than diminish the influence of reason in favour of that of nature.

As will now be seen, all the philosophers are divided into two groups: some of them assigning the good to morals and law as their content, and others basing them on utility. It is naturally asked whether a reconciliation of the two views has been ever attempted? And in fact from the remotest times it has been shown that virtue is useful because it is conformable to the eternal order of things. Epicurus himself was led to place his highest good, which was pleasure, in the mental tranquillity of the wise man. Vico says expressly that the moral element is the cause of right, and utility is its occasion. He proceeded to show this philosophically and historically, saying that man receives from God the eternal light of truth, but that ideas are awakened in him by sensations ; and therefore he first lays hold of the certain, and then of the true. The metaphysical world is followed by the civil world, or that of the nations, which is founded upon three primitive facts which are found universally among all peoples. These are the institutions of religion, of marriage, and of burial, which are called *foedera generis humani*, and which correspond to the three fundamental ideas of the human mind, namely, the existence of divine providence, the necessity of moderating the passions and turning them into social virtues, and the immortality of the soul. Vico finds his theory confirmed by the historical development of the Roman Law, which began with barbarous laws (*imitationes violentiae*). In the degree in which the plebeians acquired strength in the State the hardness of the laws came to be mitigated by jural fictions, and equity was developed in the edicts of the praetors until the complete predominance of rational right was reached under the emperors, who finally removed the exceptions of the written law, and the jurisconsults became true philosophers.[1]

If Grotius founded the science of natural right, Vico has completed it by defining natural right as " the good recognised as equal," and by showing how men attain to it by means of violence itself and material utility Montesquieu advanced in the footsteps of Vico, holding that laws consist in the necessary relationships which

[1] The work of Sir Henry Sumner Maine on *Ancient Law*, however original its views may have appeared out of Italy, only gives a develop- ment of the ideas of Vico, especially in regard to juridical fictions, testa- ments, contracts, &c.

arise from the nature of things, and analysing the external causes, such as climate and other influences, which act on legislation. Bentham took up a position away from Vico, treating utility not as an accessory element or occasion, but as the reason of law and right. The Historical School in Germany, as founded by Hugo, Hauboldt, and Savigny, returned to Vico, but it left out of view the rational element which makes history intelligible.

We concluded our review of metaphysics and ethics with Gioberti, and we now close our review of the philosophy or science of right with Vico. The true becomes the good in ethics, and the just in jurisprudence; the matter contained is the same, the relations are changed. The weakness of our mind obliges us to study these relationships in so many separate sciences, but we ought not on this account to lose sight of the whole. We have, however, gone at some length into an exposition of the doctrines which the ages have transmitted to us in order to justify our choice, and to show how here too: "Multa renascentur quae jam cecidere."

Having spent the first half of our life in combating sensualism, we gladly spend the second half of it in the defence of spiritualism. But some will say, what are we to make of a book composed according to the principles of Vico and Gioberti? Have not the moral sciences made very great progress through others? We shall only say in reply that we hope our readers will find in our work an organic unity which embraces all the progress that has been really made; and these Prolegomena may be a guarantee to them of the impartiality and fulness with which we shall expound the opinions opposed to our own, in order that students may be able to make their choice between them, as it is our desire to offer them above all things what Montaigne calls *un livre de bonne foi.*

Our work will be divided into two parts, the first of which will be designated *the Objects of Right,* and the second *the Subjects of Right.* In the first part we shall speak of the human ends: Religion, Science, Art, Industry, Commerce, Morality, and Justice, looking at them in their essence and in their modality. Property will be treated in the chapter on industry; contracts will be discussed in the chapter on commerce; beneficence will be taken up as a part of morality; and punishment and jurisdictions will naturally be connected with the discussion of justice. In the second part we shall treat of the individual and of society, beginning from the Family and rising through the *Commune* and the Province to the State, to Nations, and to Humanity.

This distribution of the subject will enable us better to show how the good specialises itself in ends, and how these are able to be attained by means of a material utility without losing any of their ethical value. As there is a hierarchy in ideas, so there is a hierarchy in goods, which leads on until the highest good, which is God, is reached. Right secures us the free attainment of some of these goods, and imposes the accomplishment of others which are more necessary to the social life, and in this consists its conditional character. Right and law are not separated from morals, but are simply distinguished from them. Social utility serves as their limit, and their sphere is therefore enlarged and restricted according to the various degrees of civilisation. In the beginning everything appears mixed up in the sphere of religion, but gradually science, art, morality, and right become distinguished from it, without losing their intimate relations with it; and this may also be observed in the case of industry and commerce.

If right is objectively the expression of the relationships of an ideal justice, it is subjectively the power which the individual or social man has to realise these relationships. Accordingly it will be incumbent on us to examine whence this power springs, what are its limits, and what is the nature of the individual, of society, and of government.

Our discussion would be incomplete if we confined ourselves to the present alone, and hence under every one of our sections, both in the first part and the second part, we shall cast a glance over the past from which the present has been historically and rationally derived. In doing so we do not consider that we are passing beyond the limits of the Philosophy of Right, in view of the close connection which Vico has established between philosophy, philology, and history.

THE OBJECTS OF RIGHT.

CHAPTER I.

RELIGION.

In our preliminary survey we have seen man thinking, feeling, and willing; but between thought and feeling there is an intermediate state of the soul which is called *Faith.* Faith is distinguished into natural and supernatural according as it depends on intelligence or on super-intelligence. The exposition of the philosophical systems has shown us that everything is not accessible to our mind, and that the creation *ex nihilo* has been introduced into metaphysics by Christianity; and the same holds good of the doctrine of grace in morals. The tendency of modern times has been to diminish gradually the supernatural even to the extent of confounding religion with philosophy. But, exclaims Véra, although the object of religion and of philosophy may be identical, namely, God or the Absolute, yet religion and philosophy differ in their mode of conceiving that object, because religion cannot liberate itself from the sphere of representation or from symbol, whereas philosophy contemplates the Idea in itself.[1] Gioberti had said more explicitly that religion looks at the obscure side and philosophy at the clear side of the idea, and that they make use of two different faculties: the first, of the super-intellect; and the second, of the intellect.

Max Müller holds a somewhat similar view. He thus expresses himself: " As there is a faculty of speech, independent of all the historical forms of language, so

[1] Véra, *Strauss, l'ancienne et la nouvelle foi.* Naples, 1873.

there is a faculty of faith in man independent of all historical religions. If we say that it is religion which distinguishes man from the animal, we do not mean the Christian or Jewish religion; we do not mean any special religion ; but we mean a mental faculty which, independent of, nay, in spite of sense and reason, enables man to apprehend the Infinite under different names, and under varying disguises. Without that faculty no religion, not even the lowest worship of idols and fetishes, would be possible ; and if we will but listen attentively, we can hear in all religions a groaning of the spirit, a struggle to conceive the inconceivable, to utter the unutterable, a longing after the Infinite, a love of God. Whether the etymology which the ancients gave of the Greek word ἄνθρωπος, man, be true or not (they derived it from ὁ ἄνω ἀθρῶν, he who looks upward), certain it is that what makes man man, is that he alone can turn his face to heaven; certain it is that he alone yearns for something that neither sense nor reason can supply. If then there is a philosophical discipline which examines into the conditions of sensuous or intuitional knowledge, and if there is another philosophical discipline which examines into the conditions of rational or conceptual knowledge, there is clearly a place for a third philosophical discipline that has to examine into the conditions of that third faculty of man, co-ordinate with sense and reason, the faculty of perceiving the Infinite, which is at the root of all religions. In German we can distinguish that third faculty by the name of *Vernunft*, as opposed to *Verstand*, reason, and *Sinne*, sense. In English I know no better name for it than the faculty of faith." [1]

How is the multiplicity of the religions to be explained? In two ways. Diderot said that all revealed religions were heresies of natural religion, meaning by natural religion that sum of truths which human reason is able to discover independently of all historical and local

[1] *Introduction to the Science of Religion*, p. 18.   1873.

influences. The existence of God, the nature of His attributes (such as His omnipotence, omniscience, omnipresence, goodness), and the distinction between good and evil, virtue and vice, with the corollary of the rewards and punishments that are to be assigned to our actions in a future life, form the substance of Natural Religion. In the beginning of the present century Paley tried to formulate methodically and scientifically what he called Natural Theology. It has not been difficult for Max Müller, by analysing the positive religions of the principal human races, to show that this Natural Theology is an abstraction. Under the guidance of philology he goes back to the time when the Aryan, Semitic, and Turanian races were not yet divided into their innumerable branches. He finds that the supreme divinity of the Aryans was called "Light" or "Heaven," a name which afterwards became *Dyaus* in Sanskrit, *Zeus* in Greek, *Jovis* in Latin, and *Diu* in German; and comparing the *Dyauspetar* of the Vedas, the Ζεὺ πάτερ of the Greeks, and the *Jovis pater* (Jupiter) of the Latins, he infers that "Heaven" was not taken merely in the material sense, but also in the sense of Providence, or as it was afterwards more clearly expressed in the words : *Our Father which art in Heaven.* The root of the name of all the Semitic divinities is found to be *El,* which signifies "the strong" or "the powerful;" and it shows us that the Semites conceived of God as the ruler of the peoples rather than as the regulator of the forces of nature. The feminine names denoted at the beginning the energy or faculties of the Supreme Being, and not female divinities. The Turanian languages cannot be said strictly to form a family ; for it has not been demonstrated that the Chinese is the point of departure of the northern branch, that is, the Tungusian, the Mongolian, the Turkish, the Finnish, and the Samoyedan, and of the southern branch, including the Tamil, the language of the Deccan and the Botigan, the languages of Tibet and of Bhutan, of the Taic, the languages of Siam, and the

Malesian, or the languages of the Malay Peninsula and of Polynesia.

Mythology confirms the original parentage of these many groups by showing the Chinese term *Tien* (Heaven) in the *Tang-li* of the Huns, in the *Tengri* of the Mongols, and even in the *Num* of the Samoyedans, in the *Juma* of the Finns, and in the *Nam* of Tibet. These names not only designated the material heaven, but also the spirit of heaven, who is the father and mother of all things, and who has in his service a great number of spirits (*Shin*), and among others, those of the dead. To Confucius *Tien*, or the spirit of heaven, was the supreme God, and he looked upon the other spirits as Socrates looked upon the gods of Greece.

The other way of explaining the multiplicity of the religions, is to regard them all as alterations of the true religion which was revealed by God to our first parents and preserved by the elect people. The Church, according to the Catholic view, has existed from the first day of the creation, and it is the ultimate terminus to which Providence will bring the whole human race by tradition and conscience. The Light has come into the world, says St. John, but men loved the darkness rather than the Light, because their deeds were evil. In consequence of sin, the idea of God became darkened, and men kneeled before trees and animals (*Fetishism*), before the stars (*Sabeism*), and before the forces of nature and personified moral qualities (*Polytheism*). More attentive observation discovers that there is almost always in these systems the subordination of the various gods to a supreme Being from whom they emanate; and hence the religions are well distinguished into two categories, according as they are founded upon pantheism or creative monotheism.

The most celebrated of the former class of religions are: 1. The Chinese Religion, which is represented in the text of the *Y-King* (*Book of the transformations*), attributed to Fou-hi, and the *Shu-King* (*Book of books*), compiled by Confucius in the sixth century B.C. In the first of these works, the fundamental principle laid down is the binary principle, abstraction and reasoning not being so far advanced as to reach unity. Fou-hi puts at the head of his categories Heaven and Earth, representing the first by a continuous line, and the second by a broken line. The heaven represents the male principle, that is, the sun, motion, force; and the earth represents the female principle, the moon, repose, weakness. Confucius takes Heaven in the more elevated sense of Providence, and makes it the sole principle of all things. 2. The Indian Religions, or Brahmanism and Buddhism. The most ancient sacred hymns contained in the *Rig-Veda* show us so many separate gods who ruled the principal forces of nature. Gradually the metaphysical conception of Brahma begins to take shape as a neutral, eternal, and inactive principle, from which are derived the other divine persons Vishnu and Shiva. The human soul derived from the great whole is destined to change its organism according to the character of its actions; and hence the great care to keep it pure from all stain so as not to make it migrate into some animal body. Buddhism passes over the problem of the origin of things, and maintains that we are born unhappy, and will be always unhappy, and that there remains for us no other resource than to shut ourselves up in a contemplative life so as to attain total annihilation. 3. The Egyptian Religion represents the infinite, in the god Amun, as the identical principle of all beings. In the prayers which are addressed to him, he is asked to come out from the darkness which envelops him and to reveal himself to men. Kneph, the good genius, is considered as the mind, the word, or love. He is represented on the monuments in the form of a man who lets an egg fall from his mouth to indicate that the world is the work of the divine word and intelligence. The passive principle or matter is represented by Athir or Athor, the mother of the gods and of men. From the egg which falls from the mouth of Kneph, there is born a fourth divinity named Phta, who is the soul of the world or the demiurge. 4. The Persian Religion resembles the Egyptian religion. The mythologists recognise Amun in Zervane-Acherene, or the Infinite, the supreme principle from which proceed good and evil, intelligence and matter, light and darkness. Similarly Kneph, the good genius, is found again in Ormuzd ; Athir, or matter and darkness, in Ahriman ; and finally Phta, the soul of the world, or the mediator between beings, in Mithra.

The social effects of the religions were different according to places and races. China, being poor in imagination, had a simple worship, and it was wholly domestic, without a vestige of hierocracy. In India, some time after the conquest by the Aryans, we see the sacerdotal class acquiring a pre-eminence, and the whole of society arranged according to castes which were supposed to have proceeded from Brahma. The Brahmans or priests were believed to have sprung from his mouth, the Kshatryas or warriors from his arms, the Vaysias or artisans from his thighs, and the Sudras or the remainder of the population who were the descendants of the conquered tribes, from his feet.

The code of Manu regulated minutely all that specially concerned the Brahmans, declaring them to be the lords of all things, which they let other men also enjoy from pure generosity. No sooner is a Brahman conceived than it is already necessary to offer a sacrifice for the purification of the foetus. When born he is made to taste clarified honey and butter. Certain rules are established conditioning the name which is to be bestowed upon him, regulating his first outgoing from the house, and how he is to be dressed. When three years old he has to receive the tonsure ; and from his fifth to his sixteenth year he must be initiated with investiture of the sacred thread under penalty of excommunication. The law regulates how this thread is to be made, and what must be the kind of wood, and what the length of the staff of the novice. The novice, when once initiated by the ceremony of the *kesanta*, can be fed on alms only. He is allowed to eat only twice a day, in the morning and evening, and sitting according to the established rules, and after having performed his ablutions. At sixteen years of age he passes under a spiritual teacher called the *Guru*, who becomes his second father, and receives no remuneration for his instruction, which may last fifteen or twenty years. The *Guru* makes the novice constantly study the Vedas, interrupting his explanations by frequent prayers. The novice watches the rising and setting of the sun, and learns to mortify his senses. When his noviciate is finished the young Brahman may become the father of a family, taking a wife of his own caste, and living principally on alms, and not eating flesh. After having procreated a family and educated them, the Brahman should separate himself from the world, and think of his eternal salvation. Having retired to the depths of a forest, and covered with the skin of a gazelle or the bark of a tree, he has to bathe morning and evening, to wear his hair long and shaggy, to let his beard, hair, and nails grow, and to live on roots or wild fruits, in some cases even refusing alms. He may take with him his old companion in life, but he must keep himself chaste as in the time of his noviciate, and bear the heats of summer and the rains of winter, and sleep on the naked earth. When he feels himself seized by an incurable malady he is to walk without stopping in the direction of the north-west until his body dissolves, living only on air and water. Often a more rigorous period closes the life of the Brahman, when he finally embraces the ascetic life, and renounces every sort of affection, becoming a *Sunyassi*. Then he no longer needs to read the Vedas ; he has to live absolutely alone, without having either bed or roof; if hunger torments him, he goes about asking alms in a neighbouring village, taking care not to tread on impure objects, and filtering the water before drinking from fear of killing the insects which may be found in it. He purifies his words with truth; and inaccessible to all that surrounds him, superior to every sensual desire, and without any other society than his own soul, he has only one solemn thought in his mind, that of uniting himself with the divine spirit. Had these prescriptions been really observed, the Brahmans would have paid a high price for their power.

But such was the corruption of the Brahmanic system that in the sixth century B.C. Sakyamuni, afterwards called Buddha, felt the necessity of a reform. He laid no importance upon caste, proclaimed equality, and prescribed common duties to all, and special duties to the religious devotees. The latter were not to be clothed with anything but rags picked up on the highways or from the dunghills or the cemeteries, according to the example which Buddha himself gave. They were to be fed only on alms, receiving in a wooden dish what was offered to them without being allowed to ask it, or to give any sign of importunity. They were to eat only once, before midday; and they were to sleep in the forest with their back leaned against the trunk of a tree, and the rest of their body stretched on a mat. Once a month they were to pass the night in a cemetery, in order to meditate on the instability of human things. They were to observe the most rigorous celibacy, and to break off all relations with their families. In the depths of winter they were permitted to take shelter in convents, which the sympathy of the people and the munificence of the kings built for them in all countries.

In Tibet, where there is a Buddhist pope, there is no secular clergy, and the Grand Lama is only the head of one of the many monasteries. Buddhism, in thus exaggerating dogma and discipline, has caused the retrogression of the civilisation which Brahmanism, notwithstanding its régime of caste, had promoted.

This reproach cannot be cast upon the Egyptian priests.

Society was divided in ancient Egypt into six or seven castes, and the individual had to follow the profession or the trade of his father. The first caste was that of the priests. They were proprietors of two-thirds of the soil, judges, astronomers, astrologers, architects, physicians, historians, preceptors, and tutors of the kings, who could not ascend the throne except by passing through a noviciate from the caste of the warriors to that of the priests. It is probable that the rules of agriculture which flourished so greatly in the kingdom of the Pharaohs were laid down by the priests, and that the works for dividing and preserving the waters of the Nile were executed under their direction. This increased their pride, and made a priest of Sais say to Solon: "O Solon, Solon, you are children; no Greek is old." But it is not right to exaggerate their science; for if Pythagoras had learned from them the properties of the triangle, he would not have sacrificed a hecatomb to the gods, as for a discovery of his own. The gigantic monuments which excite our admiration, were raised by human strength only aided by inclined planes; for we do not find in those monuments which have representations of the ordinary occupations of life, any sketch of machines, not even of a pulley.

In Persia we see classes, not castes; and at their head are found the *Mobeds* or judges of the Magi, and the *Desturs*, supervisors, or rather simple priests. The form of government is monarchical; but the king is the image of Ormuzd, and therefore he ought to protect the poor. If he showed himself unfaithful to his mission, the chief Magus, or great priest, had the right to pronounce his deposition. Polygamy is abolished in the family; and the husband or father is absolute king within the precincts of the domestic life. Life in general is represented as a warfare; nature and the soul form the field of battle, where man has to conquer his passions and the rebel forces.

The Greco-Roman polytheism transformed the gods

into so many men of a superior nature, and devoted the priests to presiding over prayers and sacrifices. The religion became an instrument of government, by means of oracles among the Greeks and auspices among the Romans.

We come now to those religions which have creative Monotheism as their basis. Modern criticism has tried to give an entirely natural explanation of creative Monotheism, denying that it was special to the Hebrews, and attributing it to the whole Semitic race. Thus Renan writes: "Nature plays a small part in the Semitic religions. The desert is monotheistic; sublime in its immense uniformity, it suddenly revealed to man the idea of the infinite, but not the feeling of that incessantly creative activity which a more fertile nature has inspired in other races. This is why Arabia has always been the bulwark of the most exalted Monotheism. It is an error to regard Mohammed as having founded Monotheism among the Arabians. The worship of supreme Allah (*Allah tôala*) had always been the basis of the religion of Arabia. Exclusively moved by the unity of the government which is displayed in the world, the Semites have perceived in the development of things only the fulfilment of the will of a Supreme Being. They have never understood the multiplicity in the universe. God is; God has made the heaven and the earth; this is all their philosophy."[1] Let us hear the reply of the celebrated orientalist Solomon Munk, who says: "The *instinct* of Monotheism has been attributed to all the Semites, but all efforts to trace it out have proved futile, as it has always concealed itself from our view, because it is founded upon the strangest philological deductions, and not upon authentic documents. We find constant exceptions in the Phenicians, the Syrians, and even the Arabians.

[1] Renan, *Histoire générale et système comparé des langues sémitiques*, vol. ii. L. i. c. 1.

For when I open the Koran I read the name of several
pagan divinities worshipped by the old Arabians. It is
asserted that the names of the Semitic divinities all indicate a certain dominion: *Baal*, the master; *Adonai*, my
lord; Moloch, the king; but there are passed over in
silence the names of Astarte, Derketo, Dagon, Chemosh,
&c. But notwithstanding this, we admit the primitive
idea of lordship, and hold that the Semites worshipped in
the beginning one God, who became multiplied by casual
contact with the Indo-European cults. The Semitic gods,
it is replied, are nothing in themselves; they represent
only the attributes of the true God, whereas the Indo-
European gods act on their own account and of their own
will. But in spite of the more accurate investigations,
I do not find the autonomy of the Indo-European gods.
Do not the Greek divinities recognise the primacy of
Jupiter? Have not the Romans their *Jupiter Optimus
Maximus?* In fact, neither the Semites nor the Indo-
Europeans were monotheists. The difference between the
two races is that the Semites, being poor in imagination,
worshipped only what appeared to the senses, such as
the sun, the moon, the planets, the constellations of the
zodiac, &c., while the imagination of the Indo-Europeans
created everywhere divinities in sublunary nature, as well
as in the firmament. . . . In a word, the Semites were
astrolaters, and the Indo-Europeans worshipped all nature.
But both of them confounded nature with God, and
neither of them were able to rise to the idea of a first
cause, absolute, unique, independent of the world, and
creative. Monotheism belongs to the Hebrews alone, and
it became theirs by the direct intervention of Providence."

The one God, the living God, revealed Himself to
Abraham, who made Him known to Isaac, and Isaac to
Jacob. The head of the family was at the same time
a priest and king; and all the worship consisted in prayers
and sacrifices. When at the exodus the family became

a people, the religion became national, and aspired at becoming universal. The God of Abraham, of Isaac, and of Jacob was made known by Moses as the God of the universe and the King of kings. That the true religion might not be corrupted it was entrusted to the guardianship of the tribe of Levi, and the Hebrew people was isolated as much as possible from its neighbours. The ark, and thereafter the temple, with the tables of the Law, were the material symbols of the alliance between God and the elect people. The solemn promise of a deliverer was taken in an entirely material sense, and hence the Hebrews did not recognise the Messiah in Jesus Christ. He developed the germs of universal charity contained in the Hebrew religion, and said: "Love God above all things, and thy neighbour as thyself; for this is the law and the prophets." In such passages of the Old Testament as the following, the same sentiment is accentuated: "The stranger that sojourneth with you shall be unto you as the homeborn among you, and thou shalt love him as thyself; for ye were strangers in the land of Egypt" (Lev. xix. 34). "If thou meet thine enemy's ox or his ass going astray, thou shalt surely bring it back to him again. If thou see the ass of him that hateth thee lying under his burden, and wouldest forbear to help him, thou shalt surely help with him" (Exod. xxiii. 4, 5).

The modern criticism has endeavoured to distinguish several periods in the founding of Christianity. The first disciples still considered themselves as Hebrews, and did not wish to admit any but the circumcised to the promises of the kingdom of God. St. Paul pleaded the cause of the Gentiles and expounded the doctrines of sin and grace. The Apocalypse was the manifesto of the Judæo-Christian party, as the Fourth Gospel was representative of the Greek philosophy. In this way the attempt has been made to show that the primitive Christianity was entirely a human work. But as Reuss, a Protestant theologian,

says, according to the traditional theology the prophets
and apostles would thus have been the merely passive
instruments of revelation, which in order to attain its
end would have neutralised and arrested momentarily or
permanently all intellectual exertion in them. On the
contrary, we think that they were the most elevated
geniuses and Coryphæi of their age, and that they had
the honour of being chosen by Providence to propagate
the new principles by making use of their natural
faculties. They were not vessels of inert matter, in
which the water which contained the germs of life was
to become stagnant; but their minds were occupied in
a free and orderly work, which the divine impulse had
excited without weakening the strength of their intellects.
The Holy Spirit prepared them to receive the heavenly
truth, purified their wills by the ministry of the word,
and thus prevented any deviation of thought or action
which might have been able to harm the cause which
they had been called to serve; and on their side they
applied to the furtherance of this cause their natural
faculties, the particular gifts of their minds, and their
knowledge and eloquence.[1]

At the outset the Christian doctrine was entirely summed
up in the expectation of the kingdom of God, of which
the Church had the keys. Its dogmas were still included
in the Old and New Testament, and were only defined
much later as it became necessary to do so. Thus it was
with the absolute divinity of Jesus Christ which was
formulated at the Council of Nice in 325, and with the
doctrine of the Holy Spirit at the Council of Constantinople in 380. In the year 1054, the first definite division
of the Church took place in the Greek schism. The
two churches differed only in reference to one dogma,
that of the procession of the Holy Spirit. Both churches
admitted the Scriptures and tradition as the sources of
the Christian faith, the infallibility of the visible church

[1] *Histoire de la théologie chrétienne au III. siècle*, p. 19. Paris, 1860.

(but not that of the Pope, whose primacy was denied by the Greeks) and the semi-Pelagian doctrine of original sin and grace; and they held the same views about the seven sacraments, purgatory, the invocation of saints, prayers for the dead, and veneration of images, although the Greeks admitted only painted images.[1]

In 1520, Luther separated himself openly from the Roman Catholic Church, and gave origin to the religious reformation called Protestantism, which produced a much deeper separation than the Greek schism. The chief differences between Catholicism and Protestantism are the following:—1. The interpretation of the Sacred Books belongs, according to the Catholics, to the clergy assembled in Council and to the Pope, whereas according to the Protestants it is left to the judgment of the individual. 2. According to the Protestants eternal salvation is attained by faith, whereas the Catholics maintain that faith is not sufficient without works. These two Protestant principles tended to emancipate the individual from authority and external practices. 3. Luther substituted the word "consubstantiation" for "transubstantiation," maintaining that the elements in the Holy Supper, without losing their proper substance, as was taught by the Catholic Church, became the body of Christ, just as red-hot iron contains the heat without ceasing to be iron. Calvin was more logical, seeing a simple symbol in this sacrament. 4. Protestantism, founding on individual inspiration, which was afterwards called private judgment, became sundered into a multitude of sects.

On the occasion of the tercentenary of the Reformation (27th September 1817), Frederick William I. of Prussia

---

[1] See for the dogmatic views the work of John of Damascus (*De la foi orthodoxe*, Paris, 1712), and for the canonical position the *Nomocarion* of Photius in the *Bibliotheca juris canonici*, Paris, 1661. As a summary, may be consulted the *Confessio Ecclesiae graecae orthodoxae a Petro Mogila composita*, Lipsia, 1595, which was approved by the Eastern Patriarchs in 1643, and sanctioned by the Synod of Bethlehem in 1672.

expressed publicly the wish for a general Union of the Protestant Churches, and at the same time he published the official scheme of a synodal constitution which was to be discussed in a future synod of the kingdom. The movement extended to the Duchy of Nassau, the Grand Duchy of Baden, the Bavarian Palatinate, and other small German States. The differences between the churches were attenuated, and a common symbol was compiled, taking the Holy Scriptures as its basis, without, however, diminishing the authority or independence of the two principal confessions, the Lutheran and the Reformed; and this union assumed the common name of the "Evangelical Church." Only the so-called Old Lutherans have kept themselves separated, in accordance with a concession of the sovereign of 1845. Gradually the other German States, with the exception of Mecklenburg, received the organisation by communities, and the synodal constitution was harmonised as well as possible with the consistorial constitution.[1]

The restoration of the German Empire in the person of a Protestant Prince took place about the same time as the passing of the decrees of the Vatican Council; and this gave occasion to a species of persecution against the Roman Church which was called the "culture-struggle" (*Culturkampf*), a word which was first used by Virchow in the electoral programme of the progressive party in 1873. The Laws of the 4th, 11th, 12th, 13th, and 14th May subjected the ecclesiastical authorities to the civil authorities, so as to render the exercise of worship impossible without the greatest abnegation. The articles 15, 16, and 18 of the Prussian Constitution of 31st January 1850, which

[1] For the doctrinal position of the Lutheran Church see the Augsburg Confession (1530), its Apology (1531), the theological treatise of Melanchthon (1521), the Articles of Smalcald (1537), and the two Catechisms of Luther (1529). For the doctrine of the Reformed Church, it will suffice to consult the *Christianae religionis institutio* (1536) of John Calvin. As regards the modern Evangelical Church, see the works of Richter (*Geschichte der evangelischen Kirche*, Leipzig, 1851), and of G. F. Schulte (*Lehrbuch des kath. und evang. Kirchenrechtes*, *Giessen*, 1886).

secured the Catholic Church as well as the Evangelical
Church by precious guarantees, were abrogated by the
Law of 18th June 1875. In the spring of 1886, the
May laws, above referred to, were mitigated in their
application, and on the 29th April of 1887 they were
almost wholly abolished.[1]

The English Church, when compared with other Protestant Churches, comes nearest the Catholic Church. Its
Thirty-nine Articles, which were approved in the London
Assembly of 1562, rejected the primacy of the Pope, the
worship of the Virgin and of the saints, and purgatory,
made the ceremony of the Holy Supper simply com-
memorative, took away the character of a sacrament from
auricular confession and marriage, &c. The Quakers, the
Moravian Brethren, and the Methodists, adopted more or
less of the mysticism proscribed by the first Reformers,
while the Armenians and the Unitarians of the present
day have come to adopt a pure rationalism.

Mohammedanism is considered by many as a heresy
of Christianity, but this view is erroneous. Islamism is
rather a return to the religion of Abraham, the gift of
prophecy having been granted to Mohammed ; and hence
its great simplicity and its tolerance of polygamy. Its
religious creed is summed up in these few words : God
is great, and Mohammed is His prophet. The Koran is
its only foundation according to the Shiites ; and it also
includes, according to the Sunnites, the sayings of the
prophet gathered by his familiar friends, the decisions of
the four first Caliphs and of the four Imams. The
Wahabites wished to reduce the worship to prostrating
oneself before the idea of the existence of God, without
the need of any intercessor ; and they profess to believe
that the destroying of the tomb of the prophet and

---

[1] See *Deutsche Reichs und Preus-* *kirchenrecht zusammengestellt von A.*
sische Staatsgesetze betreffend das Staats- Kleinschmidt. Berlin, Mai 1887.

the mausoleums of the great Imams, is a meritorious work.

Let us now look at the relations of these religions to society. The government of the Hebrews was a theocracy, and all know the words of Samuel to the elders and to the people when they asked him for a king. Nevertheless he had to concede their wish, but he did it so that the priests did not lose all their power. The faith in Jehovah, and the promise given to the seed of Abraham, constitutes the fundamental precept of the Mosaic Law: "I am the Lord thy God, and thou shalt have no other gods before me." Idolatry is compared to conjugal infidelity: "Ye are not to go a whoring after other gods;" and it is punished like adultery by stoning to death. Man is sacred because he is the work of God; the new-born child is inviolable; the slave becomes free in the Sabbatic year, that is, every seventh year. In no legislation of antiquity does there appear so much solicitude for the poor. Giving alms is called justice; and property was only emphyteutic, for in the jubilee, or after fifty years, every seller entered again into the possession of sold goods. The Levites were distributed in forty-eight cities scattered through the whole country, and they had a right to the tenth of the produce of the lands. The dignity of the high priesthood was hereditary in the family of Aaron. The prophets were a sort of inspired tribunes, who always vigorously recalled the commands of the Lord.

The modern Jews admit a tradition besides their sacred books. This tradition they carry back to Moses, and it regulates all the possible applications of the law. It has given origin to the *Talmud* (study or science), which is divided into two parts, the *Mishna* (second law) and the *Gemara* (gloss). This tradition is undoubtedly the work of the Pharisees, who had eyes and saw not, ears and heard not.

Modern criticism has found easier access to Islamism. The life of Mohammed, says Renan, is known to us like that of a reformer of the sixteenth century. He could neither read nor write; but his travels in Syria, his relations with the Christian monks, and the Biblical and Christian tradition of his uncle Waraca, awoke in him the religious vocation. Arabia was then passing through a crisis. Greeks, Syrians, Persians, and Abyssinians had penetrated into it on all sides, and had given rise to a species of religious syncretism. The ideas of a single God, of paradise, of a resurrection, of prophets, and of holy books, were introduced among the idolatrous tribes. The Kaaba was the pantheon of all the cults; and when Mohammed destroyed the images of the holy house, he found a Byzantine Virgin with the child in her arms painted on a column.

Mohammed had conceived the thought of a religious reform for Arabia alone. The idea of a universal conquest belongs to Omar. By the simplicity of its dogmas and the absence of an official clergy, Islamism resembles natural religion. Renan combats the ideas of Forster, who compares the Caliphate to the Papacy. "Whatever Forster may say, the Caliphate has never resembled the Papacy. The Caliphate has never been a powerful State, except in the period of the conquests of Islamism; but when the temporal power passed to the *Emiri-al-omra*, and the Caliphate was only a religious power, it fell soon into oblivion. The idea of a purely spiritual power is too high for the East. All the Christian branches have not been able to reach it; the Greco-Slavonic branch has never understood it; the German branch has rejected it; it is only the Latin nations that have been able to understand its value. Now experience has shown that the simple popular faith does not suffice to preserve a religion unless a consecrated hierarchy and a spiritual head watch over it."[1] Renan elsewhere[2] says: "Under the Caliphate,

---

[1] *Etudes d'histoire religieuse*, 2nd edit. p. 298–9. Paris, 1860.
[2] Under *Mahométisme* in the *Dictionnaire général de la politique.*

as under the dynasties which burst from it like clouds, one sole guarantee remained to the Mussulmans in the law which had descended from heaven. This law is placed under the guardianship of judges and juris-consults (*ulemas*), who form the first two orders of the Mussulman clergy. The interpreters of the law have often obeyed the precepts of the Koran to oppose the violation of the law; and often the Sheik-ul-Islam was as great on account of these resistances as any prefect of the praetorium under the Roman emperors. Some canonists even deny the Sultans the power to make organic laws in order to secure the execution of the sacred law. The public law of the East appears to have always conferred on the monarch an unlimited power over his functionaries, and generally over all those who have the misfortune to come near him. This cruel law of exception has its origin in the condition of the ancient ministers of the East, who were chosen from among the slaves of the seraglio; and it was also founded upon the peculiar position of the kings, who were strangers to the whole of their kingdom,—the first prisoners of the palace, as Montesquieu calls them. This deplorable policy has ruled all the monarchies of the East, and Islamism has in no way modified it. It has been wrongly asserted that the Koran does not recognise property. The property of the lands possessed by the Arabs before the conquest, and the property of lands abandoned by the infidels and divided among the faithful, are as well secured as any landed property can be in the East; and they are transmitted by sale, donation, and succession. The Koran and Sunna further recognise full proprietorship in desert lands which labour recalls to life. "If any one gives life to a dead bit of land," says Mohammed, "it is his." To the conquering Arabs there was assigned a tribute from the conquered lands, the precarious possession of these lands being left to the conquered. The old population remained attached to the soil under the surveillance of

the victorious army. These warriors were collectors of
the imposts, and were arranged in a wise hierarchy; and
they lived on vast domains such as the Europeans took
for fiefs, but they were only financial divisions, as they
wanted the most essential quality, namely, the proprietorship of the land. Islamism tempered the rigour of
proprietorship with the precept of almsgiving, which
was fixed at the tenth of the revenues; and it thus
settled the question of pauperism, which Catholicism
sought to solve by the monasteries. We now know
Islamism under its most disadvantageous aspect, saddened
as it is by Turks and barbarians; yet it is not incompatible with a certain culture, as was seen in the
eighth and ninth centuries at Bagdad, and in the tenth at
Cordova.

The true liberty entered into the world with the words
of Jesus Christ when He said: "Render unto Cæsar the
things that are Cæsar's, and to God the things that are
God's." Religion has eternal salvation in view, and consequently also mortality in the most absolute sense; while
the State has as its object terrestrial prosperity, and, consequently, right in the most human sense. Their efforts
are not opposed but convergent, since eternal salvation
does not exclude temporal prosperity, but would have
it subordinated to itself. Such subordination, however,
ought to be carried out by the free-will of the individual;
and the State is therefore obliged to secure the individual
his full liberty in matters of faith.

The worship of the first Christians is thus described by
Pliny the Younger (Lib. X. Let. 97): "The Christians
assemble on fixed days before the rising of the sun; they
sing in turns hymns in praise of Christ as a God; then
they bind themselves to commit no thefts, crimes, or
adulteries, and not to break a promise or deny a deposit; and after this, they disperse and assemble anew
to eat common and innocent food." In order to attract

the pagans they adopted some of their religious cere-
monies, such as the use of tapers, lustral water, processions, &c.

Some have thought that the whole government of the
Church was copied from institutions then existing, and
they have tried to find analogies between the election of
the magistrates and that of the bishops, between the
Church Councils and the Amphictyonic institution, without considering that new needs suffice to create new
institutions.

The ecclesiastical hierarchy really arose from the needs
of worship, and from the necessity of guarding the purity of
the faith. The distinction between clergy and laity seems to
go back to the apostolic times, as well as that of bishops,
priests, and deacons. A disciplinary authority was granted
to the churches which were metropolitan or located in the
capitals of provinces, as those of Antioch, Alexandria, and
Rome, whose primacy soon came to be recognised. The
union of the churches was maintained by the synods or
provincial councils. From the second century after Christ,
the Christian doctrine was exactly determined according
to the teaching of Jesus Christ, as attested by the Scriptures and by the tradition transmitted from the Apostles
to the uninterrupted series of their successors. However,
the Church as a whole was a depository of tradition; the
laity judged the teaching of the clergy and abandoned
the communion of the bishop whose doctrine was not
conformable to Scripture and tradition. Moreover, the
bishop was directly elected by the faithful; the priest,
the deacons, and the inferior clergy were elected conjointly
by the bishop and by the faithful, who took part in all
the affairs which concerned the internal community,
while the priests formed a permanent council at the side
of the bishop. The election, however, only designated the
individual who was to receive ordination, which the spiritual power alone conferred. There is not a single example
in the New Testament, or in the history of the Church, of

the institution of the spiritual power by means of election alone, while there are some instances in which the election is neglected. St. Paul enjoins his disciples Timothy and Titus to institute priests in the cities, that is to say, to choose those who were to preside over the worship, and to ordain them by the imposition of hands.

The government of the Church was a mixture of monarchy, aristocracy, and democracy. Monarchy was represented by the pope, aristocracy by the bishops, and democracy by the clergy and people. In the year 316, we find a canon of the Council of Laodicea which seems to restrict the popular right in elections; but it serves rather to restrict the abuse of it, since we have in the following centuries the most incontestable proofs of the intervention of the people in the elections of the clergy. The most powerful obstacles to this intervention came from the princes who desired to make themselves masters of the elections. The Church had granted them a certain right of nomination, or of confirmation in the case of the election of bishops, which, however, was to be always free; that is to say, it was to be effected by the concurrence of the bishops, the clergy, and the people. In the eleventh century the abuses of the secular power reached their height, and a long struggle began between the popes and the emperors with reference to the so-called investitures.

The Treaty of Worms of 1122 recognised the full liberty of the canonical elections, and left to the emperors only the right to give the elected bishop with his sceptre investiture in the goods attached to his church. The misfortunes of the times did not always permit the free assembling of the electoral Christian body; but Innocent III. and the fourth Lateran Council created in the Church a restricted electoral body, and entrusted the elections of bishops to the cathedral chapters, yet still leaving some traces of the intervention of the clergy and the people in such elections.[1] By the concordats of the sixteenth century, the nomination of the bishops was granted to the princes, their canonical institution being reserved for the pope.

The laity not only took part in these elections, but also in the Councils of the Church. We may quote to this effect the words of one of the latest defenders of these solemn assemblies : " The Christian society, says Monsignor Maret, rests on the authority of the First Pastors (Bishops). . . . These are the vicars or representatives of God made man, and of the primordial and infinite reason. Their government ought therefore to be a government of reason and wisdom. Reason enlightens all men, and the first pastors ought to take counsel with each other in order to their mutual illumination. But besides this natural motive there are others which arise from the very essence of the religious society. This society has received from its divine founder the deposit of the revealed truths, and preserves it in its memory and heart in order to become the interpreter of it whenever there arises a doubt regarding dogma or morals. . . . The First Pastors are the witnesses of this tradition, and show its antiquity and perpetuity by their assembly, its immutable unity by their agreement, and its charity by the tenor of their discussions. When assembled they attest the tradition of the Church, comment upon it, develop it, and propose all the laws necessary for the religious society. Thus the agreement of the chief pastors is the manifestation of Christian truth. . . . However, the chief pastors do not only agree among themselves, but call forth the councils of the Pastors of the second order (Clergy), and also of the faithful. This invitation is suggested by the great law of humility and Christian charity. Humility teaches the chief pastors that they may receive from their subordinates salutary advices, because the Spirit of God bloweth where it listeth.

[1] See Thomassin, *Discipline ecclésiastique*, t. ii.

Charity enjoins them to act always in harmony; for when
unity reigns in the souls of men, laws become more
respected and more effective, and goodness becomes
easier."[1] The same author further explains that the
clergy had a deliberative vote, and the laity simply a
consultative vote.

The Bishop of Rome was chosen like all the other
bishops until a special mode of doing this was established
on account of his peculiar importance. As the name of
Pope became a privilege of the Roman Bishop, so did the
title of Cardinal become a privilege of his presbyters.
We find in Baronius the following decree, which emanated
from Nicolas II. at the Council of Rome in 1059 : "In
primis cardinales episcopi diligentissmi simul de electione
(*pontifices*) tractantes, mox ipsi clericos cardinales adhi-
beant: sicque reliquus clerus et populus ad consensus
novae electionis accedat." A letter of Petrus Damiani,
written in the time of the successor of Nicolas II., adds:
"Sic suspendenda est causa usquedum Regiae Celsitudinis
consulatur auctoritas ; nisi, sicut nuper contigit, periculum
fortasse immineat, quod rem quandocius accelerare com-
pellat." Accordingly, the cardinals elected; the remaining
clergy and the people gave consent; and the emperor
approved the election. If the new pope was taken out
of the body of cardinals, it was not a necessity, nor is it
so to-day, but a matter of convenience.[2]

The first pope elected without the intervention of the
Roman people, was Celestine II. in 1143. The high clergy,
using as a pretext an insurrection against Innocent II.,
the predecessor of Celestine, laid claim to the right of
choosing the pontiff. The Romans complained of it, and
at the death of Celestine II. reclaimed this right arms in
hand. Lucius II., Eugenius III., Anastasius IV., and
Adrian IV. were also elected by the common suffrages of

[1] Monsignor Maret, *Le Concile général et la paix réligieuse.* Paris, 1869.
[2] Guglielmo Audisio, Diritto pubblico della Chiesa e delle genti cris-
tiane. Vol. I. Roma, 1863.

the clergy and laity: *communi voto cleri et populi electus,*
as Otto of Freisingen says in speaking of the election
of Eugenius III. But Adrian IV. finally deprived the
faithful of the electoral right, and Alexander III. was
elected in 1159 without their participation. The Romans
protested, and uniting with certain dissentient cardinals,
they elected four anti-popes. This schism induced
Alexander III. to convoke the third Lateran Council in
1179, which established the condition in principle that
the election of the popes belongs exclusively to the
cardinals.

The power of the cardinals increased along with that
of the pope. They assisted him in all affairs of importance, meeting in a public or secret consistory, whether in
an ordinary or extraordinary meeting for nomination of
the bishops, &c. The cardinals also met in temporary
or permanent commissions. The latter were instituted
by Sixtus V., some of them connected with the episcopate
of Rome for the administration of the States of the
Church, and others for the administration of the whole
Catholic world. They are the following:—1. The *Congregatio consistorialis,* founded in order to prepare the
matters which were to be discussed in the consistory. It
was rearranged by Clement IX. 2. The *Congregatio S.
Officii sive Inquisitionis,* whose office was to take note of
all heterodox doctrines. It was founded by Paul III.
in 1542, as an extraordinary commission or a supreme
tribunal against heresies. Pius IV. and Pius V. extended its authority, and Sixtus V. made it permanent.
3. The *Congregatio Indicis,* instituted by Pius V. and
Sixtus V. in order to relieve the preceding one, there
being assigned to it the examination of pernicious books.
4. The *Congregatio Sacri Concilii Tridentini interpretum,*
instituted by Pius IV. with the sole object of watching
over the execution of the decrees of the Council of Trent,
but Pius V., and then Sixtus V., added to it also the
right of interpreting them. 5. The *Congregatio sacrorum*

rituum, instituted by Sixtus V. for the liturgy and canonisations. 6. The *Congregatio de propaganda fide*, founded for the direction of missions by Gregory XV. in 1622, whose jurisdiction was extended by Urban VIII. 7. The *Congregatio super negotiis episcoporum*, and another *super negotiis regularium*, instituted separately by Sixtus V., and then combined by him into one. 8. The *Congregatio immunitatum et controversiarum juredictionalium*, established by Urban VIII. 9. The *Congregatio examinis episcoporum*, which takes due information for the nomination of the bishops. 10. Finally, the Congregation instituted by Clement IX. in 1669 to provide against the abuse of indulgences and of relics.[1]

In the gravest cases, the pope was not satisfied with the consultative vote of the cardinals, but had recourse to the deliberative vote of the Councils. Here rises the question as to the superiority of the Council over the pope, or that of the pope over the Council. There is invoked on the one side the decree of the Council of Constance, Section V.: "Sancta Synodus declarat, quod ipsa potestatem a Christo immediate habet, cui quilibet cujuscumque status vel dignitatis, etiam si papalis existat, obedire tenetur in his quae pertinent ad fidem et extirpationem dicti schismatis, et reformationem dictae ecclesiae in capite et membris." On the other side there is cited the Bull *Pastor aeternus*, approved in the fifth Lateran Council, from which we extract the following passage: "Cum etiam solum Pontificem Romanum, pro tempore existentem, tanquam auctoritatem super omnia concilia habentem, tam conciliorum indicendorum, transferendorum, dissolvendorum plenum jus et potestatem habere, nedum ex sacrae Scripturae testimonio, dictis sanctorum Patrum, ac aliorum Romanorum Pontificum etiam praedecessorum nostrorum, sacrorum canonum decretis, sed propria etiam eorumdem conciliorum confessione manifesta constat."

[1] Walter, *Manuel du droit ecclésiastique de toutes les confessions chrétiennes.* Paris, 1840.

The French clergy, being met in a representative assembly on the 19th March 1682, held to the first of these two opinions, and formulated in their famous *Declaration* the following two articles : (1) That the power of the Councils is superior to the power of the pope, according to the decrees of the Council of Constance ; and (2) That the decision of the pope is not infallible nor irreformable, except in so far as it has been confirmed by the consent of the Church. This opinion, although disapproved by the pope, continued to be taught in France, and Article 24 of the Organic Law of the 18th Germinale, anno X., which was a sort of complement of the concordat of anno IX., demanded that the qualified teachers in the seminaries should subscribe the above Declaration of 1682.

The Vatican Council has changed this state of things in declaring the infallibility of the pope in the following terms : " Romanorum Pontificem, cum omnium Christianorum Pastoris et Doctoris munere fungens, pro suprema sua Apostolica auctoritate doctrinam de fide vel moribus ab universa Ecclesia tenendam definit, assistentiam divinam, ipsi in beato Petro promissam, ea infallibilitate pollere, qua divinus Redemptor Ecclesiam suam in definienda doctrina de fide vel moribus instructam esse voluit; ideoque ejusmodi Romani Pontificis definitiones ex sese, non autem ex consensu Ecclesiae irreformabiles esse." Does the personal infallibility of the pope follow from this definition ? We give the reply of Alfonso Capecelatro. " The pope," he says, " is so united to the Church teaching (ecclesia docens) that when he speaks *ex cathedrá*, he is always bound up with the Church by the promise of Christ, and he expresses its faith. The adverse school affirms that neither errors, nor much less personal faults, can separate the Vicar of Christ from his Spouse when he speaks of religious and moral dogmas in name of the Church universal, or as head and supreme master of it to the same Church universal. In short, according to this theory, the pope is the head of a body which is called the Teaching Church; and the bishops are members of it, and are living and vigorous in so far as they are united as branches to that first and fruitful vine. When this head speaks in name of the whole body, when in name of this body he teaches all the believers, and teaches in matter revealed by Christ, or in that in which Christ radiates out His own infallibility in the Church: he is then so united, and, I may even say, so immediately identified and unified, with the body, that he always represents its faith, or, which is the same thing, the faith of Christ. This is the theory of Papal Infallibility." [1]

Let us now examine the relations of the Church with the State. In the first Christian centuries the Church was ignored by the State when it was not persecuted by it. With the Edict of Milan in 313, the Christians obtained the free exercise of their worship. Soon after, Constantine granted the Church the power to receive donations and legacies, and he gave the first example of them, and guaranteed the Church in perpetual possession thereof. He made the Christian priests share in all the privileges which the pontiffs of paganism enjoyed, that is, the right of asylum in their temples, and exemption from public burdens or from personal services, and from imposts. The least of the clergy could not be subjected to torture; and the Sunday rest became obligatory, which was a great benefit for the slaves. Such great favours were reciprocated; and the emperor even took a part in the dogmatic

[1] *Il Concilio Vaticano,* a pamphlet by Alfonso Capecelatro, formerly priest of the Oratoire of Naples, now Cardinal Archbishop of Capria. We find the same interpretation in the little work of Monsignor Fesler, Secretary of the Council, entitled *De la vraie et de la fausse infaillibilité.* The Council will therefore preserve in the future its deliberative vote, as the pope will have the right of confirmation. Dogmatic truth rests on the principle of Divine assistance, and not on the wholly human principle of the majority. After, as before the Council, the hypothesis advanced by Bellarmin of a heretical pope, is always admissible, and then the full power would reside of necessity in the Council, which could be convoked by the cardinals, or might even be assembled by the spontaneous motion of the bishops.

decisions of the Church, which were promulgated by him and made incumbent.

When the barbarians overran the empire, the Church was the only power which remained standing amid so many ruins, and it is no wonder that its power increased. Constantine had given legal force to the sentences pronounced by the bishops in the causes voluntarily submitted to their decision. Between the period of the Roman municipal government and that of the Middle Ages, we find the preponderance of the clergy in civil affairs. "And in fact," says Guizot, "it was of immense advantage that there existed a moral influence, a moral force, a force which rested only on moral convictions, beliefs, and sentiments, in the midst of that deluge of material force which broke at this epoch upon society. If the Christian Church had not existed, the whole world would have been delivered up to pure material force. The Church alone exercised a moral power. She did more; she maintained and diffused the idea of a rule, of a law superior to all human laws; she professed the belief, as fundamental for the salvation of humanity, that above all human laws there is a law called, according to the times and customs, sometimes reason and sometimes divine right, but which always and everywhere is the same law under different names." [1]

It was not enough to convert the barbarian invaders, but it was also necessary to resist their daily violences, and the still more pernicious assaults of the emperors of Constantinople who wished to act the theologian. Gregory II., surnamed the Great, sought by all means to persuade Leo the Isaurian to keep within his limits; and he did not free himself from all subjection till he assembled a minor Council in 730 in order to decree the abolition of the worship of images. Gregory III., who succeeded him in 731, tried in vain to effect a reconciliation; and when he

---

[1] See his *Histoire de la civilisation en Europe.* Deuxième leçon. Paris, 1845.

saw his territory devastated, and Rome besieged by Luitprand, the king of the Lombards, who was perhaps urged
on by Leo, he asked help from Charles Martel, and conferred upon him the honours of the patriciate and of the
Roman consulship. Pepin, the son of Charles Martel,
admonished Astolf, the successor of Luitprand : " Propter
pacis foedera et proprietatis sanctae Dei Ecclesiae ac
reipublicae restituenda jura." When the French arms
were already threatening them, Stephen likewise exhorted
the Lombards : " Ut pacifice, sine ulla sanguinis effusione,
propria sanctae Dei Ecclesiae et reipublicae Romanorum
redderet jura."

In 755, Pepin entered Italy, and did not leave it till he
had received from Astolf forty hostages, as Eginhard says :
" Firmitatis causa pro restituendis quae Romanae Ecclesiae
ablata fuerant." The Lombard king having broken faith,
Pepin crossed the Alps again in 756, and besieging Pavia
anew, he caused Ravenna, Pentapolis, and the Exarchate
to be consigned to the pope. The Lombard fidelity was
not better observed by King Desiderius, the successor of
Astolf ; and Pope Adrian had recourse to Charlemagne,
the son and successor of Pepin. Charlemagne marched
into Italy, and in 774 took King Desiderius prisoner, and
put an end to the kingdom of the Lombards, after it had
lasted 206 years. He celebrated Easter in Rome, and
confirmed and augmented the restitutions and donations
of Pepin. In order to suppress the revolts of the unsettled
Lombards, he returned several times ; and on the last
occasion he was crowned Emperor in Rome by the hand
of Pope Leo III. on Christmas day of the year 800.

What was the historical significance of the renovation
of the Roman Empire ? The peoples had trodden each
other down, but after Charlemagne the great invasions
may be said to have come to an end. The Church believed
that it might rest under the shelter of the empire. " But,"
says Cesare Balbo, " in Italy the eternal and real seat of
the pope was but a nominal seat, and was too far away

from the new emperors; and collisions immediately arose and were infinitely more felt. Every election of an emperor, and every election of a pope, was felt and was followed by troubles and misfortunes; and there arose bad and foreign emperors, and bad simoniacal and corrupt popes for more than two centuries." [1]

The juridical condition of the Church almost became the same as in the time of the Roman emperors. The bishops took a distinct place among the aristocracy, which was gradually transformed into a state of feudality. Hence it came about that the bishops depended canonically on the pope, and politically on the emperor. But the barbarism of the time did not permit the carrying out of this distinction in fact; and the simoniacal elections, with the arbitrary distribution of benefices, went hand in hand with the corruption of the habits of the clergy. Hildebrand was alarmed at the prevalence of such anarchy, and he discussed it as prior of the Abbey of Cluny with Pope Leo IV., who called him to Rome and made him a cardinal. For twenty-three years he directed the affairs of the Church under four popes, and prepared the great reform which he accomplished under the name of Gregory VII. "He proposed," says Guizot, "to subject the civilised world to the Church, and the Church to the Popes, with the intention of bringing about reform and progress, and not from a stationary or retrograde view."

The occasion of the conflict of the Church with the civil power arose in connection with the right of Investiture, a profound question, since it turned upon the issue as to whether the Church was to·dominate the State or the State the Church. Gregory VII. did not seek the simple independence of the Church, but he wished to command the sovereigns as the soul commands the body. He combated and he conquered; for he saw the Emperor Henry IV., the representative of the civil power, at his feet. But the victory was not final, because the State

[1] See *Sommario della Storia d'Italia.* Firenze, 1856.

could not abdicate its independence. Henry V., the son
and successor of Henry IV., came to terms with Calixtus
II. by means of the Concordat of Worms in 1122, in which
it was established that the pope should give canonical
institution to the bishops with the pastoral staff and ring,
and that the emperor should take part in the election,
giving the bishops investiture into the possessions which
they were to hold for the Church.

The moral dictatorship of the popes ended in Boniface
VIII., the last pope of the Middle Ages. Calamitous
times for the Church followed with the translation of
the Holy See to Avignon (which the Catholics speak of
as the *Babylonian slavery*), and the great schism of the
East which terminated at the Council of Constance, and
finally the Protestant Reformation.

The cry for reform had become universal in the Church.
The Council of Constance had shown Martin V. the
supreme need of it, and the Council of Basle was determined to follow it out, in spite of the tergiversations of
Eugenius IV. In its second period this Council proposed
to call the clergy to the observance of sanctity of life;
and it wished to put an end to the abuse of appeals to
Rome, to abolish annats and other taxes introduced by
the avarice of the Roman Court, to suppress reservations
and restore the canonical elections, and to provide for
the dignity of the sacred offices. The election of the
popes, the government of the Church, the composition of
the College of Cardinals, and their duties, were objects of
the wisest dispositions. We note in particular the canon
which restricted the number of cardinals, and prescribed
that they should be taken in a just proportion from all
the Catholic nations.[1] The decrees of reform were sent
to Pope Eugenius, with the demand that he should apply
their dispositions without delay. The pope thought it
necessary to excuse himself to the Council by special
nuncios, who said: "The Holy Father adopts as far as

---

[1] *Concil. Basil*, p. 562.

is in his power, the decrees of the Holy Council, and wishes that they be observed in the future; and if for the past it has been otherwise, this was due to insuperable circumstances." These were only words, and in fact the Council was transferred without its consent to Ferrara, which was the occasion of a new schism, and the magnificent opportunity was thrown away of avoiding the loss of seventy-five millions of Catholics.

What they would not do at Basle was done at Trent, but when too late. The first decree of this Council clearly says that one of its objects was the *reformation of the clergy and of the Christian people;* and Pope Pius IV., in confirming the resolutions of the Council, repeated that one of its ends was *the correction of morals and the re-establishment of discipline.*

But let us return to the civil relations of the Church. The Concordat of Worms, in removing the controversy as to investiture, had not regulated with certainty all the relationships of the Church with the State. There were two utopian views face to face with each other: the papal utopia formulated by Gregory VII., Innocent III., and Boniface VIII.; and the imperial utopia formulated by Dante in his book *De Monarchia.*

Gregory VII. had said in various places in his letters: "As the mother of the faithful, the Roman Church is superior to all Christendom. In this unhappy age, it supports the weight of temporal and spiritual affairs; and it commands the other churches and the members who depend upon them, including emperors, kings, princes, archbishops, prelates, and generally all Christians. Invested with the supreme authority, it institutes them, judges them, and deposes them. The sword of the prince being a human thing, ought to be subordinated to the Successor of Peter; for the seat of the Apostle depends only on God. And if resistance is offered to him, he ought after the example of the Saviour to struggle with perseverance, to suffer, and even to die, but never to abandon his post. Two luminaries, the sun and the moon, give light to the world; and two powers, the pope and the kings, govern it; but as the moon receives her light from the more luminous star, so do kings reign by the Head of the Church, who comes from God, and to whom it belongs to teach, to exhort, to punish, and to decide. The power of emperors and kings, and the undertakings of mortals, are but straw and smoke when compared with the divine omnipotence and the authority of the Apostolic Church. God has said to his Vicar: 'Thou art Peter, and on this rock will I build My church; and what thou shalt bind on earth will be bound in heaven' (Matt. xvi.). Has He made an exception for kings? Do they not make part of the flock entrusted to Peter? If therefore any one denies the sovereign pontiff, who has succeeded the Apostle, the right of commanding as ruler those who wear the crown, if he who opens and shuts heaven were subjected to mundane power, this would be as great an act of folly as if any one wished the son to command the father, or the disciple the master. Thus the Roman See being by its power so greatly superior to the thrones of the world, the kingdoms belong to Peter, and owe him tribute. What has once become the property of the Church belongs to her for ever; and even if she lost the enjoyment of it, she would not lose her right to it without a legitimate cession. Whoever is rebellious against the Lord cannot claim to be obeyed by man. Such is the end; and in order to attain it, it is indispensable that the Church shall depend only on herself. She is living in sin because she is not free; she must be delivered; and whatever may be the obstacles in the way, as the cause of the Church is the cause of God, she will conquer."

Innocent III., in sending the insignia to the chief of the Bulgarians, who had asked him to be raised to the royal dignity, thus expresses himself with regard to the omnipotence of the Holy See: "The King of kings, the

Lord of lords, Jesus Christ, to whom the Father has committed all things, putting the universe under His feet, to whom the earth belongs with all it contains and those who inhabit it, whom every creature in heaven and earth and hell obeys, has chosen for His vicar the supreme pontiff of the Apostolic See and of the Roman Church; and He has elevated him above the peoples and kingdoms, conferring upon him the power to take away, to destroy, to disperse, to build, and to plant."

Boniface VIII. wrote in his Bull *Unam Sanctam:* "We believe and confess one only Church, holy, catholic, and apostolic, out of which there is no salvation. Being one and single, it can have only one head, and not two, like a monster. This sole head is Jesus Christ, and Saint Peter His vicar, and the successor of Saint Peter. . . . We learn from the Gospel that in this Church, and under its power, there are two swords, the spiritual sword and the temporal sword. One ought to be in the hand of the Church, and therefore wielded by the pontiff, and the other in the hand of the kings and warriors, but it ought to be drawn for the good of the Church at the beck or permission of the priest. Accordingly, it is the case that the one sword depends on the other, or that the temporal authority depends on the spiritual, because the Apostle says that *every power comes from God, and all that exists is ordained by God.* Consequently we declare and say and define that it is necessary to salvation (*de necessitate salutis*) to hold that every human creature is subject to the Pope of Rome."

Dante's book, *De Monarchia,* is the manifesto of the imperial or Ghibelline party. The end of humanity, says Dante, is to develop the intellectual and moral faculties of man, and this cannot be attained without peace. Peace being a condition essential for the fulfilment of our mission, the universe ought to be ordered so as to secure us peace; and a universal monarchy alone can give us this guarantee, for where there are several equal princes, there necessarily reigns struggle and discord. On the contrary, the golden age will come again when the whole human race shall be gathered under a single head. As the poet has said: "Jam redit Virgo; redeunt Saturnia regna." Dante confesses that he had also shared the error that Rome had become the mistress of the world only by force and violence. But now he has come to see otherwise, and he holds with Cicero that Rome conquered the world not from ambition, but for the good of humanity. Unity being the goal assigned by God to the human race, the empire has been the means to it. Thus are explained the incessant victories of Rome and the death of Alexander, who might have put a stop to them. Christ was born under Augustus, was enrolled in the census, paid tribute, and acknowledged the empire. The emperor is the master of the world, but princes and nations have also their rights and their liberties. To the emperor only belongs his high jurisdiction in order to put an end to all contests. And he will be equity itself, no longer yielding either to fear or to cupidity. He should have his seat in Rome beside the pontiff; and Cæsar should exercise towards Peter that reverence which the firstborn son owes his father, in order that being enlightened by the paternal grace, he may illuminate the terraqueous globe with more virtue.

Of these two Utopias, that of Dante has triumphed. The reaction had already begun in France under Louis IX., who subjected the prelates to the judgment of the king in civil matters, and prohibited the pope from laying imposts upon the faithful in his kingdom without the express consent of the king and of the national church. If Louis IX. confined himself to resistance, his nephew, Philippe le Bel, dared to carry on the attack by imposing taxes on the ecclesiastical possessions, which till that time had been exempt from them, and by establishing an appeal on the ground of *abuse* to the lay authorities in reference to all the excesses which the spiritual jurisdiction might

have committed against the temporal. Later on, Charles
VII. assembled a national synod at Bourges, which set
forth the *Pragmatic Sanction* of 1438, into which were
introduced the principal maxims of the Councils of
Constance and Basle regarding the liberty of elections,
the provisions and collations of benefices, and the abolition
of *annats* or the fruits which Rome claimed in the first
year of the vacant benefices. Pius II. called this act
execrabilis et inauditus. To put an end to the continual
remonstrances of Rome, Francis I. and Leo X. concluded
a concordat in 1516, without expressly abolishing the
Pragmatic Sanction, which was considered as in force for
all that was not provided for by the concordat. The three
fundamental dispositions of the concordat were: the abolition of the elections of the bishops, and substitution
for them of the royal nomination with canonical institution
by the Holy See; the re-establishment of the annats, but
restricting them to the large benefices only; and the re-
establishment of appeals to the pope, but only for greater
causes, while for the others the pope was to name judges
in the kingdom.

The Council of Trent made a step backwards towards
the Gregories and the Innocents. The Council wished
that all the constitutions of the popes in favour of the
ecclesiastics should be carried out without any legal supervision, and it interdicted the appeals on the ground of
abuse against the ordinances of the prelates. The criminal
causes of the bishops were to be judged by the pope and
his delegates; and all causes of ecclesiastics pending
before the ordinary tribunal might be referred to Rome.
The bishops might punish by fines those who were guilty
of scandalous and public sin, and they might have their
sentence executed by their own officials, or by those of
the other judges. The bishops might also compel those
connected with their diocese to perform a service for their
pastor, and the monasteries might possess and acquire
immovable property. It is unnecessary to say that this

part of the decrees of the Council of Trent was not received in France.

From the Council of Trent to the French Revolution the State was always defending itself from the Roman Church. We may refer on the dogmatic side to two articles in the celebrated Gallican Declaration of 1682. The one which establishes the independence of the temporal power, declares that Saint Peter and his successors, the vicars of Jesus Christ, and all the Church, have received no other power from God than over spiritual things and what concerns salvation, and not over temporal and civil things. The king and the sovereigns are not by the order of God subject in any way to the ecclesiastical power in temporal things. They cannot be deposed either directly or indirectly by the authority of the heads of the Church; their subjects cannot be dispensed from the submission and obedience which they owe, nor can they be absolved from the oath of fidelity. Moreover, this doctrine is as necessary for the public tranquillity, and not less advantageous to the Church than the State; and it ought to be inviolably observed as conformable to the word of God, to the tradition of the holy fathers, and to the examples of the saints. The other sovereigns, such as Joseph II. of Austria, Leopold II. of Tuscany, and Charles III. of Naples, showed themselves equally jealous of their prerogatives.

The French Revolution tore up the Concordat of Francis I., and wished to give a civil constitution to the clergy (12th July 1790), for whom a political assembly was not at all competent. This constitution decreed : 1. The election of the bishops and of the parochial priests ; 2. The mode of their election, which was to be, not as in the time of St. Louis and Charles VII., by the clergy of the cathedral churches and others, but by the suffrage of all the citizens who were political and administrative electors ; 3. Canonical institution to be given by the metropolitans instead of by the sovereign pontiff; 4. The delimitation of the dioceses by the government, and not by the pope. In 1793, the French revolutionists went the length of proscribing the Catholic worship.

The Concordat of 15th July 1801 did not restore, nor could it restore, the ancient state of things. It allowed a new circumscription of the dioceses, and a dotation for the clergy chargeable to the budget of the State in return for their renouncing all their immovable goods, even those which were not sold. The nomination of the bishops continued to be made by the head of the State with canonical institution by the pope, and the nomination of the parish priests was made by the bishops with the sanction of the government. By the Concordat of 25th June 1813, which was not put into execution, the Emperor Napoleon wrested from the pope, who was his prisoner, the renunciation of the temporal power in his States, and the right to delay beyond six months the canonical institution of the bishops, in which case it would have to be performed by the metropolitan. This was the climax of the usurpations of the State over the Church. And in fact the Convention of 11th June 1817, which remained a mere project, returned to the Concordat of Francis I., as it established a dotation in immovable goods or in *rentes* for the bishops, seminarists, parish priests, chapters, &c.

The Belgian constitution raised the liberty of the Church to a canon of public right in its Article 16. " The State has not the right to intervene either in the nomination, or in the installation of the ministers of any form of worship; nor shall it be able to prohibit these from corresponding with their superiors and publishing their acts under the simple responsibility of the usual law as to printing and publication."

The Concordat of 16th March 1851 with Spain reestablished the Catholic religion with *all the rights and prerogatives which it ought to enjoy according to the law of God and the canonical sanctions.* It declared that the education in all the colleges, universities, &c., should be conformable to the Catholic doctrine, and that the bishops should not encounter any obstacle in their supervision of the youth in the relationships of morality and of the faith. It admitted the unlimited right of possessing and acquiring immovable goods, as well as in founding religious orders which might have for their object charity or the public utility. The Concordat of 7th October 1872 with the republic of Costa Rica, recognises as belonging to the Church the same rights and free communication with the Holy See in *all that concerns spiritual and ecclesiastical things*, as is enunciated in the Concordat of 18th August 1855 with Austria, which is conformable in all points to those now referred to.

We have already indicated the dogmatic differences between the Latin and Greek Churches, which were irrevocably divided from the time of the schism in 1054. We may now pause for a little on the constitution of the Eastern Church, and its relations with the State. The Emperor of Constantinople claimed to be *imperator tum et sacerdos*, and this pretension was tolerated by the popes when it turned out for the good of the Church. "Yea, of a truth," replied Gregory II. to Leo the Isaurian, "those emperors who have preceded you, namely, Constantine the Great, Theodosius the Great, the great Valentinian, and Constantine, the father of Justinian II., who took a part in the sixth synod, showed by their words and deeds what they were; with ardent zeal they studied the truth of the faith, and they aided the pontiffs in their care of the churches. These emperors, in harmonious relations and unanimity with the pontiffs, convoked synods and promoted the true understanding of the faith, and they were ornaments and supports of the Holy Church. They were emperors and priests in co-operation, and their deeds showed them to be such." In the Council of Constantinople, the bishop of the new metropolis occupied the place immediately after the Bishop of Rome, and later an analogous share of jurisdiction was decreed to him. In spite of the opposition of the pope, who combated such innovations, they were sanctioned by authority. The pope continued to be recognised as the head of the universal Church, but the pride of the patriarchs and the continual interposition of the emperors in the ecclesiastical controversies, rendered the relations between old and new Rome difficult. After the schism the power of the patriarch of Constantinople increased, and he took the title of *œcumenical* without diminishing the interposition of the emperor. The following was the ceremony for the consecration of the patriarchs, which was still in use when Constantinople fell into the hands of the Turks. The emperor, seated on his throne in the Church of St. Sofia, and having the holy senate around him, delivered the pastoral staff to the patriarch. The first court chaplain pronounced the benediction; the first chamberlain chaunted the hymn and the gloria ; the inspector of the lamps intoned the chorus: *The King of heaven*, &c. The chants being finished, the emperor then rose, holding the sceptre in his right hand, with the Cæsar sitting on his right, and the metropolitan of Heraclea on his left. The newly-elected patriarch bowed three times before the whole assembly, and prostrated himself at the feet of the emperor, and the monarch, elevating the sceptre, pronounced these words : "The Most Holy Trinity, who has given me the empire, confers on thee the patriarchate of New Rome." [1]

The Church of the East had propagated the Gospel in the immense solitudes of the north, and had created the

[1] How different is what is related of the reception given by Alexander III. to Frederick I. at Venice. The Emperor prostrated himself at the feet of the pope, who placed them on his head, quoting the text : *Super aspidem et basiliscum ;* and the emperor raising himself replied : *Non tibi sed Petro ;* to which the pope replied, *Mihi et Petro.* Balbo says this is perhaps a fable, but it shows well the manners and ideas of the time.

Moscovite Church as a dependant on itself. The metropolitans of Kieff were usually nominated by the patriarch
of Constantinople, and often they were Greeks. The
invasion of the Tartars and the removal of the capital
from the shores of the Dnieper to the basin of the Volga,
had relaxed the bonds existing between the two churches.
The metropolitan of Russia, who followed the great princes
to Vladamir, and then to Moscow, was still a suffragan
of the Greek patriarch, but he was now a Russian, and
he was elected by his clergy, and chosen by his sovereign.
After the example of her Byzantine mother, the Russian
Church showed herself from the beginning full of respect
and deference towards the temporal power. The civil
wars, and then the Tartar domination, enabled her to
acquire more influence and independence. This was
the heroic age of the Russian Church, the epoch of the
great national saints, of Alexander Newski, of Alexis, of
Sergius, and of most of the monastic foundations. The
elevation of the autocracy, along with the ceasing of the
Tartar domination, took from the Church part of her
ascendancy, but the extinction of the dynasty for a time
restored it. Ivan the Terrible humbled both the Boyards
and the clergy, and he had as metropolitan, St. Philip,
who was his Thomas à Becket. The metropolitan, the
only head of the Moscovite Church, was already too great
a personage in the eyes of the autocrat; and nevertheless
in 1589, Ivan the Terrible was no sooner dead than the
metropolitan dared to demand the dignity of a patriarch.
Good reasons for this were not wanting. Moscovy had
become a very vast State, and could not be governed from
the shores of the Bosphorus; and as Constantinople had
fallen into the hands of the Turks, the patriarch was
consequently in a position of dependence on the Sultan.
The patriarch of Constantinople, having gone to Moscow
to erect the new patriarchal see, was offered the seat
himself while preserving the title of œcumenical patriarch.
The Byzantine prelate who had come to obtain succour

for his Church, refused the offer of the Czar, and considered himself repaid by his largesses.[1] The Moscovite patriarchate was an entirely national institution, and its jurisdiction extended with the political limits of the empire. The Russian bishops assembled in council had the right to nominate their head; they chose three names, and the lot had to decide between them. The prerogatives of the patriarch remained in substance the same as those of the metropolitan, but surrounded with greater honours. Like the metropolitan, the patriarch was the supreme head of the ecclesiastical jurisdiction, and besides the affairs of the clergy and matrimonial causes, his administration of justice included cases of succession down to the time of Peter the Great. He enjoyed the revenues of certain convents and lands; his house was kept up like that of the Czar; and he had his court, his boyards, and his great officers, as he had his tribunals and his administration.

The patriarchate of Russia lasted little more than a century (1589-1700), and it is considered by the ecclesiastical historians as a providential fact. Instituted on the eve of the extinction of the dynasty of the Ruriks, the patriarchate passed through the anarchy of the usurpation, and contributed to the consolidation of the Romanoff dynasty. In the first period of its existence it contributed to save Russia from dissolution and from foreign dominion; and in its second period it communicated to the recuperative reign of the first Romanoffs a religious and paternal character, which rendered that epoch a sort of golden age in Russian history. Although the patriarchate was in full decline under Peter the Great, he believed it was an obstacle to his great reforms, and seizing the opportunity of the See being vacant, he abolished it. The ecclesiastical reform was carried out by this sovereign under an occidental inspiration which was in part Protestant. The substitution of an assembly

[1] Anatole Leroy-Beaulieu, *L'empire des tzars et les Russes.* Paris, 1881.

for a single head was not an isolated fact special to the Church; it was a general system then in vogue in the West, particularly in France, where the ministers of Louis XIV. had been superseded by the Councils of the regency. The administrative colleges of Peter the Great have been succeeded in the beginning of this century by the ministers; but the ecclesiastical college of the Holy Synod has remained. We shall glance at its composition and its prerogatives.

The Holy Synod is nominated by the sovereign, and is composed of irremovable members, namely, the metropolitans of the successive capitals of the empire, Kieff, Moscow, and St. Petersburg; and the last named, who has usually under him the diocese of Novogorod, is the president. The other members are four or five archbishops, bishops, or archimandrites, two members of the secular clergy, and two arch-priests, one of whom is usually the chaplain or confessor of the emperor, and the other that of the army. Along with the Synod there sits a delegate of the emperor under the name of Procurator-General (*Ober-procurator*). Under the Emperor Nicholas, this delegate was a general of the cavalry. He is a medium between the Emperor and the Synod, presenting to the Synod the projects of laws formulated by the government, and to the Emperor the regulations discussed in the Synod. The Synod does nothing without the intervention of the Procurator-General, who brings forward the matters of business, and is the executive of the resolutions adopted. No synodal act is valid without his confirmation, and he has a right of *veto* in cases in which the resolutions of the assembly may be contrary to the laws. Every year he presents a report to the Czar regarding the general condition of the Church, the state of the clergy, and orthodoxy. There is associated with every bishop an ecclesiastical council called the Eparchial Consistory, whose members are nominated by the Synod on the proposal of the bishop, and its resolutions are valid only if approved by the bishop. These consistories participate in the diocesan administration, and judge in the first instance the causes still assigned to the ecclesiastical jurisdiction, which causes have to terminate before the Synod. The causes subject to the ecclesiastical tribunals since the time of Peter the Great are cases of clerical discipline and matrimonial cases; and at present it is under consideration to withdraw those that concern divorce, reserving to the bishop the simple confirmation of the sentence pronounced by the ordinary tribunals.[1]

The ecclesiastical constitution of Russia served as a model to the new Kingdom of Greece. A royal declaration of 4th August 1838, accompanied with the adhesion of the bishops, withdrew the administration of the Greek Church from the patriarch of Constantinople; and the constitution of 1844 settled the superior authority in a permanent synod, consisting of five members, presided over by the metropolitan. The sovereign is represented by a commissioner who attends without joining in the deliberations, and who puts his *visa* to all the resolutions. Servia and Roumania followed the example of Greece. The Bulgarians did not wait for their independence of Turkey before proclaiming an autonomous Church. The patriarch of Constantinople replied to this at first with an excommunication, as he understood that to fix the boundaries of the young Bulgarian Church and of the old Greek Church, was the same as to determine by anticipation the share of the Slavs and of the Greeks in the inheritance of the Ottoman Empire; but in 1872 an exarch was conceded to them.

---

[1] The Greek - Slavonic Church allows divorce only on account of adultery, while withdrawing the right of a second marriage from the unfaithful spouse. It founds on Matt. v. 32, which speaks of separation and not of adultery: "But I say unto you, That whosoever shall put away his wife, saving for the cause of fornication, causeth her to commit adultery; and whosoever shall marry her that is divorced committeth adultery."

The second great scission of Christendom was a much
deeper one than that of the Eastern and Western Churches.
Luther exaggerated the supernatural by taking away
everything intermediate between man and God.   He,
however, precisely distinguished the spiritual power from
the temporal power.   The Confession of Augsburg in its
28th Article says : " The power of the keys, or rather the
commission has been given by Jesus Christ to His Apostles
to preach the Gospel, to forgive sins, and to administer
the sacraments.   This power has to do with the eternal
goods, but it is exercised only by the minister of the
Word, and is not mixed with the political administration,
which has an entirely different thing for its object and is
not occupied with the Gospel.   The magistrate protects
not souls, but bodies and temporal goods, which he defends
from all attack, constraining men by the sword and by
punishments to observe civil justice and peace.   Hence
the power of the Church is not to be confounded with the
power of the State. . . . Some have foolishly confounded
the power of the bishops with the temporal power, whence
have arisen great wars, revolutions, and tumults. . . .
The power of the Church ought not to invade a domain
which is not its own.   Christ said : ' My kingdom is not
of this world ; ' and elsewhere : ' Who has made Me a
judge over you ; ' and Paul says to the Philippians :
' Our conversation is in heaven.'   Let the Church then
not interfere in the affairs of this world ; let it not pretend to grant kingdoms, to command magistrates, nor to
abrogate civil laws.   Bishops have no other jurisdiction
and no other power than to remit sins ; and if in fact they
have any power, it comes to them not by divine right,
but by delegation from princes."   Thus the Protestants
reduced the Church to a kind of association, and they
invested the clergy with a simple power of direction as
representatives of the parishes.   Melanchthon was not
slow in apprising the multitude of his time that they were
not competent for this noble office, and he wrote (in

the *Corpus reformatorum*) as follows:—"Non debet esse Ecclesia democratia, qua promiscue concedatur omnibus licentia vociferendi et movendi dogmata, sed aristocratia sit, in qua ordine hi qui praesunt, Episcopi et Reges, communicent consilia." The Protestant minister Jurieu states that "the Reformation was accomplished by the aid of the sovereigns: at Geneva, by the senate; in Switzerland, by the supreme council of every canton; in Germany, by the princes of the empire; in the United Provinces, by the States-general; in Denmark, Sweden, England, and Scotland, by the authority of the kings and parliaments; and in France, by the authority of the grandees." The princes and magistrates were considered as principal members of the Church. The Reformers declared that God had entrusted them with the care of souls; that it was their duty to watch over purity of doctrine, to prohibit impious cults, and when necessary, to constrain their subjects to the external duties of religion. Calvin himself treats as a folly the opinion of those who wished that the magistrates should put God and religion under their feet, and should have no other concern at heart than to administer justice, as if God had set up superiors in His name to decide lawsuits, but having no care about His worship. Princes who neglect the honour of God in order to procure for men only temporal good, put the plough before the oxen. Hence the retort of Bossuet: "The advantage of the Reformation is reduced to having a lay pope in place of the ecclesiastical pope, the successor of St. Peter; and in handing over to the magistrates the authority of the Apostles." [1]

We shall describe the organisation of the Protestant Churches, beginning in order from the one which is least removed from the Catholic Church. It is a popular error that the Reformation took place in England on account of the refusal of the pope to approve the divorce of Henry VIII. from Queen Catherine. This was the occasional

[1] Bossuet, *Histoire des Variations*, L. v. p. 151.

cause and not the efficient cause, which must be sought
in the national pride of the English, which unwillingly
endured dependence on a stranger, even in matters of
religion.   It will suffice to recall the famous statute
Præmunire of the reign of Richard II., which enacted the
punishment of those who appealed to Rome, and prohibited the publication of any pontifical Bull which might
be contrary to it.   The movement of Wiclif and of the
Lollards was also a precursor of the Reformation, and it
prepared the way for Henry VIII.   In 1530, the clergy
assembled in convocation addressed a petition to the king
in which they called him the *supreme protector, lord, and
head of the Church of England* under the restrictive clause
per quantum per Christi legem licet.   The parliament
passed various acts to abolish appeals to the court of
Rome, as well as dispensations, provisions, bulls of institution for bishoprics, the payment of Peter's pence, and
annats.   There was also established an oath in favour of
the royal supremacy, which is still in force as it was
formulated in the reign of Elizabeth, in these terms:
That Her Majesty the Queen is the only and supreme
sovereign of the realm, both in temporal matters and in
spiritual and ecclesiastical matters; and that no prince,
prelate, State, or foreign potentate can exercise any
jurisdiction, superiority, pre-eminence, or ecclesiastical or
spiritual authority throughout the whole extent of the
Kingdom.   By an Act of 1559, it was explained that the
Queen did not intend to claim any authority in theological
matters, but wished to exercise her full authority over all
sorts of persons.

The English Church in separating itself from the
Catholic Church professed to preserve the *apostolical
succession of its hierarchy.* Its prelates considered themselves the legitimate spiritual heirs of those who had
proclaimed the gospel in the British Islands. The Reformation was accomplished with their concurrence, and
hence the Canon Law remained in force so far as it was

not opposed to the Common Law and to the prerogatives of the crown. The clergy having met in general assembly in 1603, published a body of canons and ecclesiastical constitutions.

The representative system has been applied to the English Church, but not self-government. In ancient times the clergy met in order to settle their own taxation, but by degrees they took part in the election of members of the House of Commons. The autonomy of taxation ceased in 1664, but the two assemblies of Canterbury and York were continued under the name of Convocations which had to deal only with ecclesiastical affairs. The convocation of Canterbury is the most important. In this convocation the bishops sit in the Upper Chamber presided over by the Archbishop, and it includes 22 deans, 54 archdeacons, and 24 mandatories of the Chapters. In the Lower Chamber there sit 44 procurators of the inferior clergy. The assembly or convocation of York is in like manner divided into two chambers, over the first of which the Archbishop presides. These two assemblies are convoked at the same time as parliament, but, as Burke says, only in form, as they confine themselves to transmitting certain conventional addresses to the Queen. No canon can be published without the royal approbation, and it is not obligatory on the laity without the authorisation of parliament.

The two archbishops as well as the bishops are, by a legal fiction, regarded as elected by the deans and the chapters; but in reality they are nominated by the sovereign, who, in case of a vacancy, and in virtue of an Act of the twenty-fifth year of the reign of Henry VIII., sends his or her *congé d'elire* to the chapter, but in the letter the person is designated who is agreeable to the sovereign, and who, if not elected, is definitely nominated in twelve days. The sovereign has the same right with regard to deans and the more important prebends of chapters.

The English Church has a right of property in extensive

domains, and gathers a Church rate which is levied even from dissenting parishioners to maintain the celebration of worship. For a long time its special tribunals have been taken away, but the Church enjoys certain purely honorary prerogatives in connection with the administration of common justice. The episcopal tribunals deal with cases of ecclesiastical discipline which may be appealed to the archbishops. Divorce is regulated by the Statute of 1857, and it falls within the competency of a special *Court of divorce and matrimonial causes.*

In Sweden and Denmark the Church is organised according to an analogous system. In the former of these two kingdoms the bishops have a consistory associated with them, and in the latter they are called general superintendents.

In Germany, the fatherland of the Reformation, Luther sought to oppose the interference of the princes with the proper administration of the Church. In 1543, he wrote as follows : " If the courts wish to govern the Church for their own advantage, God will withdraw His benediction, and things will go from bad to worse. Let the princes act as pastors; let them preach ; let them baptize ; let them visit the sick ; let them administer the communion ; in a word, let them fulfil all the ecclesiastical functions ; or ceasing to confound callings, let them occupy themselves with civil affairs, and let them leave the Church to those who honour it and have to give an account for it to God. Satan continues to be Satan; under the pope he mixed up the Church with politics, and now he wishes to confound politics with the Church." Luther established the consistorial system. We find the first instance of it at Wittenberg in 1539, where it was called together to resolve certain matrimonial questions; but its jurisdiction was soon extended. We then see consistories in all the countries of Germany, generally composed of two theologians, two legists, a fiscal or public minister, and a secretary, all nominated by the government. Under the consistory there is a superintendent who has to see to the carrying out of its resolutions, and above it there is a general superintendent whose function is to summon and direct it.

In the Calvinistic Church, which is more properly called the Reformed Church, the Presbyterian and Synodal system has prevailed. "No church," says the Old Discipline of the Reformed Church of France, "shall pretend to pre-eminence or authority over another, nor over a province or union of churches of the same province." The pastors are all equal, and even the shadow of a hierarchy disappears. Every parish has a presbyterian council or session, which is composed of the pastor and of laymen nominated by all the members of the Church. A certain number of neighbouring parishes form a presbytery, whose members again constitute the provincial synod, and certain pastors and elders belonging to the presbytery and synod sit in the national synod or General Assembly. This system flourishes in Holland, in Scotland, and in the United States of America, where two centuries ago Congregationalist Churches also were formed; and these mark the last term of independency, every church carrying on its own affairs apart from all the others.

America has the merit of having first introduced the separation of the Church from the State. Roger Williams, a Baptist minister, gave a very remarkable exposition of the principle of religious equality and freedom in a speech delivered in 1635. The ideas of Williams were also maintained by William Penn, the Quaker, and by the Catholic Lord Baltimore, until they passed into the law proposed by Jefferson, and promulgated on 16th December 1775, a law which was afterwards introduced into the constitutions of Virginia of 1830 and 1851. It bore that no one should be

constrained to profess any particular creed whatever, or
contribute to its maintenance ; that no individual should
be molested in his person or in his goods on account of his
beliefs ; and finally, that every one should be free to profess and defend his own religious opinions with arguments
without losing anything of his civil capacities. These
determinations, which were special to Virginia, passed into
the Federal Constitution with the revision of the Constitution of 1787, which declares that the Congress shall
not institute an official Church, nor prohibit the free
exercise of any religion. The constitutions of the various
States by degrees adopted these positions, and they are
formulated in the Constitution of New Jersey of 1844 to
this effect :—No one shall be deprived of the inestimable
privilege of worshipping Almighty God in the manner
corresponding to the injunctions of his own conscience.
No one under any pretext shall be constrained to attend
a religious service which is contrary to his faith and his
conviction. No one shall be compelled to pay tithes,
taxes, or other imposts to build or restore a church, or to
maintain a minister of another persuasion than the one
he believes good and with which he is associated. There
shall be no Church in the State with a preference over
any other Church. No test shall be required for admission to the exercise of official offices, nor shall any one be
disturbed in the enjoyment of civil rights on account of
his religious principles.

The government of the United States has therefore
neither *jus majestaticum circa sacra*, nor *placet*, nor appeal
ab abusu. It does not recognise the Church as a union
of the faithful, but the congregation as a civil corporation.
Its tribunals are competent when there is a case turning
on the property or the material interests of the congregation. Questions of discipline are judged by the
ecclesiastical tribunals proper. The usual mode of
founding an ecclesiastical corporation consists in nomi-
nating certain trustees who represent it, and every com-

munion has its own rules for the selecting of trustees. In the case of the Catholics of every parish the trustees are the bishop of the diocese, the vicar-general, the priest of the district, and two laymen nominated by the three ecclesiastical members. In every parish, following the example of the banks and assurance companies, the trustees require every three years to deliver to the Chancery Court of the district an authenticated statement of the movable and immovable property of the congregation. Neglect for two triennial terms to give in this account has the effect of making the corporation of the church fall from its rights. The object of this arrangement is to hinder these ecclesiastical bodies from going beyond the limit of the revenues or funded property fixed by the law in each State, which commonly ranges from £400 to £1200, but in the State of Massachusetts it may reach £20,000.[1]

Thus far we have noted four systems resulting from the relations of religion with the State: 1. Religion dominates the State, as we have seen in the East; 2. The State dominates religion, as in the classical antiquity; 3. The State and religion live in harmony, as under the first Christian emperors, and after the struggle of the Middle Ages; 4. The State and religion ignore each other, yet practise a mutual recognition, as in the Presbyterian and Congregationalist systems among the Protestants, and according to the theory which has begun to be put into application under the Belgian statute among the Catholics. Let us now see how these four systems have been formulated by the expounders of them.

The theory of the first system, or the Theocracy, emerges in the sacred books of the East, and in the papal utopia which we have already expounded. The ancient expounders of the oriental theocracy cannot be here referred to in detail, but the expounders of the papal system are

[1] Laboulaye, *La separazione della Chiesa e dello Stato negli Stati Uniti d'America.* Traduzione del Senatore Carlo Alfieri. Firenze, 1874.

abundantly accessible. Thomas Aquinas is very reserved
on the question of the relations between the spiritual
power and the temporal power. He contents himself
with saying that in regard to what concerns the salvation
of the soul, the spiritual power ought rather to be obeyed
than the temporal, but as regards civil goods it is better
to obey the secular authority. Nevertheless the two
powers are always found united in the same person alone
qui utriusque potestatis apicem tenet. The work entitled
De regimine principum is attributed to Thomas Aquinas,
and is certainly from his school. In it the pre-eminence
of the spiritual power is unfolded in the same way as in
a work under the same title by the Romanist Egidius.
Charles Jourdain has found in the national library of
Paris another work by Egidius entitled *De utraque potestate,*
in which the papal pretensions are carried to the utmost
limit. According to this writer, the Church has not only
a right to possess material goods, but has a natural
jurisdiction over every kind of such goods. The destination of temporal things, he says, is the utility of the body ;
the body is subject to the soul, and the soul to the supreme
pontiff ; and where this subordination does not exist in
fact,·from being rejected by human passions, it subsists
by right. The art of governing the peoples, he continues,
consists in co-ordinating human laws with those of the
Church, as matter is co-ordinated with form. Janet
recognises in this work that exaggeration which is usually
the sign of powers that are about to fall.

After the excesses of the French Revolution, we see
the so-called Theological School reappearing, and as a
School it seeks a fixed point in revelation and in the
pontifical authority. De Maistre, with an austere imagination and an incisive style, maintains that as all men are
born in the guilt of sin, it should not surprise us if the
just man suffers here below, since he suffers not as a just
individual, but as a man. All suffering is due to us as a
consequence of original sin, and there is no other means

of diminishing it than prayer and the reversion of good works performed by the good, which God in His mercy reckons to the account even of sinners. He regards the government of Providence as an inexorable government, and wishes that the temporal governments would imitate it. The supreme authority he attributes to the pope, on whom princes ought to depend.

De Bonald finds the nexus of all truths in a primitive language revealed to man. The Bible furnishes him with the historical proofs of this fact; and reason tells him that it was impossible for man to invent language, since according to Rousseau "speech is necessary in order to establish the use of speech." The language revealed to man by the Creator must have been perfect, and therefore must have contained true ideas. In consequence of the fall, the true language has been lost, and with it many truths have been obscured; but the Bible and the Church have preserved for us as much as God considered necessary for our salvation. Casting a glance upon the world, De Bonald finds three fundamental ideas, which embrace the order of beings and their relations, and these are *cause, means,* and *effect.* The cause stands to the means as the means to the effect. What God is in the general order of beings, the husband is in the family and the ruling power is in the State. God reigns absolutely in the universe; and the father and the sovereign should be absolute in the family and in the State. But between God and man there has been a Mediator participating in the divine and human natures, and so there should be a mediator in the family, namely, the wife; and in the State there should be an aristocracy, a body intermediate between the people and the sovereign. Domestic society should be regulated by natural religion; and political society ought to be founded on revealed religion. Thus does De Bonald attempt to demonstrate by reason and history the identity of the religious law and of the political law.

Lamennais in his first work, entitled an "Essay on indifference in matters of religion,"[1] finds no ground of trust in the senses, nor in the feelings, nor in reasoning, and he derives truth from authority, that is to say, from the testimony of a great number of persons worthy of faith which begets common consent. In the earliest times God directly governed men from the bosom of a cloud, or by means of a moral law engraven in their hearts. But He has now a representative on the earth in the pope. The spiritual power, in the largest sense of the word, pertains to the pope and to the Church. The civil governments represent only the material side of power, and they ought to depend upon the pope. Around Lamennais gathered Lacordaire, Montalembert, Gerbet, de Salinis; and after the Revolution of July, they founded the journal called *L'Avenir* in order to combat for God and liberty, and for the pope, and for the people. They were condemned in the celebrated Encyclical of 15th August 1832; and the little community was dispersed, but the seed sown was fruitful, and we shall see it bring forth fruit.

The oracles in Greece and the auguries in Rome were the most powerful religious instruments in the hand of the State. In the time of the Republic there were added to these the *pontifices*, or the five constructors of bridges, who as engineers knew the mysteries of numbers and measures; and therefore they compiled the calendar, predicted the new and full moon, fixed the festival days, and, in a word, took care that every religious or judiciary act should take place on the day and in the forms prescribed. Cicero was enthusiastic about this system, and Polybius attributed the happy results of the enterprises of the Romans to their great respect for religion.

The Emperor, in addition to all his magisterial offices, held also that of the pontificate, and he even became a god, so that both temporally and spiritually the legal

---

[1] *Essai sur l'indifférence en matière de religion.*

aphorism held good: *quod principi placuit legis habet vigorem.* Constantine, after his conversion, retained the functions of the *Pontifex maximus,* and continued from policy to take part in the pagan sacrifices and in the sanguinary plays of the amphitheatre which his new faith disapproved. The final abolition of paganism and the confiscation of its possessions, are attributed to Gratian and to Theodosius. In 384 A.D., the statue of the goddess of Victory disappeared from the Roman forum, and Christianity became the only official religion.

We have already described the relations of the Church and the Empire, and the Utopia of Dante; and we must now speak of the maintainers of the pre-eminence of the civil power. Among the first of these is reckoned William of Occam, who took part in favour of Philip le Bel against Boniface VIII. in his manifesto entitled *Disputatio super potestate ecclesiae praelatis atque principibus commissa.* In order to escape the persecution of Rome, he took refuge with the Emperor Louis of Bavaria, to whom he said: "Tu me defendas gladio, ego te calamo;" and then he wrote his *Octo quaestiones super potestate summi pontificis,* and his *Dialogus magistri Guillelmi Ockam,* extending to about a thousand pages folio. In these works he proceeds by *pro et contra,* in the manner of the Scholastics; but in the midst of infinite argumentation, he presents Christianity as a law of liberty, and the people already make an appearance behind the emperor. Marsilius of Padua, in his *Defensor pacis,* which was also written in defence of Louis of Bavaria, is more explicit. We may quote one of his conclusions, which runs thus: "Legis latorem humanum solam civium universitatem esse, aut valentiorem illius partem." He then explains how the people are not only the source of supreme power, but that they watch over it, judge it, and depose it. His intention was not only to enfranchise the State from the Church, but also from the absolute power. He goes even as far as to proclaim liberty of conscience. In the connection he says : " Ad observanda praecepta divinae legis, poena vel supplicio temporali, seu praesentis seculi, nemo evangelica scriptura compelli praecipitur."[1] Under this point of view Marsilius is the precursor of the great thinkers who advocate the reciprocal independence of the Church and the State. After the Council of Trent, Paolo Serpi resuscitated in its entirety the doctrine of the omnipotence of the pagan State, and it formed the secret inspiration of the great and unhappy Pietro Giannone. The Renaissance in general fondled this idea, which rules in Machiavelli, and glimmers also in the Utopia of Sir Thomas More and in Harrington's Oceana. Rousseau made the idea his in his *Contrat social*, which inspired the Constituent Assembly with the civil constitution of the clergy.

The Protestant writers declared themselves unanimously in favour of the pre-eminence of the State. Their common thought in opposition to the papacy was : *Cujus est regio ejus religio.* Hugo Grotius made vast researches, and concluded by attributing all ecclesiastical authority to the State. Hobbes and Spinoza incorporated the Church directly in the State, Spinoza making ample reservations in favour of freedom of conscience. But from the Presbyterians and Congregationalists other maxims could not but arise, and these were reduced to a theory by Thomasius, who would have the Church be regarded as a simple association tolerated by the State.

The Gallican writers furnish a fruitful mine for the system of concordats ; and without going back to Pithou, Coquille, and Pasquier, we shall confine ourselves to referring to the learned reports of the Minister Lanjuinais, and the Counsellor of State, Portalis, in the discussion of the Concordat of 1801 and the organic articles which followed it. The Belgian Laurent declared himself in favour of concordats in the French manner, despairing of suppressing all the power of the Church, and believing

[1] Janet, op. cit.

that its absolute separation from the State would be prejudicial to the religious sentiment.[1]

The same author witnesses to the influence exercised on the Belgian legislators by the doctrines advocated by Lamennais and the other writers of the journal *L'Avenir*. The following are briefly the aspirations of this school. "Let the clergy of France abjure in some way the old maxims of the Gallican Church as the source of equivocations and errors, as principles of a slavery imposed on religion by the political despotism, and too easily accepted in the seventeenth century by the prelates of the court, as a fatal barrier raised by profane interests between the Church and its head, as a perpetual danger of national schism like to that provoked by Henry VIII. in England, or to the one that reigned so long in the empire of the czars. Let the Church take again all her liberty both in action and in doctrines in face of the governments; let her claim those indispensable rights now denied to her by the Concordat of 1801 and the Organic Articles; let her be permitted to meet at will in provincial councils and in synods, to communicate with the sovereign pontiff without requiring permission, to found religious orders without needing the council of State and the decree of the prince, to open as many schools as may be thought necessary in the interest of religion, and to teach her doctrines in them without being subject to any surveillance by the State, and to receive her bishops only through the institution of the Holy See. But in exchange for these precious benefactions, let her make the sacrifice of all the temporal goods which the government has secured to her; let her renounce her budgets and her revenues, the official and privileged protection with which she is surrounded, and the political dignities which have been conferred on the episcopate; let her lay account only upon herself; let her hold her authority and her means of subsistence only from faith, from piety, and from the

[1] *L'Eglise et l'Etat*, p. 482 *et seq.* Bruxelles, 1858.

N

voluntary offerings of the Catholic populations; let the old alliance of the throne with the altar be completely destroyed; let there be no more solidarity between the Church and any of the dynasties which revolutions may put at the helm of the State; and let all confusion or mixing of the two powers cease. Let the Church, accepting the consequences which necessarily arise from this new order of things, acknowledge with good faith that the Catholic religion is not incompatible with liberty of worship, nor with liberty of teaching, nor with the liberty of the press, seeing that these various forms of liberty are the only power which can preserve the Church in France from a catastrophe similar to that which destroyed Catholicism in England."

In the Reformed pastor Vinet, we have an echo of these doctrines. The State, he says, cannot have any religion. And in fact, what is religion? It is a sentiment or feeling entirely concentrated in the most secret and most profound life of the soul. It regulates no other relations than those of the invisible with the visible; and the external life is to it only a means of reacting on the internal life. Men by combining into civil society make only their interests and their ideas common, but they reserve to themselves the most intimate part of their soul, their religion. Vinet does not say that the State has nothing in common with religion, since it has the morality which springs from a primitive revelation; but in the internal sanctuary every one ought to be perfectly free. The spiritual and the temporal, he adds, are distinct like law and morality, and this distinction is not an accident, but a necessity; it is not a passing phase, but the normal and definite state of society, one of the axioms of science and society. To believe that the existence of a religion is threatened by its separation from the State, is an avowal that it has no root in humanity, and no force in itself. We therefore demand this separation in order to demonstrate that religion is a need and not a habit, a conviction and not a prejudice.[1]

The formula of Cavour, *A free Church in a free State*, was the summary of these doctrines, but stripped of their exaggerations, because it was not in the mind of the great minister either to make the clergy renounce their goods, or to reduce religion to pure individual sentiment, which, carried out rigorously, would bring with it the abolition of worship and of the priesthood.[2]

Even in America, these doctrines have not been accepted in an absolute way. There the rest of the Sabbath is rigidly observed, and public-houses and restaurants are closed that they may not minister to vice. The sessions of the Federal Congress and of the special legislatures are opened with prayers led in turn by ministers of the different churches. In certain solemn circumstances, the congress, the president, and the governors of the States order fast-days and thanksgivings; and when Jefferson during his presidency raised a doubt as to the right of asking the people for prayers for the Union, he met with unanimous disapproval. In most of the States, the churches are free from imposts, and the pastors are exempted from military service and from serving on juries ; nor is this privilege in any way contrary to public opinion. The civil magistrate secures the execution of the sentences of the ecclesiastical tribunals, as is seen by an instance reported by Laboulaye. In 1869, Dr. Edward Cheney, episcopal rector of Christ Church·at Chicago, was accused before an ecclesiastical court of having arbitrarily suppressed the word *regenerated*

---

[1] See his *Essai sur la manifestation des convictions religieuses et sur la séparation de l'Eglise et de l'Etat*, printed first at Paris in 1842.

[2] The formula of Cavour certainly belongs to Montalembert : *L'Eglise libre dans l'Etat libre. L'Univers* attacked this formula because it seemed to locate the Church in the State, and hence the said writer modified it into : *L'Eglise libre dans la nation libre.* But as the *dans* continued to exasperate the too zealous journal, Montalembert and his friends were content to say : *L'Eglise libre et la patrie libre.* See A. Leroy-Beaulieu, *Les catholiques libéraux*, p. 187. Paris, 1885.

in the baptismal formula. Bishop Whitehouse interdicted
Cheney, and deprived him of his living. The congregation decided to retain their rector, and Cheney raised an
action against the bishop before the Superior Court of
the State of Illinois in order that this canonical sentence
might be annulled, as he alleged it injured his rights as
a citizen. He gained his case in the first instance ; but
when it was carried by appeal before the Supreme Court
of the State, the sentence was quashed. The tribunal
decided that whenever a particular church and its pastor
were subject to the surveillance and censure of higher
ecclesiastics, and formed part of a church whose creed
and discipline they had voluntarily accepted, then the
members that continued faithful to the communion should
be considered as alone composing the church, and as
having the right to retain its property, even although these
faithful ones might be in a minority. The majority ought
not to be allowed to abandon the communion and withdraw
themselves from the disciplinary jurisdiction and carry
away the property of the congregation ; for this would be
an act of bad faith which no court of justice could tolerate.
Here then in these microscopic proportions, the secular
arm shows itself in America. Here are cut by the root
those mixed questions which for so many ages have been
the despair of jurisconsults and canonists. Certainly it
is desirable that all controversies between Church and
State should be resolved by reciprocal agreement, including such questions as the institution of new dioceses, the
nomination of bishops, the stipends of the clergy, questions
of marriage, schools, hospices, cemeteries, processions, &c. ;
but human nature is so constituted, that the strong always
seek to oppress the weak, and hence these conflicts and
usurpations go on. But this system supposes a state of
greatly advanced civilisation, and it has therefore been
the last to appear in practice and theory.

   The great thought of Cavour was modified by his representatives and successors. Pasquale Stanislao Mancini,

late minister in Naples, by a decree of 17th February 1861, deprived the priests of the privilege of being taken to prison in a carriage. Afterwards, they were deprived of all exemption from military service, and by extreme interpretations they were allowed to marry. All civil execution is refused for the sentences of bishops who deprive their subordinates of their stipends or suspend them *a divinis*. The suppression of the religious orders has gone beyond all limit, and has violated acquired rights. The law of Piedmont of 1855 respected the religious orders devoted to preaching, education, and the assistance of the sick. The Italian suppression took effect only in the future, concentrating gradually the surviving monks in the monasteries of the order till their total extinction. The conversion imposed for economic reasons on the chapters and other ecclesiastical bodies, was left to be carried out by themselves according to an estimated state and in a determinate period of time. The law of guarantees did not break all bonds between the Church and the State; it demands the *exequatur* of the papal bulls in the nomination of bishops when they claim the temporalities.

We are far from agreeing with the maxim uttered by Odilon Barrot in a celebrated case, namely, that the law is atheistic. The modern State, answers Renan, has no official theological dogma; it is neither atheistic nor irreligious; it is even essentially religious, since it supposes right and duty, admits the taking of an oath, respects death, and believes in the sanctity of marriage.[1]

Summing up, we say that the State is the expression of the majority, and hence it should conform its conduct in whole or in part to religious rules according as there may exist one or more kinds of worship in its territory. Every one should be free to believe in his own way, but not to exhibit his religious opinions except within limits which will not injure the rights of others; and hence follows toleration, or liberty of worship, according to cir-

---

[1] See *Questions contemporaines*, p. 228. Paris, 1868.

cumstances. It nevertheless does not follow in the least that the State ought not to receive help from religion, as, for example, in relation to marriage, which may be celebrated civilly and according to the religious rites of the spouses, unless they be freethinkers; and in such a case the parties should declare it in a public instrument in order to obtain from the magistrates the permission to contract their marriage only civilly. The formula of the oath might be modified by adding to it, *On the faith of a man of honour*, which would not offend believers and would bind freethinkers. The cemeteries might be divided into various sections, one of them for freethinkers. Doctrinal teaching might be entrusted to the ministers of the various creeds, along with the primary and secondary instruction; and it might be entirely free in the higher instruction, the right being given to open the universities to whoever has means to attend them.

According to this view, religion would occupy in society the same position which it holds in the human mind, among the other ends of which we have still to speak.[1]

[1] In 1861 we discussed the relations of religion with the State in a little work entitled : *L'Italia e la Chiesa, risposta a Guizot.*

CHAPTER II.

SCIENCE.

SCIENCE separated itself slowly from religion. The separation began in the East, and was completed in Greece. In India, philosophical thought reached the production of a philosophy without God, as we have already seen in our introductory sketch. The natural sciences were almost entirely neglected by the Hindus, and the most popular work in India after twenty centuries is the Nyaya of Gotama, which lays down the rules of reasoning. But what a difference there is between it and the Organon of Aristotle, which has served as a text for so many ages, and to so many races! With all the goodwill of the Sanskritists, they have not been able to find in Gotama the theory of the syllogism.

China laid more importance on physics; and in the oldest Chinese book, the *Y King*, attributed to Fou-hi, we find as the highest categories the Heaven and the Earth, the one represented by a continuous line (—), and the other by a broken line (- -).

The first symbol represents the male principle, the sun, the light, heat, motion, force, or in a word, all that has a character of superiority, activity, and perfection. The second represents the female principle, the moon, darkness, cold, rest, weakness, or in a word, all that has a character of inferiority, passivity, and imperfection. All things arise by composition and perish by decomposition. In the *Shu-King*, there are distinguished five great elements: water, fire, wood, metals, and the earth; then the faculties; and lastly, the ethical principles, from which Lao-tse derived metaphysics, and Confucius ethics. In the twelfth century, Ichu-hi formulated the Chinese encyclopedia in the following way. The generation of the five elements proceeds immediately from the active principle and from the passive principle, which are only modes of being of the *great summit* (Tai-ki). The *Tai-ki* is the same thing as the *Li*, or the efficient and formal cause of the universe, which, putting itself in motion, generated the *Yang* (active principle), and in its repose produced the *Yn* (passive principle). The Li is manifested in man as the rational principle, which has as its contrary the *Ki* or material principle. The first represents movement, and the second repose; their union constitutes life, and their separation produces death, after which there is no more personality. Spirits and genii are only the active principle and the passive principle, or the breath of life which vivifies nature and fills the space between the heaven and the earth, and which animates man.

Society was organised in China according to the principle of generation, or on the paternal authority. The Emperor is the typical man, and he unites in himself heaven and earth, and is the father and mother of the people. He represents the universal reason, and he is crammed with all kinds of knowledge from his most tender years. After the imperial family, the Mandarins or literati form the second order of the State. The literati are divided into as many classes or grades as there are sciences; and those who know best the written signs of their science, form a council of government beside the emperor under the name of Hanlin. This council has the censorship of books, and recommends those which it believes necessary to preserve the ancient precepts and discoveries in arts having an immediate utility. The Chinese youth are educated so as to be able to manage public and private affairs in an entirely practical way. Every science is reduced to rules which are committed to memory. All undergo examination, the soldier as well as the administrator and the

lawyer. In order that the supreme college of the capital
may be the nucleus of the empire, there is established a
hierarchy among the cities, which forms an uninterrupted
chain down to the lowest village; but it is only the capital
that communicates the nobility of knowledge. After the
literati come the agriculturists, the artisans, and the
merchants, without any principle of heredity. Industry
and agriculture depend on tradition and on the police.
Before the Europeans had put their foot in China, the
Chinese were ignorant of mathematics and all the arts
that depend upon them. They were acquainted with
gunpowder, but they used it only for artificial fireworks.
They possessed the mariner's compass, but they followed
the course of the stars in their navigation; and they had
printed books, but they produced them by means of
characters cut in tablets of wood, and not by melted and
movable types.

The ancient Egyptians resembled the Chinese in their
empiricism, their spirit of tradition, and their attitude
towards the arts that are most useful for life. The
necessity of recovering their fields after the inundations
of the Nile, and the division of the land carried out by
Sesostris, led them early to the discovery of geometry.
It was, however, entirely practical, and without demon-
strations; and as they did not know the measurement
of angles and trigonometry, they made use of ingenious
methods which were adopted by the Greek and Roman
land surveyors. In astronomy, they had the merit of representing geometrically the motions of the sun, and moon,
and the five planets then known. Herodotus also asserts
that they knew the solar year 1325 years before our era.
Nevertheless, they had been preceded by the Chaldeans in
determining empirically, but with some exactness, the
periods in which the same astronomical phenomena
return. The Egyptians had the incontestable merit of
recognising the value of labour; for if the priests and
the soldiers were distinguished by great honours, all kinds

of trade were held in esteem, and it was regarded as a
crime to despise a citizen who contributed by his labour
to the public good. The division of labour was not only
applied to the mechanical arts, but also to the liberal
professions, which were all divided into guilds, so that it
was impossible for an idle man to conceal himself. Heredity was established in the arts and professions in order
to render them more perfect.

The Greeks no longer sought the laws of nature in the
theogonies, but by observation. Thales determined the
solstices and predicted eclipses. Anaximander already
drew geographical maps, and formed spheres and solar
quadrants; and Pythagoras, as by a sort of divination,
conceived a planetary system. The milky way was to
Democritus an aggregation of stars. The curves of the
orbits of the planets were considered by Plato to be
determined by attraction, while Aristotle felt as by
intuition that motion is a chief and universal fact. Hippocrates laid down medical aphorisms in spite of his physiological hypotheses and the scantiness of his anatomical
knowledge. Aristotle founded natural history, descriptive
meteorology, psychology, ethics, politics, rhetoric, and
the art of poetry, basing them on observation and
comparison of facts; and he also formulated the rules of
the deductive method, and indicated the advantages of
induction.

The founding of Alexandria, which united the West
with the East, gave an impetus to science. Astronomy
had need of trigonometry, and Hipparchus invented it.
The distance of the earth from the sun and the moon
was calculated by Aristarchus; the obliquity of the
ecliptic was determined by Eratosthenes and Hipparchus;
and Ptolemy founded a system which lasted for fourteen
centuries. While anatomy made progress, physiology
owed to Galen the discovery of the minute circulation of
the blood from the lungs to the heart; and therapeutics
found a rival of Hippocrates in Aratæus.

The Romans added somewhat to natural history by Pliny, to agriculture by Varro and Columella, and to architecture by Vitruvius, but on the whole their additions were small, as they turned all their powers to law and politics.

But what were the relations of science with religion and government in antiquity? Religion tolerated an allegorical interpretation of its theogonies, but not a direct attack, as was shown by the danger encountered by Anaxagoras and by the death of Socrates. The government left the public instruction to private enterprise, and it is only in the time of the Empire that we see schools subsidised.

Christianity was a reaction against knowing. But after having spoken to the heart, it felt the need of addressing itself to the understanding; and it entered into alliance with philosophy, and did not reject all the useful discoveries which render the practice of virtue less severe to us. In vain did Julian the Apostate wish to exclude from the schools the followers of the new religion, who were as eager to learn as to teach. In the present day the Church still interprets in an absolute sense the commission : *Go and teach all nations.*

On the invasion of the barbarians the clergy sought to save whatever they could of the ancient sciences and letters. They copied manuscripts and taught the seven liberal arts : grammar, rhetoric, and dialectic (which formed the *trivium*), and arithmetic, geometry, astronomy, and music (which formed the *quadrivium*). Charlemagne founded the Palatine Academy, which was presided over by himself under the name of David, and every member of which assumed an allegorical name. Along with this Academy, he founded a royal school under the direction of Alcuin; and it became the centre of the studies of the time, and served as a model to many others.

The Arabs were driven by their material wants to appropriate the scientific works of the Greeks; but

medicine, physics, and astronomy were so bound with
philosophy, which had embraced them all at the beginning, that the study of it was rendered indispensable.
The Arabs took to Aristotle, whom they considered to be
the philosopher *par excellence ;* and they translated him,
commented upon him, and made him known to Europe.
"But," exclaims Renan, "men often speak of an Arabic
science and philosophy; and in fact the Arabs were
our masters for about two centuries during the Middle
Ages, but only until we came to know better the
Greek originals. This Arab science and philosophy were
only a poor translation of the Greek science and philosophy. No sooner did the real Greece appear before
our eyes than these indifferent translations became
superfluous, and the philologers of the Renaissance not
without reason undertook a veritable crusade against
them. When we scrutinise it attentively, this Arab
science had nothing Arabic in it; its foundation was
entirely Greek, and among those who created it, there
was not a genuine Semite, but they were Spaniards and
Persians who wrote in Arabic. The Jews in the Middle
Ages acted as interpreters of them; and the Jewish
philosophy of that time is the Arab philosophy without
any modification. A single page of Roger Bacon contains
a larger infusion of the scientific spirit than the whole of
this second-hand science, which is worthy of consideration
as a link in the chain of tradition, but it is void of any
great originality." [1] Nevertheless, the Arabs communicated to Europe the system of numeration and the
mariner's compass, which it is said they borrowed from
the Hindus and the Chinese.

Among the most celebrated schools at the close of the
eleventh century may be reckoned the medical school of
Salerno, whose origin is lost in the night of time, and
which had even Jews and Arabs among its professors.

[1] *De la part des peuples sémitiques dans l'histoire de la civilisation.*
Paris, 1875.

In 1196, the celebrated Irnerius was called from Ravenna, where he was a judge, to Bologna, to teach the Roman Law. In the course of the twelfth century there was added to the curriculum of study the canon law, medicine, theology, and philosophy. Fourteen colleges gathered together the students of different nations; and some of these colleges were founded by popes, others by foreign princes, or by magnanimous donors. Along with them arose other colleges and corporations for examining the students and conferring the degree of doctor upon them: the doctorate in theology being conferred in name of the pope, and that in jurisprudence in name of the emperor, by the authority of whom they had been instituted. For a long time all scientific knowledge consisted in jurisprudence and theology, until literary studies were added to them. The name of Universities was given to these institutions in order to indicate that the universality of knowledge was taught in them. In the University of Naples, which was founded by Frederic II. in 1224, we find the first germs of the Faculties in the teaching of civil and canon law, philosophy, mathematics, and medicine. A student did not become a doctor in jurisprudence till after five years' study, in theology till after twelve years, in philosophy till after three years, and in medicine and surgery till after five years. The law inflicted a punishment of three years' exile on students who attended private courses; and in the other cities of the kingdom, no other study of medicine was tolerated except that in Salerno, which was affiliated to the University of Naples.

England has preserved intact the type of the Middle Ages with its twenty colleges united around the University of Oxford, and the seventeen of the University of Cambridge. The University of London, which was created by the dissenters under the royal charter of 5th December 1837, is not a teaching body. Its power extends over the whole of the United Kingdom and the colonies. It is a sort of corporation for examining students, and by an additional charter of 27th August 1867, women are also admitted to the examinations. It does not demand a fixed residence from the candidates, nor any common regulated life, nor any moral or religious discipline. But teaching is given by University College and King's College, the first of which is divided into the faculties of Arts, and Law, and Medicine, and the second into the four departments of theology, literature and natural sciences, applied sciences, and medicine. These colleges are both private institutions, the first having been founded by the Liberal party, and the second by the clerical or Anglican party.

The exact sciences and the natural sciences do not, however, owe their progress to the universities, all absorbed as they were in jurisprudence and theology. Roger Bacon was driven from Oxford because he put little account on scholasticism and ratiocination in general, which convinces without instructing, and often demonstrates error as well as truth with the same evidence. Their conclusions, he said, were but hypotheses when not verified. Experience fills up this want, and is sufficient of itself, whereas authority and ratiocination stand in need of it. Nothing dominates experience, and when Aristotle affirms that the knowledge of reasons and causes is superior to it, he speaks of the common and inferior experience employed by artisans who know neither its power nor its means, and not of the experience of men of learning, which rises up to causes and discovers them by means of observation. Bacon severely censures scholasticism, despises the cultivation of abstract logic, and prefers the *Rhetoric* and *Poetics* of Aristotle to his *Organon*. Next to languages, he wished that mathematics should be studied, which scholasticism had erred by confounding with a sort of magic. He reduced metaphysics to a sort of philosophy of the sciences, embracing the ideas which they have in common, furnishing their methods, and fixing their boundaries. To the general physics of Aristotle and the schools he preferred the alchemy which treated of the combination of the metals (not of their transmutation), and of the structure of the tissues of animals and vegetables, a subject which was not taught in the universities. He laid great value on the art of constructing houses, cultivating fields, and rearing cattle; and he had a predilection for everything that could conduce to the increase of industry, such as the construction of machines, &c.

The Renaissance carried out what Roger Bacon had anticipated. The ancient languages were better learned; texts were restored; Aristotle was studied in the original and no longer in Arabic translations; and nature was directly observed. Galileo said that the laws of nature are the simplest of all; that no one can swim better than the fishes, nor fly better than the birds; that we should rise by thought to the most perfect and simple rule, and that we would thus form the most probable hypotheses. We should follow with curiosity the consequences which mathematics will be able without hesitation to transform into elegant theorems. Geometry has studied many curves unknown to nature whose properties are admirable, but they belong only to geometry if experience has not confirmed them. In a word, to judge of principles by the verification of their most remote consequences, is the method of Galileo and the solid foundation of modern science.

By mathematical calculation and direct observation Galileo discovered the law of gravity and that of the pendulum, the hydrostatic balance, and the telescope with which he saw the satellites of Jupiter, the phases of Venus and Mars, the solar spots and the mountains of the moon. If he had given greater attention to the three geometrical laws of Kepler regarding the elliptical motion of the planets, and had investigated their mechanical principle, he might have appropriated the glory of Newton, and founded the modern astronomy with Copernicus.

Francis Bacon of Verulam in his *Instauratio Magna* set himself to find out the laws of all scientific knowledge and to describe its method, which is observation either pure or aided by experiments, and fertilised by induction. Applying this method, he himself made discoveries ; he invented a thermometer, carried out ingenious experiments on the compressibility of bodies and on the weight of the atmosphere and its effects. He had a presentiment of the force of universal attraction, and of the diminution of this force in the ratio of its distance; and he caught a glimpse of the true explanation of the tides, and of the cause of colours, which he attributed to the mode in which bodies reflect the light in virtue of their diverse texture. This same method was afterwards applied by the philosophers of the Scottish School to psychology, ethics, and social facts, and it has produced useful results.

The induction of Bacon ought not to be confounded with empiricism; for Bacon admits final causes as above efficient causes. But he recommends our stopping at the former in the natural sciences, and leaving the latter to metaphysics.

The ancients, especially the Stoics, had divided all cognitions by reference to their objects into three categories, giving the three sciences of logic, ethics, and physics. Bacon, however, divided the sciences according to the faculties from which they emanate, making history, natural and civil, arise from memory, poetry and all the arts from the imagination, and philosophy, or the science of God, man, and nature, from the reason. This division has been reproduced with new developments in the discourse prefixed by D'Alembert to the *Encyclopédie* in the last century.

Descartes, by his analytical geometry, and Fermat, with the first elements of the infinitesimal calculus, which was afterwards perfected by Leibniz, prepared the way for Newton. Newton sketched out the sidereal motions; and it required the combined powers of great mathematicians and astronomers, including Euler, Clairaut, D'Alembert, Lagrange, Laplace, and Cassini, that the sketch might become a picture.

The renovation of astronomy was followed by that of physics, which was begun by Galileo, and carried on by Volta, Oersted, Ampère, and Melloni. The eighteenth century did not remain behind the seventeenth century in chemistry, which it created through Lavoisier, and which at present threatens to absorb all the other sciences. In fact, as chemistry deals with the combinations which arise among substances, it joins hands with the sciences of life, which is a composition of substances that enter, and a decomposition of substances that are thrown out of the body. Biology, says Littré, was introduced into the world by medicine, and it lived a long time under the protection of the salutary art which undertakes to cure human sufferings; but the time has now come for its serving as a guide to medicine, and especially to pathology. The studies of the Renaissance were directed after the leading of antiquity to discover the anatomical mechanism of the living body. And thus the general circulation of the blood was discovered, as it constantly obtains air in the capillary vessels of the lungs, and loses it in the capillary vessels of the rest of the body. Thus too were the ways recognised by which the chyle passes from the intestines into the current of the circulation. And finally, in our day, there was also thus discovered the capital distinction among the nerves, some of which are destined for motion and others for sensibility, as well as that between the nerves and the brain, to which they transmit through the spinal marrow all their impressions, which the brain returns by the same channel through the motor nerves to the muscles. Bichat, at the end of the past century, thought of studying the action of remedies not directly upon diseases, which are complex phenomena, but on the tissues; but death carried him off in his thirty-first year. His work was taken up again after half a century by Claude Bernard.

From the earliest times, observers had noticed that plants obtain their nourishment from the air and from the earth, and that animals are nourished by vegetable substances, so that, in their ultimate constituents, organised bodies are composed of inorganic elements. What substances do vegetable bodies obtain from the soil? What agent is furnished by the atmospheric air to living beings? What combination do elements undergo by entering into animated bodies? What affinities are developed in these bodies? How does the juice of plants produce gums and sugars, and how does the blood of animals produce bile, saliva, and tears? All these questions remained without reply because they required a science to answer them which was not yet constituted, as the ancients had a glimpse of physiology only on the side accessible to them in anatomy. But when chemistry was created, and discovery was made in living bodies of oxygen, hydrogen, nitrogen, and carbon, which play so great a part in inorganic nature, physiology became master of the field. It is thus younger than chemistry, which arose after physics, which again had followed astronomy, which was preceded by mathematics.[1] But living beings present a sort of hierarchy, which begins with vegetables endowed only with apparatuses for composition and decomposition, rises to the lower animals that have in addition the ganglionic nervous system, and reaches the higher animals where these apparatuses and this system are found with the addition of the cerebro-spinal axis and its centripetal and centrifugal nerves. So in like manner, says Auguste Comte, the gradual development of humanity tends constantly to determine, and in fact produces an increasing preponderance of the noblest instincts of our nature. The pernicious instincts will be neutralised by the powers

[1] See *La science au point de vue philosophique*, p. 247–8. Paris, 1873. Littré would add a seventh science, extracting it from Sociology, which would gather up the external results of our æsthetic, moral, and intellectual faculties in the domain of history, and which would embrace æsthetics, ethics, and ideology.

of education and science, and liberty of thinking will yet
terminate in ethics, as it has terminated in astronomy,
in physics, &c. ; and it will thus come to be as absurd
to try to confute any rules of conduct formulated by the
new science as it now is to call in question the laws of
Newton. To this new science Comte gave the name of
Sociology.

Many objections have been made to this scientific
classification, even by the followers of the positive
philosophy. John Stuart Mill objects to the philosopher
having sacrificed in principle both psychology and political
economy. Littré answers that psychology cannot serve
as a point of departure for philosophy, as it is an appendix of biology. The material constitution of the nervous
substance is the meeting point of the spirit with the laws
of general facts, and there is no subjective science which
can be anything else than the product of the faculty
of elaboration indwelling in the nerve cells. Political
economy, adds Littré, corresponds to the theory of the
nutritive functions in biology, with regard to which,
Comte, agreeing with all good physiologists, holds that
it is of great importance as the foundation of the new
science. As the nutritive functions cannot be separated
from the action of the animal or human attributes, so the
economic phenomena of society cannot be separated from
the action of the political and moral attributes.

Herbert Spencer says that Comte endeavoured to co-
ordinate our cognitions in order that they might serve to
interpret phenomena which had not been studied in a
scientific manner ; and that he has renovated the idea
of Bacon, who tried to organise the sciences into a vast
system in which social science was to appear as a branch
of the tree of nature. The human mind, he continues, has
never ceased to seek the first cause either by religion or
by science ; and every religion is an explanation *à priori*
of the universe which science strives to explain *à posteriori*.
The whole of science represents the sum of positive know-

ledge ; it depends on the order which reigns in the phenomena which surround us, and it is not developed in series,
but on the contrary gives life to *inter-dependent sciences*
which spring up and advance together. The difference
between Comte and Spencer, says Littré, is this, that Comte
regards the sciences objectively, and hence their generality
decreases in proportion as they embrace a greater number
of objects, whereas Spencer looks at them subjectively, or
as they arise in our mind.

Before the rise of the positive philosophy, there was
another classification of the sciences by Ampère which
deserves to be mentioned. Ampère observes that human
cognitions take two special directions, towards matter or
towards thought ; and therefore he divides the sciences
into cosmological and noological. The first class he subdivides into the cosmological sciences properly so called,
or the sciences of inorganic matter, and into physiological
sciences, or sciences of organised and living matter. The
second class he subdivides into noological sciences properly so called, and into social sciences.

Ernest Renan, starting from the principle first proclaimed by Heraclitus that *Nothing is, everything becomes,*
connects all the sciences with the fact of the becoming.
In the order of reality, he recognises : 1. An atomistic
period, at least one virtually so, during which pure
mechanism reigns, but which contains the whole universe
in germ ; 2. A molecular period, during which chemistry
begins and matter already forms distinct groups; 3. A
solar period, during which matter is agglomerated in space
in colossal masses, separated by enormous distances ; 4. A
planetary period, during which in every system there
separate from the central mass distinct bodies which
possess an individual development, and during which the
Earth in particular begins to exist as a planet ; 5. A period
of individual development in every planet, during which
the Earth in particular passes through the evolutions revealed to us by geology, and in which life appears, so that

botany, zoology, and physiology begin to have an object; 6. The period of unconscious humanity, revealed to us by comparative philology and mythology, and which extends from the day in which there were beings on the earth that deserved the name of men down to the historical times; 7. The historical period, which begins in Egypt, and embraces about 5000 years, of which 2500 are well known, and 300 or 400 of which has given us the full knowledge of the whole of our planet, and of all humanity.[1]

This system differs from that of Comte and his followers, because it puts chemistry before astronomy, and makes no mention of physics. It agrees with Comte's system regarding the uselessness of metaphysics, a science which can only gather together the manifestations already reached. God is here synonymous with the total of existence; He is even more than the whole of existence, because He is the absolute which seeks Himself. Hence it appears that the system of Renan is only that of Hegel turned upside down.

According to Hegel, the general exists before the particular, of which it is the foundation, or rather its substance. Science is only the deduction *à priori* of all that is contained in the idea of being. The only scientific method is the speculative method, which transports us with a bound into the absolute, and which, starting from a first induction, descends by a series of antinomies and syntheses from the general to the particular, or from the abstract to the concrete, according to necessary laws. . The Idea is the universal principle, of which things are manifestations; and hence, in order to study these in their source, it is necessary to consider the idea in itself, which gives the science of logic; out of itself in nature, which gives the philosophy of nature; and when it returns into itself in the spirit, which is the object of

---

[1] See *De la métaphysique et son avenir*, Revue des Deux Mondes, 15th Jan. 1860.

the philosophy of spirit: a tripartite division which comprehends the whole of knowledge. Logic, according to Hegel, is the system of pure reason, of the truth in itself, the science of God considered in His eternal essence, and independently of His physical or moral realisation. It is divided into three parts: the science of *being*, the science of *essence*, and the science of the *idea*. The philosophy of nature is also divided into three parts: mechanics, physics, and organics, which are each sub-divided into three sections. This is the weakest part of Hegel's work, because it is the most arbitrary. The philosophy of the spirit is also tripartite. The first part, entitled *subjective spirit*, is subdivided into anthropology, phenomenology, and psychology; the second part, which has for its object *objective spirit*, is divided into three sections: right, morality, and customary practice. Finally, the third part, whose object is *absolute spirit*, leads us to the ultimate developments of the spirit in art, in religion, natural or revealed, and in philosophy. The history of philosophy and the philosophy of history form the complement and conclusion of this gigantic work.

Gioberti deduces the whole encyclopedia from the ideal formula. The subject, the idea of Being, gives origin to the ideal science, that is, to philosophy, which is conversant with the intelligible, and to theology, which studies the super-intelligible made known by revelation. The predicate furnishes the physical or natural sciences, and the mixed sciences, such as æsthetics and politics. The copula which expresses the conception of creation furnishes the matter of mathematics, logic, and ethics, which express a mediate synthesis between Being and the existent, the intelligible and the sensible; that is to say, it furnishes matter to mathematics when we descend from being to the existent, and take in time and pure space; and it furnishes matter to logic and ethics when we remount from the existent to Being by finding the conceptions of science and of virtue.

The encyclopedic sketch which Enrico Cenni, in his valuable work on *Italy and Germany*, draws from the works of Vico, presents considerable analogy with the one just considered. Alongside of dogmatic theology, the foundation of the *scibile*, he puts ethics as the basis of the *agibile*. Metaphysics, which starts from this, consists in the doctrine of the ideas seated in the eternal Word that has created the world by them, and which are therefore the efficient and final causes of the universe, without which no science is possible. Hence flows the doctrine of the immortality of the soul, the only real basis of psychology; and psychology in conjunction with the doctrine of ideas generates logic and her daughter criticism, along with æsthetics or the science of the beautiful. And, on the other side, she rears the science of jurisprudence or the philosophy of right, which is the substance of all the juridical and social sciences, namely, civil, criminal, and public law, the foundation of politics, which again embraces the science of the government of the State, and the sciences of international relations and public economy. Then comes mathematics with all its branches, from which we descend into physics, this word being used to signify the science of the sensible universe in all its varied provinces.[1]

We may also mention the division of the sciences worked out by Gioacchino Ventura according to the method by which they are treated, namely, authority, reasoning, and observation.

We come now to the question as to what ought to be the attitude of the State towards science? We have seen how the universities arose in the Middle Ages. They entitled themselves the "first-born daughters of the king," in order to indicate that science wished not to be oppressed by religion. In fact, when the Middle Ages were drawing to their close, the divorce of science and religion became

---

[1] *L'Italia e la Germania*, p. 154. Firenze, 1884. Flint's *Vico*, 1884.

always more patent, till it was definitely pronounced by
the Renaissance. It is marvellous how the popes themselves, dazzled by the splendour of the restoration of
antiquity, took part in the movement. But it was not
long till men of great genius like Descartes, Pascal,
Leibniz, and Vico began to show the agreement between
science and religion; and this was confirmed by Galileo,
Bacon, and Newton. In the eighteenth century the
struggle recommenced, and religion appeared extinguished
for ever; but we see it rising again from its ashes in the
beginning of the nineteenth century. The French Convention closed all the universities in France, and then by
the law of the year 2, it renounced all interference on the
part of the State with education, putting teachers, male
and female, under the immediate surveillance of the
municipality, of parents, legal tutors or curators, and all
the citizens. Then studies began to perish from want of
aliment, until a decree of the year 4 established the central
schools: that is to say, in every canton of the republic
there was established one or more primary schools, whose
directors were to be examined by a jury of instruction;
and in every department there was instituted a central
school, whose masters were to be examined and nominated
by a jury of instruction under the approbation of the
departmental administration. Those cities which already
possessed colleges had the power given to them to found
at their expense supplementary central schools and special
schools for the sciences, antiquities, and arts, the arrangement of which was to be regulated by particular laws.
And, finally, the National Institute of the Sciences and
Arts was established at Paris, and it belonged to the whole
Republic.

This arrangement was found insufficient, and under the
Empire there was created the monopoly of the University,
which substituted the spirit of government for the principle of incorporation. The academies which succeeded
the provincial universities, and whose limits of jurisdic-

tion were concurrent with the courts of appeal, were only sections of a great administration. Laferrière says that Napoleon created the University of France from the thought that in our modern society, so sharply separated from the religious corporations, there was needed a teaching body of a lay kind, which should cover with its greatness and dignity the obscure existences consecrated to the laborious duties of teaching. He wished this body, to which he conceded all the guarantees of existence and of jurisdiction, to be under the immediate action of the head of the State; and in consequence he created a Grand Master, who was his delegate and his representative, and a council of the University, which had as its superior in matters of regulations and of high jurisdiction the Council of State, which was often presided over by the Emperor. This Grand Master was responsible only to the head of the State. Napoleon had made the University a branch of the public administration, and at the same time a corporation that was large and strong from its unity; but in order to give to this his creature a powerful and vigorous life, he restricted the legal right of families, and the right of religious beliefs and of liberty. He made the Catholic dogma the basis of the teaching; and the University, a glorious monopoly placed under the action of the government, absorbed in its bosom all the private institutions. His thought is clearly expressed in these words which he addressed to the first Grand Master, De Fontanes : " I wish a teaching body, because a body never dies, but transmits its spirit and its organisation. I wish a body whose doctrine may be safe from the little fevers of the time, which shall always march although the government falls asleep, and the administration and institutions of which shall become so national that they shall not be able to be lightly changed." [1] By the ordinance of 21st February 1815, the government of the University was assigned to the University; but there

[1] See *Cours de droit public et administratif*, 4th ed. 1854.

was a long way yet to go before reaching the law of the liberty of the higher teaching, which was passed with difficulty on 12th July 1875.

The German universities were founded on the model of the ancient University of Paris, which had been copied from the Italian universities. They are corporations in which the State is represented by a curator, who supplies their wants when their special revenues do not suffice. On account of this aid, the minister of public instruction nominates the professors out of three candidates proposed by the academic senate, which is composed of the rector for the time, the rector of the preceding year, and a certain number of ordinary professors chosen by their colleagues, and by the university judge. The university maintains a correctional jurisdiction and a police over the students, and this jurisdiction is exercised by the said academic judge. The faculties regulate their instruction according to the best of their judgment, assigning to their constituent members the courses of lectures that have to be delivered in accordance with the latest advance of science. The *Privat-docents* may choose the subject of their prelections from among the matters belonging to the faculty with which they are connected. The faculties alone have the right of conferring the university degrees, although they do it in name of the university as such. The State in Prussia reserves to itself a special examination called the *Staatsprüfung*, to which it subjects those who aspire at exercising a liberal profession. The students are free to attend the lectures of any professor, and to arrange the order of their own studies, on the condition of paying the professors.

A German university embraces many branches of education which in other countries are relegated to special schools, such as engineering in bridges and roads, forestry, polytechnic instruction, &c.; and it possesses also a part of the normal schools in the so-called seminaries for future professors. The Leipsic Senatus states that the characteristic of the university is to offer to every student the opportunity of considering every branch of human science in its living connection with the other branches of science, and to appropriate it freely more in the spirit than in the letter.[1] "Our universities," says Von Sybel, "are superior to other universities, just because they are not simply schools, but so to speak *laboratories* of science ; and because continuous scientific production has to be the soul of their teaching. For this purpose the State calls men of the greatest scientific capacity in the country to the universities as professors. Hence such a fact as seeing an eminent scientist without an academic post, as is commonly seen in France, almost never happens with us. As regards the nomination of a professor, the first importance is laid upon his scientific capacity, and it is not a fatal objection that he should possess but a small degree of the facility of teaching. If he is capable of producing genuine scientific work, he is believed to be fitted for fulfilling the principal function of our university teaching. Undoubtedly we also demand that the young men shall be prepared in our higher institutions for a certain number of professions, but we do not wish this to be done mechanically and perfunctorily. We do not wish to cram into the memory of the student in the briefest and most convenient way possible, a heap of formulae and notions necessary for examinations and for the first year of his probation. . . . The fundamental aim with us is to initiate the alumnus in the proper method of the science studied by him, and to put him into a position, not to be himself a scientist, but to exercise afterwards his own profession scientifically. He has to learn first of all what science is, how scientific work is done, and what is meant by the term scientific production. The professor, in so far as weak human powers allow it, ought in every lecture to unfold some new and original problem, and to familiarise the student while listening to take a part in the work of the intellec-

[1] Hippeau, *L'instruction publique en Allemagne.* Paris, 1873.

tual process. Whatever may be afterwards his profession, the student in his youth should be the disciple of science and nothing else: for the acquisition of a certain scientific maturity and elasticity of mind is the best preparation for any profession."[1] That is how the question has been resolved in Germany as to whether the university should be scientific or professional.

In Italy the question is still being studied. Some wish to reduce the universities to provincial institutions for general culture and to professional schools. Thus they would concentrate into a few institutions of a finishing kind the high culture, and such institutions should also have to serve as normal schools. According to this system the monopoly of the State would remain in the sphere of the higher instruction which requires large resources and exceptional capacities. Others again would prefer to form the universities into corporations, with property and statutes of their own, and with full authority over the higher studies. In the view of the former, liberty of teaching consists in the conditions of impartiality granted by the State to all scientific opinions, while the latter regard it as consisting in the absolute independence of the teaching corporations. In the United States of America the latter system prevails, and it presents no inconvenience, as the State is able to take away from these corporations their civil personality whenever they do not fulfil satisfactorily their proper office. In such a system the State examination would be in place as a constant test of the excellence and efficiency of the teaching.

Besides the universities there are other scientific bodies, such as academies, which aim at the advancement of the sciences, which deserve to have a recognised personality in the State.

Positivism has tried in our time to make the relations between science and society closer. Moved by the inconveniences of too great a division of material and scientific

---

[1] From his Inaugural Discourse to the University of Bonn in 1868.

labour, Auguste Comte, advancing on the footsteps of his master Saint-Simon, has sought for the basis of a true spiritual power which only science can lay. A large and liberal education of the youth which should prepare them for all the professions, arts, or crafts, is a remedy, but it is not sufficient. Hence Comte demands the institution of a distinct power which would impose on all classes, and in the whole course of their life, respect for the supreme rights of general interest. In other words, he demands a moral and intellectual authority which might serve as a guide to the opinions of men and enlighten their conscience: a spiritual power whose decisions in all questions of great importance would be received with the same respect and deference as the judgment of the astronomers in a matter of astronomy. The conception of such an authority in moral and political matters would seem to imply that thinkers have arrived, or are about to arrive, at a certain unanimity, at least on essential points, as in the other sciences. To this the methods of positive science are tending ; and the uncontested authority which the astronomers enjoy in astronomical matters would in great social questions be common to the positive philosophers, who would possess the government of minds under these two conditions : that they should be in their spheres wholly independent of the temporal government, and that they should be peremptorily excluded from that government in order to be able to give themselves solely to the guidance of public education.

In no system, however, is the interference or surveillance of the State restricted to the higher instruction. We have already seen how the colleges, which were instituted to provide an asylum for poor students, gradually took on the teaching of the universities, making use of their professors. During the religious wars, they had much to suffer, and then they had to bear the competition of the Jesuits. In France, after the expulsion of the order in 1762, the University of Paris again took

possession of the colleges, which it opened only after
the Revolution.

The instruction given in the colleges was not adapted
for all the citizens, as is shown by the following words
of Saint-Marc de Girardin. "Every time that the course
of events has given origin to a new society, occasion is
given for a new education to arise; for education always
forms the social state. Have you in the Middle Ages a
society that is wholly religious?. Then the education will
be theological. In the fifteenth century, society eman-
cipates itself, and it becomes secular and temporal. After
the French Revolution, there is born a new society, a
commercial and industrial society, [which demands an
appropriate education. Our education has the defect
of being too special, too exclusive; it is good for forming
learned men, literati and professors who are no longer
theologians, as was the case in the fifteenth and sixteenth
centuries. To-day, we need merchants, industrialists,
agriculturists, and our education is not fitted to form
them."[1]   .

In the course of the eighteenth century various
attempts were made to found schools in which the
teaching of things (realities) should be substituted for
the teaching of words. The first of these was instituted
by Councillor Hecker at Berlin in 1747; but it failed.
The creation of the *Realschulen* or *Burgerschulen* was reserved for our century. In 1829 Spilleke reorganised the
school of Hecker, giving it the character which still
forms at present the basis of technical instruction. He
was the first to understand that such institutions ought
to preserve a scientific character, and not to be merely
mechanical and empirical, and that they should serve
as a preparation for the purpose of practical life as the
gymnasia do for the so-called liberal professions. England,
which holds so tenaciously by its traditions, has had to

---

[1] *De l'instruction intermédiare et de son état dans le midi de l'Allemagne.*
Paris, 1835.

establish quite recently middle class examinations; and even the Universities of Oxford and Cambridge confer a diploma in most of the subjects of the faculties: " Tum in litteris Anglicis, in historiis, in linguis, in mathematica, in scientiis physicis et in caeteris artibus quae ad juventutem educandam pertinent." France was slower in accepting the new teaching, but it finally instituted it by the law of 21st July 1865, under the title of *Enseignement secondaire spéciale.* The reaction in favour of classical study and the Imperial University, had rendered the intentions of the convocation vain. Italy preceded France in establishing technical teaching by the law of public instruction of 13th November 1859.

But is there not a way of co-ordinating secondary technical instruction with classical teaching ? A mode of doing so exists in the United States, where the common schools embrace primary instruction at all its stages, as well as that given in the German Realschulen, and a part of that which is given in the Italian gymnasiums and lyceums. The pupil passes successively from the first rudiments to grammar and arithmetic, not neglecting drawing and music. The Grammar School and the High School add the ancient and modern languages, literature, history, geography, geometry, algebra, chemistry, physics, and natural history. In this system of study, the ancient languages do not occupy the centre of knowledge as in the gymnasiums and lyceums; but mathematics, the physical and natural sciences, history, geography, the language of the country and foreign languages, form more the basis of the instruction. Greek and Latin, which are taught in the Grammar Schools and the High Schools, are made the subject of study both on account of the beneficial influence which they exercise on the understanding, and because they form part of the examinations for admission to colleges and universities. In the colleges there are carried on studies in humanity and rhetoric, and the bachelor's degree is conferred.[1]

At the basis of the educational pyramid both in Europe and in America is the primary instruction. Luther wrote a celebrated letter on this subject to the municipal councils of the cities of Germany, which runs as follows:—

"DEAR SIRS,—Since we daily spend so much on guns, streets, highways, &c., in order to procure peace and worldly prosperity for a city, we ought for far better reasons to spend something for the poor youth by keeping one or two schoolmasters for them. The whole power and strength of Christianity lies in posterity, and if the youth are neglected it will go with the Christian Churches as with an uncultivated garden in the spring. There are people who serve God with the strangest practices, by fasting, wearing a penitent's shirt, and doing a thousand other things from piety; but they are lacking in true religion which consists also in training the children well. They do like the Jews who left their temple to sacrifice on the summits of mountains. But believe me, it is much more necessary to instruct our own children than to get absolution, or to pray and make pilgrimages and fulfil vows. In my opinion the authorities should take steps to compel the subjects to send the children to school. . . . If they can compel healthy subjects to carry lance and musket, to mount the ramparts and to perform all sorts of military services, how much more ought they to impose the duties on the subjects of sending their children to school, because there is a worse war with Satan to be carried on. And if I could or were compelled to give up my office of preaching and my other occupations, I would take up no vocation rather than that of a schoolmaster or teacher, because I believe that next to preaching this is the most useful, the greatest, and the best calling; and indeed, I don't know to which I should give the preference."

[1] Cf. Hippeau, *L'instruction publique aux Etats-Unis*, 2nd ed. Paris, 1872.

We do not wish to take the position of maintaining that Catholicism is hostile to the school; yet it is certain that after the Reformation, and especially since the French Revolution, it has regarded it with a certain distrust; and whereas in the Protestant schools the master is a half-pastor, the teacher in Catholic countries always assumes more of the lay character.

Ought the State to follow the opinion of Luther and make elementary instruction obligatory? The French philosopher Cousin gave his judgment for the affirmative in his report to the Chamber of Peers on the law of primary instruction of 1833. "A law which would make primary instruction a legal obligation has not appeared to us more above the powers of the legislator than the law in reference to the national guard, or the one which you have just passed with regard to forced expropriation for the sake of public utility. If the reason of public utility is sufficient to entitle the legislator to lay his hands on property, why should not the reason of a much higher utility suffice to entitle him to do less, namely, to require that the children shall receive the instruction indispensable to all human creatures in order that they may not become hurtful to themselves and to the whole of society." An absolute necessity would excuse the legislator for having recourse to coercive measures when he had exhausted all the means of persuasion, as would be subsidies to municipalities for the founding of numerous schools and prizes for the poor children who attended them. This is the system followed in England, while in many States on the Continent recourse is taken by preference to penalties. The Articles 326–329 of the Italian law of 13th November 1859 already referred to, declared that primary instruction was obligatory; and if fathers, or those who exercise the paternal authority, neglected to send their sons to the communal school, without providing effectively in another manner for their instruction, they were threatened with being punished according to the penal laws, which, however, had assigned no penalty in particular for this offence. But this is provided for by the Articles 3 and 4 of 15th July 1877, regarding the obligation of elementary instruction. The first article authorises the syndic to exhort, and then to admonish negligent parents; and the second article subjects them to a fine ranging from 50 centimes to 10 francs, which may gradually be applied in consecutive years.

What are the relations which the State ought to maintain between religion and science ? We answer, their complete independence, but without this degenerating into hostility. In the preceding chapter we have seen that it is impossible to confine religion within the precincts of the Church, and it is equally impossible to exclude it from the school. Religious instruction ought to be given in the schools and colleges by the ministers of the Church of the majority, the right of keeping away from it being reserved for dissenting pupils. In the universities, faculties of theology ought to be maintained with the consent of the ecclesiastical authority, and chairs ought to be founded for the principal cults in the State. Under a system of liberty of teaching, where instruction is given at all stages, whether supplied by private individuals or by corporations, the State should maintain its part as supervisor and custodian of the law, in order that religion and science may not commit usurpations.

CHAPTER III.

ART.

THE true is the Idea considered in itself as thought; but when the Idea appears blended with the external reality, and is perceived by the mind without being carried back to its abstract generality, it may become the beautiful. The imagination produces the beautiful by uniting together a sensible form taken from the external world and an intelligible type furnished by the reason, through means of a mental individualisation which it takes from itself, and which, conjoined with the other two elements, constitutes the ideal type. When the Idea overpasses the form, we have the sublime; when it is in a certain equilibrium with it, we have the beautiful. We see the sublime appearing first in the arts, because it is nearer to the Idea.

The positivists attack the beautiful, as they have attacked the good and the true, by their theory of the relativity of our cognitions. They maintain that the beautiful is but a play of our faculties, an illusion of the mind. Some years ago, writes Herbert Spencer, I read in a German author whose name I do not now remember, that the æsthetic feelings spring from the impulse to play. The proposition has remained in my mind, because if it does not contain the whole truth, it is the germ of it. Grant Allen, in his *Physiological Æsthetics*, goes back directly to sexual selection as the source of the æsthetic pleasure, just as Littré had made every kind of altruistic sentiment spring from it. In his application

of this theory, however, Herbert Spencer does not fail to
note what is special to the beautiful, as he wishes to
exclude from it all that is necessary or even useful to life,
as well as every interested desire. Then returning to his
fixed idea of play, he foresees the abdication of art in
favour of science, that humble Cinderella hitherto hidden
by the domestic hearth, but destined yet to eclipse her
proud sisters and to reign as a queen. Strauss, on the
other hand, shows himself less severe, asserting that
poetry and music will be able to co-exist with science,
occupying, however, the place of religion.

How did the beautiful arts arise? Were they an
imitation, or a creation? A poetical writer says that the
forms of the mountains are the architecture of nature;
the peaks, furrowed by the lightning, are her statuary;
the shadows and the light are her painting; the murmur
of the wind and the waves, her harmony; and the whole
together, her poetry. Art sought to imitate inanimate
nature by architecture, and animated nature by sculpture
and painting. Music served as a passage to the arts of
speech. The end of art is not imitation, but the representation of the beautiful, the revelation of the universal
harmony. Art arouses in us feelings that are calm and
pure, and incompatible with the gross pleasures of the
senses. It elevates the mind above the common life, and
predisposes it for generous actions by the affinity which
reigns between the ideas of the divine, the true, and the
beautiful, from which its social influence arises.

Art begins as the interpreter of the religious ideas, and
expresses through symbols the relations of the invisible
principle with the objects of nature. The symbol is an
image which represents an idea, and is distinguished from
the signs of language in that there is a natural and not
an arbitrary or conventional relation between its image
and the representative idea. Thus the lion is the symbol
of courage; the circle, of eternity; the triangle, of the
Trinity. But the symbol represents the idea only on one

side, and is ambiguous in its nature; nor can it express that equilibrium between the idea and the form which is the characteristic note of the beautiful. Much has been said of oriental art as being symbolical by its nature; but this was done in the ardour of discovery; and thereafter it was reduced to its just value.

In oriental art Hegel sees imagination in the state of ferment, or thought which is vague, and confused. The principle of things is not yet grasped in its spiritual nature; the ideas as to God are empty abstractions, and the forms which represent Him bear a character that is exclusively sensible and material. Still immersed in the contemplation of the sensible world, and having neither measure nor fixed rules wherewith to value the reality, the oriental imagination is lost in vain endeavours to penetrate into the general meaning of the universe, and it is not able to use for the expression of its profoundest thoughts anything but gross images and representations, in which is manifested the crudest opposition between the idea and the form. The imagination thus passes from one extreme to another without guide and without purpose, and it presents us at the same time with combinations the most grand, the most whimsical, and the most grotesque. Hegel likewise finds in the Indian poetry scenes of human life that are full of sweetness, of graceful images and tender feelings of nature; but as regards its fundamental conceptions, the spiritual is overwhelmed by the sensible. Thus in it we often find the lowest triviality alongside of the noblest situations, and an absolute lack of proportion and precision. The sublime is only the unmeasured; and as regards the basis of the myth, the imagination, seized by vertigo, and incapable of regulating the movement of thought, loses itself in the fantastic, and produces only enigmas that are void of any element of reason.

Hegel shows more severity towards the Chinese art, which he excludes from his *Æsthetics*, for reasons which we transcribe from his *Philosophy of History*. "Generally," he says, "this people have a great aptitude for imitation, which they have applied not only to the common things of life, but also to art. Yet they have not succeeded in reaching the beautiful. Their painting lacks perspective and shading, and they even reproduce European pictures according to this method. A Chinese painter knows well how many scales there are on the back of a carp, and how many indentations are found on a leaf; he knows the various forms of the trees and the bending of their branches; but his dexterity is not founded on the sublime, the ideal, and the beautiful."

India has left us not only her interminable poems, but also her temples, many of which are hollowed out in the sides of mountains, and are supplied with artificial pillars of wood which imitate the trunks of trees with their branches. Works in beams of wood distinguish the Aryan peoples. The Semites, not having forests nor trees fitted for construction, erected monuments with stones well or ill joined together, and without any cement. The Turanian races used smaller stones, and sometimes bricks, and they invented cement in order to hold them together.

Tradition points to the tower of Babel as the first monument, and the latest erudition is showing us Turanian and Semitic races prior to their division in possession of those regions which afterwards became Chaldea and Assyria. We may cast a glance on the remaining monuments of those races in order to follow the progress of art. In the level plains of India, the temples consist of small edifices which are identical in structure, and which are heaped on one another in order to attain the desired mass. Through all the East, architecture is the art *par excellence;* and sculpture is only a vast hieroglyph which recalls the attributes of the divinity. The gods and heroes are represented large, and the secondary spirits smaller; the divinities possess as many heads as they have qualities, and as many arms as they have functions. Painting consists solely in coloration, and is symbolical.

The god Shiva, who represents the sun or the fire, is painted red; and Vishnu, who represents the moist element, water, is painted azure.

The Assyrians and Persians constructed palaces which also served as temples and as national archives. They are built of bricks coated with stucco and with bas-reliefs in stone or gypsum, which represent the national history, which is also illustrated by numerous inscriptions. In their ancient buildings the Egyptians began to use clay and reeds, for which they afterwards substituted stone. The most recent researches have put beyond doubt the almost exclusively Semitic origin of the Egyptians.[1] They practised the worship of death, and their principal monuments are tombs in the form of pyramids. There is found in them evidences of a very great observation of nature, and a certain artistic discernment. Under the twenty-third dynasty the Egyptians adopted a column which seems to have originated the Doric order. With the Greeks sculpture and painting ceased to be simple accessories of architecture, and they introduced into it a new element, the art of grouping personages together, or what we call composition. The Greeks besides created style and taste, that is to say, they perfected the expression of created things without taking account of the hieratic types; and they acquired that attitude and habit which conduces to a reasoned choice. This is explained when we reflect that in Greece the works of art were not as in the East entrusted to servile hands, nor were they destined merely to satisfy the need of the beautiful felt by certain social classes, but they were produced by artists and artisans freely associated together, and were destined to give pleasure to all the citizens. The Romans, occupied with politics and administration, sought for usefulness in the beautiful arts. In architecture, they preferred the arch to the architrave; they constructed magnificent bridges,

---

[1] Maspero, *Histoire ancienne des peuples de l'Orient*, p. 16, 4th ed. Paris, 1886.

aqueducts, and cloacæ, and they invented special kinds of edifices, such as baths and amphitheatres.

In the Greco-Roman art, the lines are straight and sometimes monotonous in their simplicity; they do not rise to any great distance from the soil, but constitute a sort of horizontal architecture, or a style in length. On the contrary, in Persia the ancient Assyrian architecture made progress; its lines preferred to run in curves and shot upwards towards the heaven, forming a sort of perpendicular architecture, or a style in height. Some distinguished authors maintain that the Byzantine art was descended from the Persian art. The foundation of Constantinople was a reconquest of the East which had already made its influence felt through Christianity. The conical form predominated in the Byzantine architecture, and was adopted by the Mussulmans.

In the West, the Churches continued to be bad imitations of the basilicas of the first Christian emperors. The roof was supported by a framework visible in the interior; but towards the year 1000, the model began to be altered. For the framework the arch was substituted; buttresses were added to the walls to support them, and the relations between the elevation and divisions were changed. The form of the church was modified into a Latin cross with a large nave, flanked by two smaller ones. The new style was called the *Romanesque*, and it was generally used in the south down to the fourteenth century. The north was not satisfied with it, and it added to it the ogive form and the thousand arrows that seem to dart to heaven. The style of architecture which is improperly called the Gothic arose in France in the eleventh and twelfth centuries along with the *Chansons de geste*, scholasticism, and the communes. It was a product of the Roman style as the Arabic architecture was of the Byzantine style. The two styles were closely allied. The ogival had remained a long time in the East in a sporadic state, and certainly the great builders of the twelfth century did not go thither to get it. The Gothic architecture, however, was an effort of abstraction, and the architects, enamoured of their designs, weakened the mass of their buildings.

The Renaissance of the ancient literature recalled attention to the still existing monuments of antiquity, and Italy produced a band of great artists who adapted purity of design to massive greatness. Society enlarged its basis more and more; and architecture lost its fine taste, sacrificing beauty to utility. In sculpture, Greece remained incomparable, having reproduced the human form with greatest perfection. It is enough to cast a glance on the sarcophagi of St. Constance and St. Helena, discovered in the excavations of the Nomentan and Labican ways, and transported into the Museum of the Vatican, to be convinced of how much Christianity had caused sculpture to retrograde. These two sarcophagi are in porphyry, and of rose colour. On the first genii and angels are represented as gathering and pressing the grape; and on the other horsemen are triumphing over their enemies. The vine and Bacchus serve as a transition to the new mysteries, whose characteristics are completed by the representation of corn, sheaves, and bread. But how clumsy are these angels and genii when compared with the Dionysuses of the beautiful days of the ancient art, and what decline is not marked by these cavaliers of the age of Constantine! In the Middle Ages more attention was given to expression than to execution, but this was corrected by the Renaissance, although in the last works of Michael Angelo there is seen a strong development of muscle, which has been further exaggerated by the modern realistic school.

The Greeks began to make use of painting in order to give greater relief to the forms of architecture, but it was not long till they also used it to imitate nature, and also to reproduce human facts. Coming down the course of ages and arriving at Herculaneum and Pompeii, we find two distinct elements in painting. One of these is purely conventional and decorative, and it is represented by a single colour and a combination of tones in order to please the eye; and the other, which we shall call naturalistic, aims at reproducing animated scenes and complete landscapes. These two elements seem to be mixed up in that kind of painting which is called *Arabesque,* and which Vitruvius considered a corruption of art. In the pictures of Herculaneum and Pompeii, we find perspective, well-modelled figures, and a dramatic effect carried even to exaggeration in the mosaics. Visiting the catacombs, we find no longer perspective, difference of planes, or well-modelled figures; and composition itself seems to be wanting. On the contrary, we observe an immovable hieratic form, a tendency to suppress the effects obtained from the Greeks and from the Greco-Romans, in order to attain to naturalism and to painting on the large scale. This return to the past commenced among the Greeks of the East, where it still subsists, and it also laid hold of those in the West, where it lasted till the fourteenth century.

All the traditions of ancient art, however, were not then extinguished. Duccio of Sienna and Cimabue of Florence fixed their attention on the ancient designs, studying them from the side of perspective and of anatomy. Rhumor says they understood the value of these, and applied themselves to soften the leanness of those bony figures which had been drawn with all possible geometrical rigidity. Giotto, in order to imitate nature better, no longer varnished his colours with wax, like the Byzantines; and he thus preserved their brilliancy and truthfulness, so as, according to Boccaccio, even to produce illusion by them. Masaccio gave greater roundness to his figures, and Beato Angelico of Fiesole gave them more feeling. Leonardo da Vinci acquired the secret of the forms of the human body, and he attained that serenity of expression which arises from the perfect balance of our faculties. Perugino transmitted to Raffaello all the depth of feeling characteristic of the Florentine School, and he united with it the purity of design characteristic of antiquity, thus bringing art to its final perfection. Correggio by the magic of chiaroscuro, and Titian by the richness of his colouring, brought ideality always nearer and nearer to reality.

Reality is the dominant characteristic of the Flemish and Dutch Schools of painting. But common life has also its poetry, and the excellence of the artist consists in seizing it. The two Van Eycks filled up their pictures with a thousand accessories, which, however, were always expressive, and did not diminish the importance of the principal subject. Rembrandt is entirely impregnated with the Protestant faith, and on his canvas he draws the human rather than the divine. The other nations took their models from Italy and from the Netherlands.

The arts of speech followed the same course of development. . Language, as used by poetry, was full of images, to which metre was soon added, which then brought with it rhyme. "Among all the arts," says Hegel, "poetry has specially the power of revealing to consciousness the spiritual life, the passions which agitate the soul, the ideas which predominate in the mind, the course of human things, and the divine government of the universe. Hence it was the teacher of humanity, and its influence was universal."[1] Poetry first presents us with a picture of the moral world in its external existence, and represents it under the form of a great action in which gods and men take part. This kind of poetry attaches itself to the figurative arts, revealing to us the objective impersonal

[1] Hegel, *Cours d'esthétique,* traduction de Ch. Bernard, vol. iv. p. 150. Paris, 1851. Hegel's system of Æsthetics has been summed up by Professor Michelet of Berlin, one of his most faithful disciples, and Michelet's summary along with Hegel's Introduction has been translated by W. Hastie into English, with much facility and elegance. Edinburgh, 1886. [The Philosophy of Art. An Introduction to the scientific study of Æsthetics, by Hegel and C. L. Michelet. Translated from the German by W. Hastie, B.D. Edinburgh, 1886.]

side of existence in the sense that the action takes the form of an event entirely extraneous to the poet, and is completed independently of the human will by an external fatality. Many of the lower kinds of poetry, such as the epigram, the ancient elegy, the gnomic poetry, the cosmogonic and philosophical poems, may be considered as belonging to epic poetry, inasmuch as the idea which informs them is expounded in itself without the poet uniting to it his own reflections and personal feelings. Thus we have the expression of a complete fact in the epigram, or a succession of maxims and sentences in gnomic poetry having the object of setting clearly forth a moral truth, or again a description of the great scenes of nature, a narration of the genesis of beings and of the cosmic revolutions, and a poetical exposition of the laws of the universe and of the first discoveries of science. Lyrical poetry, on the contrary, has a personal and subjective character. The poet does not relate, but he enjoys, suffers, and often rebels against the external reality. And when the struggle is not limited to complaints, but is changed into action, which the various actors carry on under our eyes, then arises dramatic poetry, which describes the conflict of human liberty with fate, as in the ancient dramas, or with the passions, as in the dramas of modern times. Or lastly, it shows us the contrast between the will and the petty accidents of life which produce no evil but beget laughter.

In order to express its proper conceptions in words, art does not always require metre and rhyme, but may even use the manner of common language. Thus we have the various kinds of narrative, descriptive, oratorical, and didactic. The first two are on the confines of poetry when they trace out the vicissitudes of the human heart, as in the novel and the romance ; or they depict battles and other great events, as in history, when treated artistically; or they describe the various beauties of nature, as in travels. Eloquence is excluded by many from the beautiful arts, because it has a purpose of utility; but in order to attain it, it is often obliged to move the affections, and always to connect its ideas in such a way as to induce persuasion in the minds to which it is directed, and this persuasion cannot be obtained without artistic dexterity. The same may be said of the didactic kind of composition, of which we have also essays in verse which both delight and instruct.

Summing up, we may say that, in the figurate arts, the East distinguished itself in architecture, Greece in sculpture, and Italy and the Netherlands in painting. The ideal of the peoples of the East was supernatural and overwhelming force, as revealed in the great phenomena of nature ; the ideal of Greece was man contemplated in all his physical and moral vigour, as the hero ; and the ideal of modern times has been the soul, which, without despising its terrestrial limits, aspires to heaven. Thus in poetry, the East has given us the Ramayana, Mahabharata, Shahnameh, the poems of Antar, and the Book of Job, which all belong to the epopee, and, exceptionally, the Psalms of David, the Indian Sakuntala, and certain Chinese dramas. Greece began with Hesiod and Homer, and then produced Pindar and Anacreon, Aeschylus, Sophocles, Euripides, and Aristophanes. The modern times start with Dante and Petrarca, but find their complete expression in Shakespeare, Molière, Ariosto, Cervantes, Schiller, Goethe, Lamartine, Victor Hugo, Manzoni, and Leopardi.

Sounds variously combined were also adopted to express the various affections of the soul. Thus we find among all peoples musical instruments employed to give the signal of battle, to excite the courage of the combatants, and to animate all kinds of religious and civil assemblies. Among the Greeks, music was of peculiar importance. Pythagoras invented the three-footed lyre in imitation of the tripod of Delphi. It consisted of three lyres harmonised, the one according to the Dorian measure, the other according to the Phrygian measure, and the third according to the Lydian measure; and they were held together upon a movable base which the player made to turn with his foot, thereby substituting one lyre for the other without any one perceiving it.[1] To Pythagoras is also attributed the discovery of the musical proportions, and the mode of determining the depth or height of tones by the greater or less rapidity of the vibrations of chords, as well as the invention of notes, although this seems to belong to Terpander. Music and poetry were inseparable companions in Greece. Archilochus of Paros is regarded as the inventor of lyrical poetry, only the heroic hexameter having been used before him. He introduced the accompanying recitative, which was adopted by the tragic and dithyrambic poets. The Greek drama was composed of monologues, dialogues, and choruses. The first two were declaimed, and the chorus was chanted in a measured rhythm. In the time of Aeschylus, there were as many as twenty in the chorus, but they were reduced by a law to fifteen. Every ode was divided into strophe, antistrophe, and epode. The first was chanted when the chorus turned to the right; the antistrophe when it turned back to the left; and the epode when it stood still. The odes of Pindar were chanted in the same manner; and all the poets understood music and themselves regulated the chanting of their verses. The Greeks were not acquainted with harmony in the sense given to this word now, but they knew how to direct and lead vocal and instrumental masses.

The music of the Romans was similar to that of the Greeks, and Vitruvius says expressly that musical science being obscure in itself, remained entirely unintelligible to those who did not know the Greek language. Horace

[1] The Greeks had besides the Ionian measure, intermediate between the Dorian and the Phrygian, as also the Æolian, intermediate between the Phrygian and the Lydian. The Lydian measure was specially sweet and voluptuous, and the Ionian was also pathetic and soft.

called it the friend of the temple; and the first Christians
were accustomed to sing psalms without the aid of any
instrument, until organs were introduced in the seventh
century. Ambrose developed the art of singing in the
churches of the West; Gregory the Great effected various
reforms upon it; but the title of creator of church music
must be assigned to Giovanni Palestrina. He exhibited
such majesty and style, such truthfulness in expression,
and such a noble simplicity in modulation, that he has
only been equalled by Handel and a few other masters.
The use of oratorios became common in the sixteenth
century, especially in the Catholic States of Germany;
but the Protestants continued to sing psalms, and admitted
no other instrument into their churches than the organ.
The origin of the composition of these oratorios goes
back to the popular mysteries or moralities, just as the
origin of the lyrical drama may be traced to the madrigals
which were sung in friendly gatherings, their motive
being taken from the verses of Petrarca and of Tasso.
The first application of the chanted declamation of the
Greek tragedy to the profane lyrical drama, seems to
have taken place in the representation of the Orpheus
(*Orfeo*) of Angelo Poliziano in 1475. The Daphne, written
by Rinuccini, and set to music by Peri, obtained a great
reputation. Carissimi perfected both sacred and profane
music, and after him Scarlatti, Porpora, Paesiello, Cimarosa,
and Pergolesi prepared the way for Rossini, the real
creator of modern music. In Germany, instrumental
music got the upper hand, and Mozart, who had much of
the Italian school, was succeeded by Beethoven, Weber,
Meyerbeer, and lastly by Richard Wagner.

We have seen how Greece freed itself from the symbols
of the East in order to live in a just equilibrium between
spirit and matter. There is no atmosphere more favourable to art. In place of a theocracy and a hierarchy of
castes, or even a monarchy, the Greeks founded the city,
which produced other cities even to the number of three

hundred, such as Miletus, which spread its colonies over all the shores of the Black Sea. Taine has put the question: "How did they live in such a city?" And he answers it thus: "A citizen worked very little, as he usually received his support from subjects or tributaries, and he was always served by slaves, the poorest of them possessing at least one of these domestic servants. Athens counted four of them for every citizen; and other cities, like Ægina and Corinth, possessed some four or five hundred thousand of them! On the other hand the citizen had no great need of being served. He was sober, like all the refined races of the south, and he could live on three olives, a morsel of garlic, and the head of an anchovy. His clothing consisted of a half shirt, a large cloak like that worn by shepherds, and a pair of sandals. His house was a narrow building, badly constructed, and far from solid. Robbers penetrated into it by making a hole in the wall. It was, however, sufficient to sleep in; and a bed and two or three elegant jars were its principal furnishings. The citizen, having few wants, passed his time in the open air. As he had neither to serve king nor priests, he was sovereign in his own city. He chose his own magistrates and pontiffs, and was also capable of being raised to these offices; and although but a tanner or a blacksmith, he judged in the courts the gravest political causes, and deliberated in the assemblies on the greatest affairs of the State. He spent his life in the public squares discussing the best means of preserving and aggrandising his city, in reviewing its alliances, treaties, constitution, and laws, in listening to the orators, and in perorating himself, up to the moment when he had to go on board to start for the conflict. The young men passed the greatest part of the day in the gymnasiums, exercising themselves in wrestling, boxing, leaping, running, throwing the discus, and strengthening their muscles and making them supple. They wished to have the body as robust, as well developed, and as beautiful as possible, and no other education has better attained this end. From these habits of the Greeks, there sprang quite special ideas. The ideal personage in their eyes was not the thinking mind, or the delicately sensitive soul, but the naked body, sprung from a good race, and of beautiful growth, well-proportioned, active, and dexterous. This mode of thinking was manifested in a thousand ways. In the first place, while the Carians, the Lydians, and their other barbarous neighbours were ashamed to show themselves naked, the Greeks threw off their clothes without hesitation, in order to wrestle or to run. In the second place, in their great national festivals, the Olympian, Pythian, and Nemean games, it was the nude man who triumphed. The youth of the first families gathered at these games from all points of Greece and from the most distant colonies, prepared by long exercise according to a particular rule of life and by constant labour for engaging in them ; and there, under the eyes and amid the applause of the whole nation, being divested of their garments, they wrestled, engaged in boxing, hurled the discus, and competed in races on foot or in chariots. The victorious athlete in the foot-race gave his name to the Olympiad; and the greatest poets celebrated it. Pindar, the most illustrious lyric poet of antiquity, has sung only of the chariot races. When the victorious athlete returned to his home, he was carried aloft in triumph, and his strength and agility became the pride of his country."[1]

Sculpture was the Greek art *par excellence*, architecture and painting serving only as its accompaniments. The temple awaited the god who was to inhabit it, and sculpture created for it the most beautiful form of living beings. Painting, so long as it did not acquire an existence by itself, was reduced to a simple colouring of the statue or of the materials of architecture. The arts of articulate or inarticulate speech were developed parallel

[1] *Philosophie de l'Art*, p. 102. Paris, 1865.

to the arts of design ; and in the great national festivals of Greece, athletes, sculptors, painters, musicians, poets, and historians were crowned.

The Dorians, the founders of the Olympian games, excluded the contests in music and poetry which took place at the beginning at the Delian festival and at the Olympian games. Lycurgus, following the rigorous prescriptions of the Dorian genius, prohibited the beautiful arts, excepting music, dancing, and a severe poetry. In like manner, Pythagoras founded his school on meditation and silence, without prohibiting poetry, and leaving a large field for music. Plato exaggerated the Doric tendency when he banished the poets from his State. This is how he wrote in this connection in Book III. of his *Republic:* "If ever there should arrive in our State a man skilled to represent many parts, and capable of all kinds of imitation, and should wish to recite to us his poems, we would pay him homage as we would to a sacred being who is marvellous and enchanting ; we would say to him that in our State we have no one like him, and after having sprinkled his hair with perfumes and adorned his head with fillets, we should send him away." In Book X., he gives his reasons for such exclusion as follows : "We say of all the poets beginning from Homer that their fictions, whether they have virtue or any other thing as their object, only imitate phantasms, and never reach reality. When a painter draws a shoemaker, he understands nothing of his art, and yet when the people look at his colour and sketching, they believe they see a real shoemaker. Furthermore, in order not to be accused of hardness and coarseness towards poetry, we may say that this accusation about it, is of ancient date (and here he quotes various passages). Nevertheless, if imitative poetry (for he admits lyrical poetry) could prove to us by good reasons that it ought not to be excluded from a well-governed State, we should receive it with open arms." With the same rigour, he excludes the Lydian and Ionian measures in music, and he admits only the Doric on account of its earnestness, and the Phrygian which was employed in religious hymns.

The beautiful arts held the place of national institutions in Greece ; for every one felt himself happy to speak the beautiful tongue of the Greeks, thereby distinguishing themselves from the barbarians, and to take a part in the intellectual combats. The initiative, however, was entirely left to the individual, as the State maintained neither museums, nor academies, nor schools of the beautiful arts. The Romans, on the contrary, showed themselves at first averse to the fine arts. " The Klephte," says Michelet, "after the combat, sings on the solitary mountain. The Roman, having returned to his city with his booty, cavils with the senate, lends out at usury, litigates and pleads. His habits being those of a jurisconsult, he grammatically interrogates the law, or tortures it by dialectic to make his case out of it. Nothing is further from poetry, which began in Rome with the patrician disciples of mute Etruria, which in her feasts prohibited singing and only permitted pantomime. Being magistrates or pontifices, the *patres* had to preserve in their language that solemn conciseness proper to the oracles, which we admire in their inscriptions. As to the plebeians, they represented in the city the principle of opposition, of struggle, of negation, or of interest, and all this had nothing poetical about it. If there were popular songs at Rome, they belonged to the clients who attended the banquets of their patrons and combated for them and celebrated the common exploits of the *gens.*"[1] Among their clients and slaves, after the second Punic war, the patricians received various Greeks, for the instruction of their children and themselves. Paulus Æmilius, an austere pontifex and a scrupulous augur, had in his family Greek pedagogues, grammarians, sophists, rhetoricians, sculptors, and painters.

---

[1] *Histoire de la république romaine,* o. vi. p. 372. Bruxelles, 1840.

Scipio Africanus had as a client and panegyrist, the famous Ennius, who was born in Magna Graecia, and who imitated the Greeks with some originality. The national poet of old Italy was Naevius of Campania, who preferred the Saturnine verse to the Greek hexameter, and wrote many popular satires against the patricians, by whom he was persecuted.

But men like Paulus Æmilius and the Scipios were exceptions; for when Mummius took Corinth, and the king of Pergamos offered him a hundred talents for a picture, he said: "There must be something magical in that canvas," and he sent it to Rome. To those who had assigned to them the task of transporting the pictures and statues he had seized, he said: "Take care not to damage them, for if you do, you shall be condemned to make them again!"

Fashion introduced into Rome the luxury of the fine arts, and we find in the Theodosian Code that the emperors were wont to assign rooms in the public buildings to painters and sculptors, both to work in, and to exhibit their productions.

Christianity radically changed the conception of life by sanctifying pain, poverty, humility, and ugliness. The artistic opposition between paganism and Christianity is beautifully expressed in Goethe's poem, "The Bride of Corinth." Christianity enlarged the basis of society; and the little cell in which the statue of the Greek god was enclosed, and the portico under which the procession of the free citizens wound, were no longer sufficient. The multitude needed an enormous building which they also used for civil purposes, and it was provided with immense arches and colossal pillars, which were constructed by several generations of workmen who believed they were labouring for the salvation of their souls. With the Renaissance came the alliance of Christianity with ancient art, and it produced marvellous masterpieces. After the French Revolution the basis of society was enlarged anew. *Comfort,* a thing unknown in the ancient world, rendered our habits prosaic; scepticism made inspiration more difficult; and the governments, by founding museums, schools of fine art, and periodical exhibitions, undertook to further the arts of design, while those of speech were maintained and advanced by the industry of the publisher.

CHAPTER IV.

INDUSTRY.

HITHERTO we have looked at the mental development of
man without taking account of the necessities that surround him. But he cannot apply his mind to worship, to
science, or to art, without sustaining his body. The earth
only brings forth when it is bathed with the sweat of his
brow. Labour, however, was not a malediction but a rehabilitation. The earth was really cursed only to Cain,
to whom God said: "When thou tillest the ground, it
shall not henceforth yield unto thee her strength." Nevertheless the Lord permitted him to build a city, to which
he gave the name of Enoch, from whom was born Tubal
Cain in the sixth generation, "who was the instructor of
every artificer in brass and iron."

Leaving the Semitic traditions for the Aryan traditions,
we find that the cultivators and the artisans sprang from
the thighs of Brahma, while the priests were brought forth
from his mouth, and the warriors from his arms. Many
centuries before our era, history shows us the Pelasgi
spread over all the shores of the Mediterranean from
Etruria to the Bosphorus, in Arcadia, Argolis, Attica,
Latium, and perhaps also in Spain, where they left everywhere indestructible monuments in walls formed of enormous blocks of stone without any cement. "We are
astonished," says Michelet, "to see a race that was spread
through so many countries disappearing in history. Its
various tribes perish; they are absorbed among foreign

nations, or, at least, they lose their names. There are
no other examples of a ruin so complete. An inexpiable
malediction is attached to this people; all that its enemies
tell us of it, is ill-fated and bloody. To them belong the
women of Lemnos, who slaughtered their husbands in
one night; they were the inhabitants of Agylta, who
stoned the Phocean prisoners. Perhaps this ruin of the
Pelasgi, and the hostile tone of the Greek historians with
regard to them, may be explained by the contempt and
the hatred inspired in the heroic tribes for the agricultural
and industrial populations which had preceded them.
In fact, this was the character of the Pelasgi. They
worshipped the subterranean gods who guarded the
treasures of the earth; as agriculturists or miners they
tore open its bosom, in order to draw from it gold or corn.
These new arts were odious to the barbarians; every
industry they did not understand was regarded by them
as magic. The mysteries of the initiations which the
various corporations of artisans practised, lent appearance
to the most odious accusations. The magical worship of
flame, that mysterious agent of industry, that violent
action of the human will upon nature, that mixture and
soiling of the sacred elements, those traditions of serpent
gods and of dragon men of the East who worked by fire
and magic: all this terrified the imagination of the heroic
tribes. They had only the sword to use against the
unknown powers of which their enemies disposed; and
everywhere they pursued them by the sword. It is related
that the Telchines of Sicyon, of Bœotia, of Crete, of Rhodes,
and of Lydia, poured at will the water of the Styx on
plants and animals. Like the magicians of the Middle
Ages, they predicted and raised tempests. They pretended
to heal diseases; and could they not also smite any one
at will? The Cabiri of Lemnos, of Samothrace, and of
Macedonia—the same name designating the gods and the
worshippers—were forgers and miners like the Cyclopes
of the Peloponnesus, of Thrace, of Asia Minor, and of

Sicily, who, with a lamp fixed on their forehead, penetrated into the depths of the earth." [1]

Max Müller expresses the opinion that the Turanian or Tartaro-Finnic race had preceded the Semitic and Aryan races. Wherever these two races penetrated, they found savage peoples which they exterminated, but whose memory survived under the representation of giants, of magicians, or of animals. Some of these peoples attained to civilisation; as the Cushites and the Hamites in Western Asia and in Africa, and the Chinese in Eastern Asia. This primitive civilisation had a materialistic character, with a religious and poetic instinct that was little developed, a feeble sentiment of art, a tendency to elegance and to refinement, a great aptitude for the manual arts and for the applied sciences, a positive spirit inclined to commerce, to comfort, and to amusement. It had no political life, but instead of it an administration so complicated that it has not been equalled in Europe, except in the Roman Empire and in modern times. The traces of the Cushite and Hamite civilisation disappeared at the contact of the Aryan civilisation, but the Chinese form of it still subsists in our day.

Labour supposes property: (1) in our own faculties, and (2) in the matter to which they are applied. This is evident in the case of material labour; but all doubt will also cease in regard to intellectual labour, whenever it is considered that the artist is master of the marble which he sculptures, and the writer of the pages to which he entrusts his ideas, as in like manner the professor and the physician are masters (at least for the moment) of the attention of the scholar and the body of the invalid.

Property, like society, is natural to man as endowed with liberty. Liberty consists in the full possession of oneself, in the capability of developing the proper activity of one's own talent, and enjoying its fruits.

---

[1] *Histoire de la république romaine,* c. iii. p. 283.

The free man labours, and then possesses. Property involves the right to labour, to form capital, to exchange, and to donate. As property is not extinguished with death, so when a person has not disponed, the positive law dispones for him according to his presumed will. In principle, then, all men have implicitly the right to use external things for the rational ends of life. But as these are not separate external things sufficient for all, society has established rules according to which the individual may acquire, preserve, or lose the immediate power over them. The State, which represents society, has not divested itself on this account of all right of interference, but has always a supreme dominion (*dominium eminens*) over property, which it exercises by means of the protection, the guarantee, and the rules which regulate the use of it, as is specially the case with forests and mines. By its imposts, it assigns to itself a part of property, and reserves the right to dispose of it by means of expropriation for the public utility. Accordingly the State, with its eminent dominion, represents the social side of property, and establishes the organic bond that binds it to the various generations when it determines the modes of transmission and of succession.

It was only slowly that this comparatively perfect form of property was reached. The investigators of positive Law have explored all the corners of the earth in order to find the transitions from one form of it to another. It may suffice to refer to Sir Henry Sumner Maine (*Ancient Law; Lectures on the Early History of Institutions; The Village Communities of the East and West*) and M. Emile Lavelèye (*De la propriété et de ses formes primitives*), and to indicate their conclusions.

Sir Henry Sumner Maine, in the works referred to, shows that the family and ownership of property were organised in an identical manner among the old Aryan peoples from Ireland to India.—The population was divided into clans or tribes whose members believed themselves to be connected by a family bond as the descendants of a common ancestor. At the head of the clan there were found chiefs, whom the Irish traditions called "kings." When the clan was numerous, it was subdivided into groups, whose members were united with each other by a bond of kinsmanship, and subject to a chief whom the Anglo-Irish legists designate under the name of "*capita cognationis*." These groups corresponded to the Roman *gens*, to the Greek γένος, and to the *gentes* or *cognationes hominum* of Germany, among whom, as Cæsar relates, the soil was divided every year. The juridical and political unit in the social order was not, as in the present day, the isolated individual, but the family group, denominated *Sept*, which corresponds exactly to the *Zadruga*, a family community which the Germans more properly designate *house-communion*. The *Sept* resembled those family groups, societies of *companions* or *frarescheux*, the confraternities which in the Middle Ages assembled in France in one large house (the *Sella*), and which cultivated the soil in common, and divided its products among each other. India, even in our day, offers us in the *joint-family*, as the English call it, the exact image of the Celtic *Sept* of Ancient Ireland. The joint-family forms a moral person which acquires property, and has a perpetual duration like all corporations of *mortmain;* and it offers the perfect type of that archaic mode of undivided enjoyment which is found in all primitive agricultural societies. It embraces all those persons who might have participated in the funeral sacrifices of the common ancestor. It resembles the agnatic family of the Romans, which comprehended all those who might have been subject to the authority of the common progenitor, if he had been still alive. According to the decisions of the courts of justice in India, no member of the family has a separate right to any part of the common property, but its products ought to be put in charge, and then divided according to the rules of an undivided enjoyment.

The members of the family are united, as it is said in India, by their *food*, their *worship*, and their *land*.—The Irish tribe constituted a civil person which was maintained by itself, as is said in the *Brehon Laws*. At first it was perpetuated with the possession of the land—" the land is a perpetual person;"—but it was also able to subsist without cultivating the soil, by the exercise of some industry. A part of the territory of the tribe, probably the arable land, was divided among the different families of the *clan;* although these quotas were subject to the control of the community. "Every one," says the law, "ought to preserve his land undiminished without selling it, without burdening it with debts, and without giving it away in payment by right or contract." As in all the ancient customs, alienation was permitted only with the consent of the whole community, and so it is still practised in India. The obligation to follow the same rotation of crops in the order of cultivation—the *Flurzwang*, as the Germans call it—is in this system as strict as in the Russian *mir*, and in the old German *village*. The words of Tacitus: *Arva per annos mutant*, are well interpreted in this sense by Belot. The annual abandonment of the settlements was caused by the nature of the soil, the scarcity of manure, and the insufficiency of the agricultural instruments.[1] In another passage Tacitus had laid emphasis on the nature of the proprietorship, stating : *Agri pro numero cultorum ab universis in vices occupantur quos mox inter se secundum dignationem partiuntur.* This division was no longer annual, as in the time of Cæsar, but it was made at indeterminate periods. The phrase of Tacitus, *apud eos nullum testamentum*, is applicable, not only to the Germans, but to the Irish Celts, and to all the primitive peoples.

Lavelèye remarks that "so long as primitive man lives by the chase, by fishing, and by the gathering of wild

---

[1] Cf. Nantucket, *Étude sur les diverses sortes de propriétés primitives.* Paris, 1884.

fruits, he does not think of appropriating the land, and he' considers as his own only the objects he has captured or fashioned by his hand. Under the pastoral *régime*, the notion of territorial property begins to dawn. It is attached, however, only to the space which the herds of each tribe habitually range over; and frequent quarrels break out on the subject of the limits of these ranges. The idea that an isolated individual could claim a part of the soil as exclusively belonging to himself, does not yet occur to any one; the conditions of the pastoral life are absolutely opposed to it. At the moment at which the Romans and the Greeks appear in history, they had arrived at a state of civilisation which is more advanced and more modern than that of the Germans of Tacitus. They had already passed for a long time from the pastoral *régime ;* they cultivated corn and the vine, and nourished themselves less on flesh. It was agriculture which furnished them with the greatest part of their subsistence. Nevertheless there still remained very recognisable traces of the primitive *régime* of the community. Thus cattle would not have been able to serve as a means of exchange, had not the greatest part of the land been a common pasturage, to which every one had the right to send his herds and flocks. The two customs are so closely connected, that the one cannot be conceived without the other. With individual and limited proprietorship I cannot receive oxen in payment; for how shall I nourish them? If cattle are used as instruments of exchange, it may be inferred from the fact that a great part of the soil is collective property." [1]

Leaving the Greeks aside, we shall accompany Mommsen in his exposition of the origin of property in the soil among the Romans. " Among the Romans the land was for a long time common good, and the ownership of immovable property is very recent. At first the owner- ship of property was limited to the possession of slaves

[1] *De la propriété et de ses formes primitives*, p. 4, 151. Paris, 1882.

and cattle (*familia pecuniaque*). . . . *Mancipatio*, the first
and universal form of sale, springs from the ancient period
in which ownership did not yet extend to the earth,
because it took place only in reference to those objects
which the hand of the acquirer could seize. The possession
of lands was originally a common possession, and it was
undoubtedly divided among the different family unions;
only the products were divided according to households.
In fact the agrarian community and the city, constituted
by family unions, were connected by close relations with
each other; and long after the founding of Rome, we still
meet true communists who lived together and cultivated
the soil. The language of the old laws shows that riches
at first consisted in herds and real rights, and that it was
only much later that the soil was divided as private property among the citizens. The original land estate was
called *heredium*, from *heres*, and it contained only two
jugera (about one acre and a third), a space like the extent
of a garden, and little greater than the small field enclosed
by hedges among the Germans. If the two *jugera* did
not suffice to support a family, it received a part of that
common land of the tribe or State, which was the original
ager publicus, and which gradually grew through the conquests of the kings and of the republic, and which was
very soon usurped by the patricians. This usurpation
was the occasion of the struggle of centuries between the
patricians and the plebeians, till the time of the emperors;
and to the plebeians it was a question of life. A group of
families which formed a *clan* inhabited a village (*vicus* or
pagus), the union of clans constituted the nation (*populus*)
or the State (*civitas*); and the State had, as its centre, a
fortified place or a citadel, which was always situated
upon a height."

In its development property followed the status of the
persons connected with it. At first the only proprietors
were the *cives optimo jure*. Their property was called
dominium quiritarium, and they were able to vindicate

it from any one. The necessities of life compelled the recognition of another species of property, called that *in bonis*, or *dominium bonitarium seu naturale*, to which the ancient law did not concede any right of action. The praetor supplied this by the *actio Publiciana*, which took the place in this connection of *vindicatio*. The citizens no sooner became all equal under the empire, than these old distinctions disappeared, and the right of property consisted of these three elements : (1) The right to use the thing without otherwise appropriating its fruits, that is, to apply it simply to one's own use, advantage, and enjoyment *(Jus utendi)*; (2) the right to gather the fruits produced by the thing *(Jus fruendi)*; (3) the right to draw from the thing a utility by changing it, transforming it, and even destroying it *(Jus abutendi)*, which, in the juridical language of the Romans, did not mean to make a bad use of it, as it is written in the Institutes : *expedit reipublicae ne sua re quis male utetur*.

Under these free proprietors lived the cultivators or farmers and the slaves. The former were also called *rustici, originarii, adscriptitii, inquilini, tributarii, censiti*, words which all indicated a class of men who lived on the land and were engaged in agricultural labours. They were not slaves ; they were able to marry at will, and to have recourse to magistrates on occasion of grave injuries to their persons, or in reference to exactions that went beyond use and wont. They constituted a part of the estate like the cattle *(servi terrae glebae inhaerentes)*, and they were not entitled to abandon it under any pretext, the proprietor having a right to reclaim them even from among the ranks of the clergy. The fruits of the land belonged to them, and they owed to the proprietor only an unalterable proportion in commodities *(redditus annuae functionis)* fixed by custom. The slaves possessed a *peculium*, but it was always at the disposal of their master.

The Germans—as we are told by Cæsar, Tacitus, and

Ammianus Marcellinus—had likewise agriculturists and slaves. The former were hereditary cultivators of the lands which were conceded to them for a regulated consideration; the latter were bound to domestic services or to the cultivation of the lands reserved for the daily uses of the family. In the bosom of the families were formed the *bands* which elected a chief for some distant expedition. Tacitus says: " If a tribe languishes in the idleness of a long peace, the principal youths go to the nations which are at war, because repose is irksome to this people. The warriors become illustrious in the midst of dangers; and it is only by means of war that they can preserve many followers." [1]

The Roman Empire was invaded by these bands, which brought with them the organisation of the tribe, with the addition to it of the bond of military subordination. The chiefs spread themselves over vast domains, where they lived along with a few companions in arms. The organisation of the tribe could not but be altered by their change of place. In Germany the sovereignty in relation to general affairs belonged to the assembly of the heads of families or proprietors; and in reference to particular affairs, to every single head of a family. This last species of sovereignty had a double origin and a double character. On the one hand, it had the bonds and the customs of the family, the proprietory head being the chief of the clan, surrounded by his relatives, down to the most distant grade, and in every kind of condition ; and on the other hand, it was founded upon conquest and force, a part of the territory having been occupied with arms in their hands, and the conquered having been reduced almost to slavery. After the conquest the reunion of the common assembly became always more difficult ; and consequently there remained only the second form of sovereignty, which extended itself, not only over the cultivators and slaves of the Roman world, but also over the free men who had

---

[1] *De morib. Germ. c. xiv.*

come from Germany. Guizot accordingly says : " How was it possible for those who were living beside a chief who had become a great proprietor possessed of a thousand means of influence, and whose superiority increased every day, to preserve long that equality and that independence which the companions of the same band formerly enjoyed ? Evidently this could not be. Those free men who, after the invasion, still lived for some time around their chief, were not long in becoming divided into two classes : some received benefices, and, having become proprietors in their turn, they entered into the feudal association ; others, always fixed in the interior of the domains of their ancient chief, fell either into a condition entirely servile, or into that of cultivators working a part of the land under obligation to discharge certain services or performances." [1]

Three centuries had passed from the time of Tacitus, and temporary possession had become converted into proprietorship. The first act by which the barbarian invaders affirmed their power over the conquered Romans was the partition of the lands. Thus arose the feudal system (*feodum*, from *fe* or *fee*, wage, and *od*, possession), which ruled property during the Middle Ages. However, by degrees, the kings from *grands fieffieux* became really heads of the nation, and claimed for themselves all the sovereign prerogatives. Nevertheless, those thousand abuses did not cease which had confused the persons with the land, to the shame of all the powers of the legists, who strove to bring about the triumph of the conception of the Roman proprietorship and of absolute monarchy, which attributed to the king not the *dominium eminens*, but full proprietorship in the goods of their subjects. It so appears in this passage in the Instructions written by Louis XIV. for the Dauphin : "Everything that is found throughout the whole of our States, of whatever nature it be, belongs to us by the same title. You ought to be persuaded that kings are absolute lords, and have

---

[1] *Histoire de la Civilisation en France*, Leçon xxxiii.

full right of disposal over all the goods possessed by ecclesiastics and laymen so as to use them at any time."[1]

The French Revolution of 1789 limited the powers of the king, and removed all confusion between persons and possessions. In the celebrated night of the 4th August, Feudalism was abolished, all personal servitude being made to cease without any compensation, and facility being given for redeeming every real servitude. By personal servitude, says the Instructions of 15th June 1791, is meant a subjection imposed on the person, and which he has to bear only because he exists or dwells in a particular place. The report of Merlin adds: "There are abolished without possibility of restoration personal servitudes and the rights which are derived from them or which represent them; that is to say, such as are not sprung from contracts of infeudation or from taxation, and which are due only from persons independently of all possession of the soil, and which have as their basis only the bold usurpations of feudalism maintained by the power of the lords of the soil, legitimated by the *law of the strongest.*"[2] These wise restrictions were set aside by the Legislative Assembly, which respected only the rights resulting from a primitive concession of the soil, rights which, however, were not respected by the Convention.

After a long course of centuries, the notion of property returned to what it was in the Roman Law, to which corresponds, in the main, Article 544 of the French Civil Code, which became Article 436 of the Italian Code, and which runs as follows: "Property is the right to enjoy and to dispose of things in the most absolute manner, provided that there is no use made of it which is forbidden by the laws and the regulations."

Among the other non-Aryan races property passed through nearly the same changes. The Mosaic law for

---

[1] Henri Martin, *Histoire de France,* t. xiii. p. 259, 4th ed. Paris, 1854. *droit français,* vol. ii. p. 94. Paris 1859.
[2] Laferrière, *Essai sur l'histoire du*

maintaining property in the same tribes and in the same families, cancelled debts every seven years, and commanded the restitution of alienated lands every forty-nine years at the great Jubilee. Among the Arabians, property consisted in movable objects and in cattle; and even in the present day the land in Algeria belongs in common to the members of the *douar* or village, to whom it is distributed by the Cadi. After the Mohammedan Conquest the lands abandoned by the infidels, and divided among the believers, constituted a real individual property which was transmissible by sale, donation, and succession. The Koran and the Sunna acknowledge full proprietorship in desert lands that have been rendered fruitful by labour. "If any one gives life to a dead land," says Mohammed, "it belongs to him." Nevertheless, the free proprietorship, called *mulk*, is an exception in Mussulman countries. Fabrics and trees form objects of property, but not the land that supports them—called *emerié*—which belongs to the State, and is given in simple enjoyment to private individuals. The Christians are simple tributaries, the hereditary possession of the land belonging to them on condition of labour and of tribute. Originally such tribute was assigned to the Arab chiefs in certain given territorial circumscriptions, which have been erroneously compared by writers to feus, although, as Renan points out, the most essential element in the feudal system, the land, was wanting in the arrangement.

Of the nations belonging to the Turanian race, China has practised all the systems of ownership in property from complete community to equal division of the soil; and this latter arrangement has been carried so far as to demand that every possessor should cultivate his share with his own hands, a refinement not yet reached by the modern socialists. Nevertheless, according to Eugène Simon, formerly French consul in China, a portion of the property is inalienable in the case of every family. At the beginning, this inalienable part extended to thirty

hectares (about seventy-four acres), but now it is reduced
on the average to three or four *hectares*, and is called the
patrimonial field. Of 330 millions of hectares which
constitute the territory of China, from 70 to 75 millions
are found thus restricted. The patrimonial field represents
the whole tradition of the family. It is there that we
find established their habitation and their burying-ground;
in it rises the hall where twice in the month the family
assembles to judge the delinquencies and the offences and
shortcomings of the members of the family; and it is
there where the family archives are preserved. According to Simon, this system keeps the inhabitants in the
country instead of turning their minds from cultivation,
and driving them into the cities, as is the case in Europe.

America was peopled by a northern offshoot or branch of
the Turanian race. To the greater part of the population
of the new continent the land was common to the tribe
for the purposes of the chase and fishing; and custom
recognised only movable property. However, the two
empires of Peru and Mexico raised themselves to a certain degree of civilisation. Here is what Robertson writes
regarding the system of ownership in property: "The
state of property in Peru was no less singular than that
of religion. . . . Neither individuals nor communities had
a right of exclusive property in the portion set apart for
their use. They possessed it only for a year, at the ex-
piration of which a new division was made in proportion
to the rank, the number, and exigencies of each family. . . .
In the Mexican Empire the right of private property was
perfectly understood, and established in its full extent.
Every person who could be denominated a freeman had
property in land. . . . The tenure by which the great
body of the people held their property was very different.
In every district a certain quantity of land was measured
out in proportion to the number of families. This was
cultivated by the joint labour of the whole; its produce

was deposited in a common storehouse, and divided among them according to their respective exigencies." [1]

Facts, the sons of the free will, had an influence upon ideas, the daughters of reflection. Minos and Lycurgus reduced to laws the Dorian customs that prevailed in the island of Crete and at Sparta. Pythagoras raised them to a doctrine in the maxim: " Everything is common among friends." It is still disputed as to whether Pythagoras wished to found an institute of education for wise men and statesmen, or set forth a social ideal. The first hypothesis is the most probable; and thus his communion would only have been voluntary, and limited to a certain period of life.

Plato, in the *Republic*, set himself to formulate this ideal by abolishing individual property and the family. He was not long in perceiving that he had gone much beyond the mark; and, wishing to take account of the prejudices and of the weakness of his compatriots, he delineated in the *Laws* the plan of a society less perfect but more adequate to the ideas of his time. However, the dream of community of possession always followed him. Here is how he expresses it in Book ix.: "I declare, in my quality of legislator, that I do not regard either yourselves or your goods as your own, but as belonging to all your family, which with all its goods belongs to the State." Under the guidance of these principles, he divides the territory into 5,040 portions, a number equal to that of the active citizens, that is, of those who have the right to participate in the administration of the State and to carry arms. Each of these portions is inalienable and indivisible ; and they are distributed by means of the lot. The use of the precious metals and borrowing at interest, as well as the industrial and commercial professions, are severely interdicted from the active citizens. The trades are exercised by slaves under the direction of free artisans,

---

[1] *The History of America*, Book vii.

who are devoid of political right; and commerce is left to strangers, choosing out the *least corrupt* among them. Every active citizen is to be entitled to transmit at his death to one of his sons the portion of land possessed by him ; but the laws are formally opposed to allowing more than one portion to fall into the same hands. The citizens might possess movable riches up to four times the value of their lands ; but how were they ever to acquire them, not being able either to work, or to use monies in gold or silver, or to borrow on interest, or to carry on trade ? Perhaps by booty acquired in war. All the citizens were to be fed at one table, at the expense of the State. In order to maintain the balance between the number of citizens and the portions of the land, the magistrates were from time to time to interdict generation ; and if this remedy turned out insufficient they were to think of founding a colony abroad. As to women, they are not to be common as in the Republic ; but they are to take part in the labours of the men, as also in the dangers of war.

Aristotle observes that property is an essential part of the Family and also of the State, because men have wants, and ought to have wherewith to satisfy them. He maintains against Plato the utility and the legitimacy of property; considering it, however, as a fact, the origin of which it is idle to investigate. The law, agriculture, and booty appear to him three modes of acquisition, equally legitimate. Occupancy, even by means of force, seems to him the useful beginning and principle of property. And indeed in antiquity, property could not appear but as a violent fact, protected afterwards by the law, which modified it arbitrarily every day. Nothing was more common among the ancients than the intervention of the Government in the distribution of properties, division of lands, abolition of debts, and the prohibition of any abandonment of one's patrimony. All these provisions which we regard as contrary to right, were very frequent in the republics of Greece ; and Aristotle cites various examples of them.

Christianity tempered the rigour of property by charity. We bring all that we possess, says Justin Martyr, and divide it with the needy. Everything is common among us except the women, says Tertullian. St. Peter had expressly acknowledged the right of property; for, in the passage of the Book of Acts, in which Ananias and his wife are shown to be punished with death for having concealed a part of their possessions, we read these words: "Whiles it remained, was it not thine own? and after it was sold, was it not in thine own power?"

The community of goods was, therefore, entirely voluntary, and the Fathers of the Church explain to us how that riches and poverty exist in order to furnish the rich with occasion for their liberality, and the poor with occasion for patience. It will suffice to cite the passage of the letter of St. Augustine to Hilary, in which he recalls the fact that Jesus Christ, in His answer to the rich man who asked Him what he should do in order to be saved, did not say, "Go and sell all that you have," but only "*Keep the commandments.*" And he adds that the Redeemer, when He says that it is very difficult for a rich man to enter into the kingdom of heaven, does not condemn riches, but the immoderate love of them. Then, coming to the text in the Gospel which says, "If ye would be perfect, go and sell all that you have, and give to the poor," St. Augustine proves that these words contain an advice, and not a precept. "Jesus Christ," he says, "distinguishes precisely between the observance of the precepts of the law and a more elevated perfection; because, on the one hand, He teaches if ye would attain to eternal life, keep the commandments; and, on the other hand, if ye would be perfect, go and sell all that you have." Why then, exclaims the sainted doctor, should the rich who do not attain that degree of perfection, not be able to be saved if they keep the commandments; if they give that it may be given to them, if they pardon that they may be pardoned? This attitude and contention of the Church have never been belied : for in the first century it condemned the communism of the Nicolaitans ; in the second, third, and fourth centuries it repudiated the communism of the Gnostics ; in the fifth century, that of the Pelagians ; and in the Middle Ages, that of the Cathari, the Paterini, the Fraticelli, the Lollards, and others.[1]

In modern times not a few attacks have been directed against individual property. Sir Thomas More, Lord Chancellor of England, when a young man, wrote his *De nova insula Utopia*,[2] in imitation of Plato's *Republic*. He admitted slavery, to which those who were condemned for grave crimes and prisoners of war were to be reduced. Its only variation from Plato's conception consists in all classes, including even the magistrates, being obliged to apply themselves for some hours to manual labour, which was then beginning to be held in esteem, and in admitting liberty of conscience, the need of which was being strongly felt. The impress of Plato's mind is still more clearly seen in the *Civitas Solis* of Thomas Campanella, in which there is advocated promiscuity of women, and their perfect equality with men both in rights and in duties. Old men and matrons, under the surveillance of the chief physician and the triumvir Amor, provide for the satisfaction of the desires without ever losing sight of the perfection of the race. A supreme head assigns labour and rewards it.

A century later, Morelly published "The Code of Nature" (*Le Code de la nature*, 1755), of which the following are the fundamental laws :—

" I. Nothing in society shall belong as property to any one individual except the things of which he may make use at the moment for his wants, his pleasures, and his daily labour ;

---

[1] Thonissen, *Le socialisme dans le passé*, ch. iv. p. 93. Bruxelles, 1850.
[2] *Utopia*, new edition, with Lord A. Saint-John. London, 1852. Bacon's *New Atlantis* and an analysis of Plato's *Republic*, and Notes by I.

"2. Every citizen shall be considered a public man, and maintained at the expense of the State;

"3. Every citizen shall contribute to the public utility according to his powers, his talent, and his age; and by this standard his duties shall be regulated conformable to the laws of distribution."

Rousseau a few years before had said that "Society is the universal and sovereign proprietor of all that is possessed by its members;" and elsewhere he says again that the fruits belong to all, and the land to nobody.[1]

Whatever may have been the influence on the French Revolution of Rousseau and the other writers of the eighteenth century, such as Diderot, Mablay, Linguet, and Bissot de Warville, who were all opposed to individual property, yet the Convention put the declaration at the head of the Constitution of 1793 that property is "the right which belongs to every citizen to enjoy and dispose of his goods, his revenues, and the fruit of his labour, or of his industry." Nevertheless, in 1797, after the fall of Robespierre, Babeuf founded the *Sect of Equals*, whose conspiracy was discovered just at the moment when it was about to take action. In their manifesto to the French people it was written that if the Constitution of 1793 was a step towards equality in fact, there was needed another revolution, and the last in order to make all social difference disappear. May all the arts perish if need be, if only we attain to actual equality. Various projects of decrees had been designed to bring this desire to effect. We may note that which instituted national workshops.

The unsuccessful attempt of Babeuf was taken up again by Louis Blanc in 1848. He had been preceded by Fourier and Saint-Simon, the first of whom had developed the idea of attractive labour sketched by Sir Thomas More, all the inhabitants of a State being divided into so many groups of 3,200 persons each, which would

---

[1] *Contrat social, Discours sur l'origine de l'inégalité.* Dijon, 1751.

have to absorb all capital and industries; and the latter
had taken from Campanella the idea of a supreme head,
the distributor of labour and of its reward according to
the work done.

The last and most violent adversary of property was
Proudhon, who wished to reduce it to an indefinite possession. Property, he said, has a just foundation, which
is the liberty of the labourer to possess the fruit of his
labour; but property became unjust by becoming capital.
On the other hand, community, although it springs from
a just idea, is the most odious of the forms of injustice,
because it ignores personality. How is this antithesis
to be reconciled? The synthesis is furnished to us by
the idea of mutuality. The ideal society is an association
of free workers who are independent, who live in families
without any other capital than their instruments of
labour, and who exchange their products according to
the principle of mutuality, which is thus formulated:
"Equal wages for an equal time of work." The State
will be made up of these associations of workers; and
there will be no idle consumers, no political government,
almost no magistrateship or police, except such as shall
be spontaneous, special, and local. Hence Proudhon's
system has taken the name of *Mutualism* and *Anarchism.*
There is still another system called *Collectivism,* which
consists in taking possession (according to some, by means
of purchase, or, according to others, by force) of the
material instruments of production, in order to put them
at the disposal of the manual labourers.

Let us now cast a glance at the views of those who
maintain individual property. Thomas Aquinas reproduced the theory of Aristotle, explaining that property,
if not a natural right, is not contrary to natural right,
to which he adds "per adinventionem rationis humanae,"
or by law. Grotius could not rise in regard to property
above what was taught by the Roman jurisconsults. He

sees the origin of it in occupation, and he acknowledges
the part belonging to work in mobiliary and industrial
accession.

Locke was the first to find the origin of property in
labour. What is the principle, he asks, by which,
without convention and without the intervention of
authority or law, man becomes proprietor in the universal
community? This principle, he answers, is labour; for
although the land and the lower creatures are common,
yet every one has a particular right to his own person.
The labour of his body and the work of his hands are ·
undoubtedly his own property: whatever he has removed out of the state of nature by means of his toil
and his industry belongs to him, for as this toil and
industry are his own exertion, no other ought to appropriate the fruits of it, and all the more when there
remain for others similar common things. He adds,
treating specially of property in land: "But the chief
matter of property being now not the fruits of the earth
and the beasts that subsist on it, but *the earth itself,* as that
which takes in and carries with it all the rest: I think
it is plain that property in that too is acquired as the
former. As much land as a man tills, plants, improves,
cultivates, and can use the product of, so much is his
property. He by his labour does, as it were, enclose
it from the common. Nor will it invalidate his right
to say everybody else has an equal title to it; and
therefore he cannot appropriate, he cannot enclose, without the consent of all his fellow-commoners, all mankind.
God, when He gave the world in common to all mankind,
commanded man also to labour, and the penury of his
condition required it of him. God and his reason commanded him to subdue the earth, *i.e.,* improve it for the
benefit of life, and therein lay out something upon it
that was his own, his labour. He that in obedience to
this command of God, subdued, tilled, and sowed any
part of it, thereby annexed to it something that was his

property, which another had no title to, nor could without injury take from him."[1] Locke concludes that the limits of moderation should not be exceeded, and that in appropriating a quantity of things greater than our wants, we in a certain way take what belongs to others. It is the great question of the limitation of the right in property which thus presents itself to his mind.

The later writers, except those who, like Montesquieu, founded the right of property on the law, have done nothing but clear up and amplify what was indicated by Locke. The political economists from Quesnay to Turgot patronised the theory that property is derived from labour; and in recent times Carey and Bastiat maintained that all revenue or rent from land had its origin in labour.[2] Beaudrillart called the first occupiers not the privileged holders, but the martyrs of property. "This expression martyrs, which has escaped from me," he adds, "I will not withdraw, but I shall maintain and explain it. Often people do not know what they are speaking of when they speak of the naked land. The naked land is the bramble and the reptile; it is the pestilential marsh; it is struggle and suffering under the most painful forms; it is often death coming in consequence of horrible privations and maladies which slowly consume the heroic pioneer of culture and civilisation, and upon whom sophists afterwards will call down a malediction as all their reward. People believe that it is the land which made the primitive proprietor. The truth is that the proprietor became such only after having made the land: made the land, I say, not doubtless as regards its matter, in regard to which man creates nothing, but as regards its value, the only mode of creating which has been given to man."[3]

[1] *Two Treatises of Government*, II. c. v. 5th ed. London, 1728.
[2] See Bastiat's *Harmonies of Political Economy*, translated with notice of his life and writings by Patrick James Stirling, LL.D., F.R.S.E., 2nd ed.; and especially Dr. Stirling's note at p. 274.
[3] *Discours d'ouverture du cours au College de France.* Paris, 1858.

The philosophers also have been inspired by the words of Locke already indicated, namely, that the labour of his body and the work of his hands are man's patrimony. Labour, says Cousin, is only a continuous and regular application of human liberty, or of the active and voluntary force which constitutes our *ego;* it is only a prolonged occupation. Labour makes property sacred, but it is the respect due to the person which renders labour itself sacred.[1]

Kant had already maintained that specification gave rise to a sort of provisory property, which, in order to become definite, needed the consent of all the members of society. Accordingly contract, not the respect due to the human person, was the origin of the right of property, according to Kant.

Fichte held by the doctrine of natural right, declaring it to be a personal right of man in relation to nature that he ought to possess a sufficient sphere of action in order to draw from it his means of subsistence. This physical sphere ought to be guaranteed by the social activity in order that it may be made profitable by labour. Thus all ought to labour, and all ought to have wherewithal to labour. The younger Fichte, in his *System of Ethics,* says that the right to possess is an immediate and inalienable right which precedes all law. Property is possession conformable to the right guaranteed by the State, and it is instituted for the general good. Whence it follows that the proprietor is bound juridically to use his property well. "We shall yet come," he says, "to a social organisation of property which will lose its exclusively private character by becoming a true public institution. Then it will no longer be sufficient to guarantee to every one property legitimately acquired, but it will also be necessary to enable him to obtain the property which comes to him as the result of his legitimate labour. . . . Labour is a duty towards oneself and others, and he who does not

---

[1] *Histoire de la philosophie morale au XVIIIme Siècle.* Leçon vii.

labour does injury to others, and therefore deserves to be punished."

Ahrens, in his *Cours de droit naturel*, adds that property is the realisation of the means and conditions necessary for the development, physical or spiritual, of every individual, in the quality and quantity conformable to his rational needs. For every man property is the condition of his life and of his development. It is based on the very nature of man, and ought therefore to be considered as a primitive and absolute right, not resulting from any external act, such as occupation, labour, or contract. As the right is directly derived from human nature, it is enough to be a man to have a right to a property.

It is evident that the three last mentioned authors have confounded potentiality with actuality, and right with its realisation; and we reserve for the second part of our work on the Subjects of Right, the determination of the exact limits between the individual and society.

The limitation of the right of property has greatly exercised the mind of the philosophical political economist John Stuart Mill. "It is no hardship to any one," he says, "to be excluded from what others have produced: they are not bound to produce it for his use, and he loses nothing by not sharing in what otherwise would not have existed at all." Mill thus acknowledges a free activity anterior to labour, and he respects its effects. But his ideas become less precise when he treats of property in land. *The land* he represents as *the original inheritance of all mankind.* "When the 'sacredness of property' is talked of, it should always be remembered, that any such sacredness does not belong in the same degree to landed property. No man made the land. It is the original inheritance of the whole species. Its appropriation is wholly a question of general expediency. When private property in land is not expedient, it is unjust."

There are certain things, Mill says, which cannot enter

into commerce without necessarily becoming a monopoly, among which is the land, which gives a revenue to the proprietor as the price of his monopoly. Mill would leave intact the produce of labour and of capital, but he is of opinion that the State may and ought to put a special tax on the rental, which would restore to society the part which belongs to it in the individual property. He would give the proprietors the choice of giving up their land to the State at the current market price, supposing they were not willing to submit to the special tax.[1]

Others again propose the legal redemption of all immovable property.[2]

It is not surprising if this theory, known as the *Nationalisation of the Land*, has been proposed only in England, where from many historical reasons which we cannot here enter upon, the land is found in a few hands, and where it has become almost impossible to acquire it. But the International, an association of workmen, has wished to extend this operation also to the Continent, where the land circulates in the market like any other ware, and is oftener offered than asked.

The conclusion Laveleye comes to in the work already referred to, is more logical. He would restore gradually the primitive village community, which still exists in some of the cantons of Switzerland under the name of *Allmenden.* Such property would be divided into several categories according to the nature of the land, and would thus give forest, meadow, and arable lands. Every family would have the use of the forest, of the meadow, and of a portion of the other lands, under the obligation of cultivating it so as to draw from it its greatest possible produce. The partition would be revised from time to time in order to preserve the limits of equity, and to make room for new families. Thus the potentiality of proprietorship

---

[1] J. S. Mill, *Principles of Political Economy*, Book ii. c. ii.
[2] See Fawcett on the difficulty of applying such a project to England in his *Manual of Political Economy.* London, 1874.

would be combined with its actuality; and by equality in fact being made to hold place with equality in right, all social revolution would be rendered impossible.—In order to attain this ideal without violent commotions various means are proposed. These are the following: 1. To establish a maximum in material possessions; 2. To reduce to the fourth degree, or at most to the seventh, successions *ab intestato;* 3. To restrict the power of bequest by will to such persons only as are included within the said degrees of relationship; 4. Finally, expropriation for the public utility. As the lands might return to the community they would be distributed to the most indigent families, to which there ought likewise to be furnished a sufficient capital. The methods of cultivation ought to be prescribed by the commune, from which machines would also be held. In a word, co-operation is to be substituted for individual interest.—It is not considered that in such a system liberty would be sacrificed without advantage being obtained, unless emigration were to be imposed in order to keep up at a level of equality the number of those participating in the system. Besides, this is applicable only to small villages, as it is not possible to divide into infinitesimal fractions the lands which surround the large cities.

But is individual property not to have any corrective ? The laws ought to provide that it may be accessible to all, and that it shall not accumulate in a few hands. A good system of beneficence of which we shall speak in Chapter VI. should come to the aid of those who cannot obtain it under any form. The field is open to all, and the less fortunate cannot complain of not finding a place except by paying, since it is due to the capital accumulated by the labour of those who have preceded them that they find an extensive public domain, both material and intellectual, and that they are put into a condition for developing their faculties.

Thus far we have seen the basis of property in the

respect due to the human personality, its origin in occupation or labour sanctioned by conventional law, and its collective or individual form according to the different stages of civilisation. It now remains for us to consider it under the aspect of quantity and quality. Viewed in reference to quantity, we have exclusive property, or co-proprietorship (*condominium*), according as a physical or moral person possesses the rights of ownership over the whole thing, or over an ideal part of it, as for instance a sixth, a third, &c. The co-proprietor has all the rights included in ownership, but he cannot exercise them isolatedly. Under the point of view of quality, proprietorship may be full and whole, or incomplete and divided. Ownership is full when all the rights are exercised by a physical or moral person. It is divided when one has the right to dispose of the thing and the other to enjoy it, provided, however, that it be possible to obtain a consolidation of such rights, as occurs between the proprietor, the usufructuary, and the user, as well as between the *dominium utile* and the *dominium directum* in emphyteusis. The Roman laws also admitted the right of surface, which consisted in the buildings constructed on the soil, or on the area of a lower story, or in plantings made on the soil of another. The right of surface is not found in the French Code, nor has it an equivalent in the Italian Code; but theory and jurisprudence have retained it and qualified it as a species of *dominium utile*. In practice, we find that public administrative bodies grant building areas under the obligation of their restitution after an assigned period of enjoyment. The permission obtained to build on the foundation of another is no longer considered as a right of surface. Ownership in property may undergo dismemberments by necessary or conventional servitudes, and it may obtain increments by means of accession immovable, or movable and industrial. The first arises from alluvion, or by a piece of land removed by instantaneous force. The rule of alluvion is contiguity, and that of insular accession is proximity, except when this happens by instantaneous force, in which case the proprietor of the ground removed preserves his ownership, Movable accession arises from conjunction or union, specification, and mixture or confusion. When two movable things belonging to different owners come to be united in such a way as to produce a single whole, to which of the two do they belong? If they can be separated without perceivable deterioration of the one or the other, with the right of separation each one regains his own thing. But if they cannot be separated without deteriorating either the one or the other, the accessory follows the principal. But if the accessory thing is much more precious than the principal, the latter follows the former. Such is the general rule.

Industrial property is guaranteed in Italy by the Law of 30th August 1868, which secured the exclusive use in commerce of distinctive trade-marks and signs. It is encouraged by the exclusive right which is wont to be granted to discoverers and inventors. The oldest law of this kind is the English Statute of 1623, suggested by Lord Bacon. The American colonies imitated the example. The French Law of January 1791 followed. It was adopted in the law now in force of 5th July 1844, which served as a model for the legislative decree of 30th October 1859, regarding industrial patents, and it was extended to the whole kingdom by another law of 13th February 1864.

Movable property was the first to arise and the last to be developed. It has been developed by means of industry, man beginning to employ his muscular energy, then using that of the animals, and finally directly adopting natural agents. What a difference there is between the sharpened stake of the savage and the perfected plough, between the hollowed trunk of a tree and the steamboat, between the spindle and the domestic loom, and between the spinning-wheel and the power-loom!

Society feels the benefit of all industrial progress, and mechanical contrivance promises to reduce man to the simple director of material labour, making the forces of nature to labour for him. This beneficent influence is not restricted to the mode of production, but it extends also to the consumption of the products, because as the products cost less, a greater number will be able to use them, and thus industry will not only have abolished slavery, but it will also abolish misery. Thus the economist, F. Passy, exclaims : "Industrial property, instead of taking anything from the fund of the community, is just the constant agent which forms this fund; and the price when it is freely agreed to, is not an obstacle to the exchange of the gifts of nature, but facilitates it by rendering them accessible to all."

What are the relations of industry with religion, science, and art? If in the past religion assigned it a very subordinate place, yet it did give it a place in the social organisation in Italy and in Egypt. The *collegia opificum* of the Romans resembled the confraternities of the Middle Ages, when industry put itself under the protection of a Saint. Now that the great factories are substituted for domestic industry, the intervention of religion becomes always more necessary. Who knows whether we shall not see the religious corporations rising again under an industrial form? Day-nurseries and infant asylums take the place of the domestic hearth in the absence of the mother; but by what shall these be animated, if not by the spirit of religion? Science, again, is often occupied with the interests of industry; for it would return to its rudimentary state without the aid of mechanics, physics, and chemistry. Art adds taste to industry, that special quality which renders the commonest objects of life so valuable.

The State cannot deny to industry those guarantees which it concedes to religion, science, and art, as it also constitutes a legitimate end of human activity.

CHAPTER V.

COMMERCE.

INDUSTRY cannot be conceived as existing without Exchange. Even in the patriarchal state, the individuals produced for the family, and not each one for himself. Commodities then formed almost the only product, and services were regarded rather as a form of work than as a matter of exchange. By degrees wants increased, and it became necessary to provide things required for the use of the clan, of the village, &c., and the effect of competition began to make itself felt.

It is not only products or services that are exchanged for other products or services, but almost every human relation may *sensu lato* be called an exchange. Thus the Romans were in the habit of including in the *jus commercii et connubii* all the civil right which by degrees came to be conceded to the Plebeians. Vico thinks that in the earliest times all the clients were called *nexi*, as being *bound*, for the word "nexum" signified obligation, as appears from the text of the XII Tables: "Cum nexum faciet manicipiumque," &c., and the contractors were called *nexi*.

Modern society is distinguished from that of the early ages by the great number of its relations of Contract. In primitive times the individual did not enjoy any separate right by himself. He obeyed certain rules of action which were imposed upon him by the conditions under which he was born. The individual members of a family could not enter into contracts, because the family would

275

not have taken any account of the obligations which might have been imposed upon them. The heads of the family were able to undertake obligation for it; but it happened very rarely, and with such formalities, that the slightest inobservance of them produced the nullity of the obligation. Examples are to be found in the history of the Roman Law, which show us how the Romans began to dispense with one part of the ceremonial, and how the other parts were simplified, and how it was allowable to pass entirely from them under certain conditions. Thus it came about that certain contracts could be made without any ceremony, and they were properly those on which the activity and energy of the social relations depended.

The Roman scholars defined the "nexum" as *omne quod geritur per aes et libram.*[1] The first use of the *nexum* was to give solemnity to the alienation of goods, and it then came to be applied to the contract, which was considered as an incompleted sale. When the subject of the contract was not to be forthwith executed, the *nexum* was regarded as artificially prolonged in order to give time to the debtor. From the *nexum* four forms of contracts took origin: Verbal Contracts, Written Contracts, Real Contracts, and Consensual Contracts. It was only to these four classes of contracts that obligatory force was given, and in the case of any of the first three it was necessary to observe certain formalities, as the simple consent of the contracting parties did not suffice. In the verbal contract the *vinculum juris* was established by means of a stipulation, that is, a demand and a reply; the demand came from him who received the promise, and the reply came from him who promised. In the contract by writing an inscription was entered in the account-books of the families

<hr>

[1] "*Nexum* Manilius scribit omne quod per libram et aes geritur, in quo sint mancipi; Mucius Scaevola, quae per aes et libram fiant, ut obligentur, praeterquam quae mancipio dentur. Hoc verius esse, ipsum verbum ostendit, de quo quaeritur. Nam idem quod obligatur per libram, neque suum sit, inde *nexum* dictum."—VARR.

and on tablets, and in the real contract it was necessary that the delivery of the thing should be a subject of preliminary agreement.

In the course of time Real Contracts were distinguished into *Nominate*, as *mutuum, commodatum, depositum, pignus,* and *Innominate*, according to the formulae, *do ut des, do ut facias, facio ut des, facio ut facias* : many contracts of this kind receiving such special names as *permutatio, precarium,* the *contractus aestimatorius,* which consisted in a commission to sell a subject, and the *contractus suffragii,* the purpose of which was to obtain some favour from the prince by means of remuneration given to a courtier or to another person of high position who was not obliged by his office to perform the act in request.

Four Nominate Contracts—*mandatum, societas, emptiovenditio, locatio-conductio*—belong to the class of consensual contracts, the consent of the parties being sufficient to render them complete without the need of any formality ; and on this account they were derived from the right of nations (*jus gentium*).

Besides Contracts there were also *Pacts* in use, which did not induce civil action. Many of these, however, obtained civil authority from the Praetors (*pacta praetoria*), from the Imperial Constitutions (*pacta legitima*), or sometimes they were immediately adjoined to contracts of good faith (*pacta adjecta*).

The Roman Law has always distinguished Obligation from Convention. It defined the former thus : *Obligatio est vinculum juris quo necessitate astringimur ad aliquid dandum vel praestandum vel faciendum vel non faciendum ;* and it defined the second : *Conventio est duorum pluriumque in idem placitum consensus.* Looking to the origin of Obligations, they were divided into three classes, according as they arose *ex contractu, ex delicto,* or *ex variis causarum figuris.* The last class was subdivided according to the analogy which they have with a contract or a delict into obligations *quasi ex contractu et quasi ex delicto.*

They arose from a reason of natural equity acknowledged
by the law, as when the captain of a vessel binds the
owner, the agent, the merchant, &c. The Quasi-contracts
comprehend the carrying on of the affairs of others
(*negotiorum gestio*), tutory (*tutela*), curatory (*curatela*), the
acceptance of a succession (*additio hereditatis*), the administration of a thing which has accidentally become
common or of a succession still undivided, and the payment of a debt not yet due. The Quasi-delicts are acts
of negligence which result in harm to others.

Some more recent Jurisconsults make obligations spring
ex facto, ex lege, seu ex aequitate, and they include the
contract, as also being a fact, in the first class.

Among the interpreters of the Roman Law, it will be
enough to refer to Domat and Pothier, who have freed
this part of the Roman Law from the rubbish of the past,
and have introduced into it as much of Customary Law as
was necessary. The compilers of the French Civil Code
only reduced their treatises to Articles.[1]

According to the French Civil Code, conventions are
obligatory by the simple consent of the parties, without
its being necessary that there be delivery of the thing or
the execution of the act on the part of one of the contractors, or any extrinsic formality.[2] In principle this is
contrary to the Roman Law, according to which, as a
general rule, the consent of the parties is not sufficient to
render a convention civilly obligatory (§ 2, *Inst. de Oblig.*
3, 13).

Contracts are divided in the Civil Code into *unilateral*
and *synallagmatic* (*sensu lato*), according as one of the
parties is bound by obligation to the other without that

---

[1] See in Locré's *Législation civile,
commerciale et criminelle*, the dis-
courses of Bigot, Préameneau,
Favard, Joubert, and Moricault.
Vol. vi. Bruxelles, 1836.

[2] The French Code requires a
notarial act for donations, contracts
of marriage, constitutions of hypo-

thec, and surrogation without the
consent of the creditor. The Italian
Civil Code—wholly like the French
Code as regards the matter of contracts — requires the notarial act
only for donations and nuptial
deeds.

other party being bound, or according as the two parties are bound reciprocally towards each other. These Synallagmatic Contracts are subdivided into *perfect* and *imperfect*, according as the prestations to which the parties are bound are or are not considered to form the equivalent of each other. The perfect Synallagmatic Contracts are commutative when the equivalent consists in a certain advantage for each of the parties ; they are aleatory when the equivalent consists either only in reciprocal probabilities of gain or loss, or in a probability connected with an advantage that is certain for one or other of the parties.

Contracts are also distinguished into contracts with an *onerous* title, and contracts with a *gratuitous* title, or contracts of beneficence. Contracts are of an onerous title when the advantage which they procure for one or other of the parties is obtained only by means of a prestation that is executed or promised. Contracts are of a gratuitous title when they secure to one or other of the parties some advantage independent of any corresponding prestation. Synallagmatic Contracts are all, and necessarily, of onerous title; but Unilateral Contracts are not always contracts of beneficence.

Contracts are called Contracts of Acquisition or of Guarantee, according as their object is to increase or simply to guarantee the patrimony of the two parties, or of one of them. They are nominate or innominate, according as the law does or does not indicate them under a special denomination. The rules established by the Civil Code for contracts in general are applied to all contracts, whether they be nominate or innominate; but the rules that are particularly laid down for the various nominate contracts are applicable only by analogy to innominate contracts.

The Quasi-contracts are licitous (allowable) and voluntary facts, from which there result, of full right, either certain unilateral obligations on the part of him who performs them, or certain reciprocal obligations towards those to whom such facts have brought damage or advantage. The Civil Code in respect of quasi-contracts speaks only of the *gestio negotiorum,* or the receipt of *indebitum.* Nevertheless the administration of a particular thing still undivided among several persons who are not united by a social relationship of contract, when it is taken up without mandate by one of the beneficiaries, presents all the marks of a quasi-contract. The other quasi-contracts found in the Roman law are embraced, according to the classification of the French and the Italian Civil Codes, in the category of Legal Obligations.

Every human activity may be the subject of contract, as a prestation may consist either in the prestation of a thing or in the accomplishment of an act. A contract which is without a subject, or which has in view a prestation that is physically impossible, is considered as non-existent. The subject ought to be determined at least in its species, and it ought to offer some pecuniary advantage to one of the two contractors, without which the execution could not be demanded in court, as all questions of doing resolve themselves into questions of giving. Finally, the subject ought to be licitous, or, in other words, it ought not to be contrary either to moral custom or to public order. The cause ought to be true and licitous. The existence of the contract is proved by testimonies or by titles, according to the amount of the sum and the circumstances in which it was instituted. All the subjective conditions requisite for the validity of contracts, will be treated in the sequel.

Almost contemporaneous with the compilation of the French Civil Code, Kant was occupied with the classification of contracts from the purely philosophical point of view. "All Contracts," says Kant, "are founded upon a purpose of acquisition, and are either—A. Gratuitous Contracts, with unilateral acquisition; or B. Onerous Contracts, with reciprocal acquisition; or C. Cautionary

Contracts, with guarantee of what has been already acquired. A. The Gratuitous Contracts are—1. Deposition; 2. Commodate; 3. Donation. B. The Onerous Contracts are—I. Contracts of Permutation or Reciprocal Exchange, including—1. Barter; 2. Purchase and Sale; 3. Loan. II. Contracts of Letting and Hiring. C. The Cautionary Contracts are—1. Pledge; 2. Suretyship; 3. Personal Security.[1]

Kant's classification has been retained by Hegel, by Ahrens, and by Gans, but Gans observes that it does not contain the contract of Association. Trendelenburg, in his *Naturrecht*, has tried to give another simpler Classification of Contracts as follows : " In relation to their objects Contracts have principally in view either a donation (where there is an advantage without a counter-exchange), or a simple exchange (permutation by prestation and counter-prestation), or an agreement with regard to a common affair (association). These three Species of Contracts have this in common, that they represent originally an agreement of different wills. In contrast to these there is a species of contract which aims at resolving a plurality of claims which have already arisen in a commercial relation, and which consequently tends to a division (transactions)."[2]

Hitherto we have used the word *Commerce* in its widest juridical signification. But it is also employed in a more limited acceptation, to indicate the relations which arise from the Exchange of present or future values,—relations

---

[1] See Kant's Classification more fully in the English translation of his *Philosophy of Law*, p. 122. (T. & T. Clark, 1887.) Excepting the last contract, which belongs to international law, these are the Nominate Contracts of the Civil Law. Warnkönig truly remarks : Illi ipsi scriptores si quis eorum doctrinas examinaverit, NIL FERE NISI JURIS ROMANI REGULAS de obligationibus repetisse cernuntur, et raro quid sane docent, ubi ab illo jure recedunt. Neque hoc mirandum : nam sublato certo obligationum fundamento, quod ipsorum negotiorum natura ex juris civilis sanctionibus constituitur, fragmenta tantum et inanes definitiones tradi necesse est. *Doctrina juris philos.*, p. 158.

[2] *Naturrecht*, Th. ii. c. 1.

which constitute the object of Commercial Law, properly so called. Such Exchange forms the habitual occupation of certain individuals who buy in order to sell again, and it requires to be regulated in a special manner. The positive laws, following the guidance of reason, have modified in behoof of these persons the rules of certain contracts, such as Sale, Location, Mandate, Security, and Association; and they have created certain special contracts in this connection, such as the Letter of Exchange, Bottomry, and Maritime Insurance. Commercial Sale is distinguished by the speciality that it can be carried out in regard to a thing of which the seller is not the owner, and that the purchaser can obtain compensation at the expense of the seller when he is not punctual in the execution of delivery. The hire of work in the matter of Commercial Contracts is called Commission, and has special rights and duties, as when it is applicable to transports. Mandate is often transformed into a contract of commission, and the commissioner does not bind the committer, but only himself, towards third parties. Commercial guarantee necessarily requires a written act after it amounts to a certain sum; and the permission of the judge is required for the sale, which has to be carried out by public auction, except in the case of Banks authorised by their statutes to receive deposits and to give advances. The subject may not remain after valuation in the power of the creditor, as is the case with the civil pledge.

The contract of association or society in Commercial Law has undergone the greatest modifications. In the Civil Law, certain persons associated themselves together without a bond of copartnery, for a particular matter of business,—mostly in relations of patrimony,—and third parties were obliged to call them severally before the competent tribunal. In Commercial Law, on the contrary, such persons are bound altogether (*conjunctim*) and for all their goods in such a way that they form a juridical being with a fixed domicile, and the act constituting its existence is to be drawn up in writing, and accompanied with all the guarantees of publicity. This species of association is called by a collective name, and we find some examples of it in ancient times, especially at Rome, where they were formed for military supplies and for the collection of the taxes, with a capital divided into shares which were transferred by public or private acts. There is a second kind of association, in which some of the members are held responsible to third parties with all their substance, while others are bound only for the capital they have invested; the former being called *Commanditanti*, and the latter *Commanditari*. Troplong sees the origin of this kind of association in the contract of *Cheptel* (in cattle), of which an example is already found in the last period of the Empire. It was, however, in the tenth and eleventh centuries, and through the operations of Italian merchants, that this mode of association assumed its commercial form. The prejudices against interest on money, and the dread of staining the nobility of their house by appearing as merchants, induced many to adopt this plan of association. The latest kind of such association was the Anonymous Company, which is a simple association of capital. The credit transactions of the association are only binding on the acting administrators of it; but its formation, as well as the regulation of the shares, is subject to the approval of the civil tribunal as a matter of voluntary jurisdiction. The Association or Company with a limited liability has been introduced in England and France under the form of the anonymous association, and it does not require the approval of the Government. A last form of such associations is that which is called the "Society with variable capital." Its statutes make entrance or withdrawal free to members, but under the condition that the common capital must not be altered by more than a tenth of the whole. It has received legal existence in France and in Belgium.

In 1844 certain weavers of Rochdale—afterwards called

the *Equitable Pioneers*—entered into combination, in order
to obtain the means of living at a cheaper rate. Their plan
was to purchase sugar and tea in bulk, in order to sell
them retail to themselves and others at the current prices,
then dividing the profits among all the members of the
association at the end of the year. The same principle was
likewise applied to production, by giving the workmen an
interest in the success of an undertaking, from a certain
part of their wages being invested in shares. Germany
made a happy application of the co-operative principle to
credit by means of Advance Societies (*Vorschuss-vereine*).
They soon became People's Banks (*Volksbanken*), the
founder of which was Schulze-Delitsch, in 1851. He
united industrious operatives into societies, so that by
paying a trifling sum at entry, and with a small monthly
contribution, they accumulated reserve funds. The society
then borrowed money at interest under the collective
guarantee of all its members, and distributed it among
those who applied for it. In this way every industrious
operative who obtained admission into one of these
societies was sure to find the sum which he required to
carry on his little industry.

The new Italian Code of 1882 allows every kind of
society or association to take the co-operative form. But,
in order to render these associations accessible to all, it
is enacted that the share shall not exceed one hundred
francs. To hinder any one who has subscribed for a large
number of shares from imposing his own will upon the
other members, the Code interdicts the holding of shares
to more than five thousand francs, and it prescribes that
in the meeting of shareholders a vote shall be given to
every person without taking account of the number of
shares held. Finally, in order to avoid speculations on
'Change, it is laid down that the shares shall be nominated,
and that it shall not be allowable to cede them without
the consent of the council of managers or the meeting of
shareholders, according to the conditions provided in the

statute. The voluntary withdrawal of members is permitted, but they remain bound to third parties for a period of two years for the operations current, and up to the amount of the shares held.

We come now to Contracts of a purely Commercial origin, namely, the Bill of Exchange and Maritime Exchange or Bottomry. In Athens the idea was already formed of a Bill payable to order, and the Letter of Exchange was not entirely unknown. In a harangue of Isocrates against Pasion, we find that a certain Stratocles, when about to set out for Pontus, preferred to leave a sum with a young man of that country then residing in Athens, receiving a letter to his father that he should pay him it in Pontus, and the banker Pasion guaranteed the contract. Cicero, writing to Atticus, asked him if he should convey a sum to his son in Athens by way of exchange or in kind. In ancient times, transference by endorsement was unknown, so that it is rightly held that the Bill of Exchange was invented in the Middle Ages, and probably by the Jews. The German Law of Exchange does not recognise any difference in the legal effects of a Bill of Exchange and of a Note payable to order, regarding them both as by their nature acts of commerce. This principle is adopted in the new Commercial Code of the kingdom of Italy of 1882. The Letter or Bill of Exchange is defined as a commercial obligation to make payment at a definite place and time of a sum to the order, mediate or immediate, of the possessor of this obligation. On the other hand, the Note payable to order is an obligation to pay at a determinate time a certain sum to the legitimate possessor of the claim. Both are transferred by endorsation.

Transactions in Bottomry or Maritime Exchange (*foenus nauticum*) were known to the Romans, and Cato was able to make large profits by them. In the Contract of Bottomry, the debtor is discharged from repaying the capital and interest if the ship perishes in the course of the voyage. On the contrary, if fortune favours it, he has to restore the sum borrowed at "nautical interest," which is much higher than the ordinary rate. After the invention of the compass and of navigation by steam, the dangers at sea were greatly diminished, and this contract began to fall into disuse.

The last of the Commercial Contracts is that of Marine Insurance, which consists in undertaking the risks that may be run by a vessel and its cargo during the voyage. By paying a small premium, security is given against all accidents at sea. Marine Insurance has served as a type to all other kinds of insurance.

The merchant is favoured by special privileges in regard to the means of proof at law. He is entitled to establish his proof by the commercial books in which all his obligations are regularly entered, and these are valid against him as evidence, and may be used as valid evidence against third persons, provided they are merchants having transactions with him; he can also establish his proof by the books of public officers regularly kept; and finally, by the oral testimony of witnesses, without limit as to the amount, whenever the judicial authority believes it convenient. By making a declaration of his bankruptcy (which, however, must neither be fraudulent nor culpable), a merchant may be released from all obligations to his creditors. Moreover, a majority of the creditors, who represent three-fourths of the claims, by drawing up an agreement, are able to compel opposing creditors to accept it, and to avert the bankruptcy. A special jurisdiction, with adequate knowledge of the commercial usages, will have to decide all differences that may arise.

It may be asked, What have the other branches of human activity done for commerce?—Even from the most remote times religion came to the aid of commerce. Commerce took its start in the wallet of the pilgrim and on the back of the camel. The most celebrated temples of antiquity, of which some were founded in the oasis of the desert, and were places of rest and refreshment for the caravans, became the centres of the greatest markets. In Africa, such were the temple of Jupiter Ammon, and of Meroë and Assum in Abyssinia; and in Asia there were Manoraba or Mecca in Arabia, Palmyra in Syria, and Pataliputra (the *Palibothra* of Megasthenes, now *Patna*) in India.

Commerce was carried on by land, and with much difficulty, so that only goods of great value could be transported, such as the precious metals, pearls, perfumes from natural products, and byssus (the finest tissue of Indian cotton), the superfine woollen tissues of Thibet, some of the silks of China, and of the works in ivory from India.

By degrees the commerce of the coasts sprang up, and it stretched from the Arabian Sea, touching the Persian Gulf, and on to India, and perhaps to China. In the Mediterranean Sea, the Phœnicians, who came, according to Herodotus, from the Red Sea, occupied the coasts of Asia and of Africa, and, advancing by the columns of Hercules, spread themselves over the shores of Spain. They found rivals in the Greeks, who covered with their colonies the Euxine Sea, the Palus Mœotis, and Magna Græcia, founded Cyrene in Africa, Marseilles in Gaul, and lastly Alexandria, the greatest emporium of antiquity. With the development of maritime commerce there were transported, not only objects of luxury, but also commodities, and especially corn. The Romans were not a commercial people, but their highways, their harbours, and their maintenance of so many different nations in unity, indirectly aided the progress of commerce.

The Arabs may be called the successors of the Romans, if regard is given to the extent of the empire of the Caliphs, which stretched from the Tagus to the Indus. Europe groaned under the barbarian invaders, but by degrees the ancient Roman cities rose again, first in Italy, then in Germany along the Rhine, and others were founded in Flanders and on the Baltic, which were bound in league among themselves. This great movement had been aided by the Crusades, which poured the West upon the East, erected a Latin empire at Constantinople which lasted fifty-four years, and a kingdom at Jerusalem which lasted eighty-six years. The North carried into Italy its products in wool, hemp, flax, and building timber, in order to exchange them for the products of the East. Silk was raised by means of the few silkworms which two monks brought in their staffs to Justinian; and the cultivation of it spread into Greece, Italy, and France. Navigation was rendered more secure by the use of the compass and the astrolabe.

The course of commerce was disturbéd by the founding of the Ottoman Empire in the thirteenth century, and more than ever by the conquest of Constantinople and of Egypt. The need was then felt to find a new way to India and China. The Portuguese succeeded in finding it by sailing round Africa, and discovering the passage of the Cape of Good Hope, and they made Lisbon the emporium of the Eastern commerce. Voyages of discovery were then multiplied, and Christopher Columbus, going in search of the Indies by the western ocean, found a new world. Science likewise came to the aid of commerce. Doria taught how to take advantage even of contrary winds; and Galileo having discovered the satellites of Jupiter by means of observations on their eclipses, showed the way to determine the latitude of any particular place. Railways and the electric telegraph have now turned the whole earth into a common market-place.

Art did not advance commerce, but it was greatly aided by commerce. The Medicis at Florence co-operated by their riches in creating many masterpieces; and the Flemish and Dutch schools were really born in the bosom of trade.

Industry thus furnishes the material of commerce, and if its first development took place in the East, this arose from the fact that production, both natural and artificial, had its cradle in that favoured land of the sun. And now that iron and coal play the principal part in industrial production, commerce shows its predilection for the North.

In ancient times the State did not show itself in any way particularly favourable to commerce any more than to industry; but neither did it oppress it with special burdens, as it has been shown superabundantly that customs tariffs were then mere fiscal imposts. The errors of the mercantile system, which made wealth consist principally in the precious metals, generated the prohibitive system, and thereafter the colonial system, which, instead of aiding commerce, injured it, as it did not supply the consumers with all that they desired. Men came to understand that wealth consisted in all kinds of products and was born of labour; yet prohibition did not therefore cease, but was transformed into protection. It is only since the first quarter of the present century that the State has restricted itself to its mission of guardianship in relation to commerce, and has been gradually reducing the customs tariffs to simple fiscal dues.

CHAPTER VI.

MORALITY.

In distinguishing ethics from jurisprudence and morality from right, we explained that the former considers the internal forum, and the latter the external forum. However, we added "that the internal ends of morality are the moving forces of right."[1] Society cannot leave to the caprice of individuals the whole of morality, although it is now accurately distinguished from legal right.

History shows us public power rising from the household, and in the ancient States various institutions safeguarded private morality. At Sparta, it may be said that private life in a manner did not exist, as the whole time of the citizens was there regulated. At Athens there was entire liberty, but the Areopagus watched over the habits of the people, and jealously scrutinised the conduct of all candidates for public offices. At Rome two magistrates were appointed in the year 444 B.C., to whom were entrusted the material and moral supervision and censorship of the republic. They watched the public revenues, drew up the list of the senators and knights, marking with disgrace whoever had in any degree forfeited the public esteem. Under the Empire, they became instruments of the rancour of the emperors. By degrees the Church appropriated the censorship of morals, and the ecclesiastical decisions became also of civil authority. After the French Revolution, the State became secular, and certain great moral principles were formulated into

[1] *Prolegomena*, p. 121.

articles of law, such as: "The son, whatever may be his age, ought to honour and respect his parents;" "The law grants no action for payment of a debt contracted at play, or for a wager." The guardianship of other principles was entrusted to a discretionary power called *police,* the ideal of which is traced in a circular by the minister Fouché in 1815 as follows: "Calm in their movements, prudent in their investigations, everywhere present, and always protecting, the police ought to keep an eye on the progress of industry and of morals, for the sake of the happiness of the people and the repose of all. It is instituted like justice in order to secure the execution of the laws and not to infringe them, to guarantee the liberty of the citizen and not to attack it, to secure the safety of virtuous men, and not to poison the source of social enjoyments. It should neither extend itself beyond what the public or private safety demands, nor check the free exercise of the faculties of man and of his civil rights by a violent system of precautions." According to the scope of these principles, the police have an immediate authority over public places, and especially over public exhibitions and shows, public women, &c.

Beneficence is a private virtue, but society cannot remain entirely strange or indifferent to the misfortunes of the citizens. It leaves associations to take action; but on great occasions, such as a flood or a conflagration, it intervenes directly. The principal argument advanced to keep the Government away from works of beneficence, is that the State has no goods of its own, and to give to one anything in the way of relief, would be to take from others as a tax. The same objection might be raised against several of the public services, but it does not prevent the Government from discharging such services as are really of general interest. The fundamental principle of all society is that every one ought to provide for his own wants and for those of his family by means either acquired or inherited; for all activity would cease if men were to count on anything else than their own labour. But in the case of sudden and immediate misfortunes a germ of love has been placed by God in every breast, and in all civilised countries there are not wanting benevolent foundations supported by common contributions or endowed by rich benefactors, to which the State has been ready to grant a civil personality.

The Constitution of the French Republic of 4th November 1848 sought to determine in its preamble the relations of the citizens and of the State in the matter of beneficence as follows: "The French Republic is democratic, one, and indivisible. It recognises rights and duties, anterior and superior to positive laws. It has as its principles liberty, equality, and fraternity; and as its basis the family, labour, property, and public order. . . . Reciprocal duties are binding on the citizens towards the Republic, and on the Republic towards the citizens. The citizens ought to love their country, to serve the Republic, to defend it at the cost of their lives, and to share in the burdens of the State in proportion to their fortune; they ought to secure the means of existence by labour, and in foresight to provide resources for the future; they ought to co-operate for the common well-being by aiding each other fraternally, and promote the general order by observing the moral laws and the written laws which regulate society, the family, and the individual. The Republic ought to protect the citizen in his person, his family, his religion, his property, and his work, and to put within the reach of every one the instruction indispensable to all men. It ought by fraternal assistance to secure the existence of the necessitous citizens, either by procuring for them work within the limits of its resources; or in default of the family to which they belong, by giving aid to those who are not in a state to work."

The commentary on this somewhat too elastic declaration is found in the General Report presented to the Assembly by Thiers in the sitting of 24th January 1850, in the name of the Commission of Beneficence and Public Provision. The reporter lays it down as a principle that the State is not an abstract and insensible being, that there are isolated and accidental evils for which private beneficence is sufficient, but that there are also general evils which afflict whole classes of citizens which require collective and social beneficence. He maintains, however, in several places the spontaneity of such acts of beneficence, whether public or private, wishing them to be free, but co-ordinated as far as possible. In the first period of life, he says, it is necessary to take up and nourish the child which the mother abandons from shame or insensibility, to succour the mother who has the courage not to abandon it, to watch over day-nurseries or infant homes, to prevent the tender powers of youths from being abused by labour, to take care if they fall into crime that the correction shall not become the occasion of greater perversion, and in fine, to protect them in the first stages of their life. In the adult age, the man is responsible for himself, and the State can only reserve a good part of the public works for times of crisis, keeping ready the plans of such works and the means of executing them. Societies for mutual help are the most appropriate means of avoiding disasters, and poorhouses should serve only for temporary reception of strong men till there is found work to employ them. For cases coming under disease and old age, provision should be made by hospitals and hospices, and especially by banks of deposit in which a small annual contribution is applied to provide a pension for old age. The reporter wished to see such banks administered by the Government and constituted on the tontine principle, that is to say, that the share of the one who dies first should go to the benefit of the survivors.

Let us see how such ingenious institutions are constituted. Chateaubriand asks: How did the ancients do without hospitals? And he answers that they had two means of getting rid of the poor and of the unfortunate, which the Christians no longer possess, namely, infanticide and slavery. This statement has been found too absolute by recent writers, who have remarked that the Mosaic legislation, with its Sabbatic year and its jubilee, was all inclined in favour of the poor. In pagan antiquity we likewise find consoling maxims, as in Homer's verse in the Odyssey, which says that "guests and the poor are under the protection of Jove," and in the passage of Cicero, beginning " hominum caritas et amicitia gratuita," &c. The institutions of the patronate and of hospitality, the *leges agrariae*, the *leges anonariae*, the *largitiones* or *congiaria*, the *epulae* and *sportula*, were directed to relieve the people from their distress. There were not wanting societies of mutual help, such as the φρατρίαι at Athens, and the *sodalitates* at Rome. In the time of Hippocrates the Greeks caused the sick to be carried into the temples of Æsculapius in order to invoke the favours of the divinity and the aid of his ministers. At Rome the temples likewise served to receive strangers who fell sick, and slaves who had been abandoned by their masters. At Athens, the Cynosarges, an ancient temple dedicated to Hercules, was destined for the reception of illegitimate children, who were reared at the expense of the republic. Augustus granted help to parents with a numerous offspring; and Nerva wished that in all Italy, orphans should be nourished at the public expense. In many Greek cities there arose public edifices, named γεροντοκομεῖα, devoted to keeping old men who deserved well of the country ; and at Sardis, the house of Crœsus served as an asylum for old men who had become unable to work. Various laws in the Digest imposed on the cities the duty of consecrating the surplus of their revenues to the support of children and of indigent old men.

With all this, paganism cannot be called charitable. It deified force, beauty, and pleasure, and held that the unhappy had somehow merited the wrath of the gods. The institutions above enumerated had almost all a political origin. The struggle of the rich and poor was fierce in the ancient cities. The first drew almost all the things necessary for their wants from the labour of the slaves, and the second claimed a right to idleness in order to attend to public affairs. Dionysius of Halicarnassus says that Romulus having put a great distance between the patricians and the plebeians, and having excluded the latter from the senate and from all public offices, required for the sake of the security of the State to find a means of bringing the two orders together and uniting them by some tie; and therefore he ordered that every plebeian should choose a protector among the patricians. The continual wars of Rome compelled the plebeians to neglect their fields and fall into debt. The little farm was very soon eaten up by the accumulation of interest, and the person of the debtor was made responsible for the rest. The law of the XII Tables says: "Let the rich man be surety for the rich man; and whoever will, let him be surety for the poor man. The debt being admitted and the cause adjudged, let there be thirty days' respite. . . . If no one become surety for him, let the creditor take him with him and bind him with ropes or chains, which may weigh fifteen pounds or less if the creditor so wishes it. Let the prisoner live at his own expense, or let there be given to him a pound of meal or more at pleasure." Happy was it for him, exclaims the historian Michelet, if by a prudent emancipation, he was able to preserve his sons. · And the same writer adds, although all the kings of the earth came to pay homage to the Roman people represented by the senate, this people was rapidly extinguished, being consumed by war and by devouring legislation. The Roman, spending his life in the field beyond the sea, did not return to visit his little estate. A constant exchange took place between Italy and the provinces, the former sending her sons to die in distant countries, and receiving in return millions of slaves, some of whom, attached to the land, cultivated it and fattened it with their bones, and others, crowded in the cities, ministered to the vices of their masters. The emancipated slaves and their offspring ended by forming the Roman people, and in the time of the Gracchi they almost alone filled the forum. One day, Scipio Æmilianus, exasperated by their interrogations, uttered these memorable words: "Taceant, quibus Italia noverca est; non efficietis ut solutos verear, quos alligatos adduxi."

Appian describes to us the remedies that were vainly tried to save the middle class. The following are almost his words: In the successive conquests of the various countries of Italy, the Romans used one part of the territory for building cities, or founding in the already existing cities, colonies of Roman citizens. The part of the territory of which the right of war had made them proprietors was distributed to the colonists if it was already cultivated, or sold, or farmed. But if, on the contrary, it had been devastated by war, as often happened, they put it up to auction in the state in which it was found for an annual return in kind, that is to say, for the tenth of the produce if it was adapted for being tilled, and for a fifth if covered with trees. The pasture lands were subject to a tribute in great and small cattle. It was the design of the Romans to increase the Italian race, which had now been broken by all kinds of labour, and to procure for themselves national auxiliaries. It turned out quite the contrary, because all its citizens adjudged to themselves the greater part of these uncultivated lands, and in the course of years they were declared immovable proprietors of them. They acquired often by main force the neighbouring estates, and entrusted their lands and herds to the management of slaves, the freemen having been often summoned to military service. Hence it came about that the large proprietors became very rich, that the rural districts were populated with slaves, while the freemen diminished, in consequence of their misery, the imposts, and the military service, and more than all, from the preference given to the slaves. This state of things excited the discontent of the Roman people, who saw the Italian auxiliaries diminishing and their power compromised in consequence of the great multitude of slaves. The remedy for so great evils was not easy, since it was not absolutely just to strip the citizens of their possessions which they had aggrandised, improved, and covered with buildings, seeing that they had enjoyed them for long years. The tribunes of the people had with very great trouble got a law adopted which prohibited the possession of more than 500 jugera of land, and a herd of more than one hundred in large animals, and fifty small ones. The same law had enjoined the proprietors to employ a certain number of freemen as overseers and inspectors of their estates. This law was accepted under the religious obligation of an oath, a fine having been fixed for those who contravened it. The surplus of the 500 jugera was to be sold at a low price to the poor citizens; but neither the law nor the oath was observed. Some citizens to preserve appearances transferred the lands under fraudulent contracts to their friends, but the greater number defied the law.

From the year 260 from the foundation of Rome, the consuls had begun to buy corn in Etruria and Sicily in order to sell it at a lower price to the poor citizens. In time, Sicily did not suffice, and Sardinia and Africa became the granaries of the empire. In the time of Cæsar, the legally entitled poor who received *tessara frumentaria* were 320,000! To celebrate his triumph, 22,000 tables were spread in Rome, each with three couches, on which reclined 198,000 guests from among the populace and the soldiers. The Falernian wine was distributed in jars, and the Chian wine in profusion. Augustus made frequent distributions of money after the death of Cæsar, giving at one time 600 sesterces a head, 400 after the victory of Actium, and later even 800. Cæsar had reduced the *tessarae frumentariæ* to 150,000, but under Augustus they reached the earlier number. The clients under the empire lost their moral character. This is how the Count de Champigny describes them : " It is still dark, and the poor man is busy brushing his old toga in order to hasten to the heights of the Carinae and of Coelius. As the client of everybody, he goes to knock at every gate; he crowds in the street before the threshold of every rich man, elbows and reviles his companions in servitude, feels himself threatened by the rod of the ostiarius, struggles into the courtyard, and by bribing the slaves penetrates into the atrium, sees passing before him friends of the second or third class, whispers to the nomenclator a name which that slave mangles, obtains a languid smile from the patron, a sleepy glance, a disdainful salute which looks like a yawn, and as the reward of so much trouble puts into his basket a little sausage, or the magnificent largess of twenty-four solidi." [1]

The true and real beneficence did not arise till later in the time of the Antonines, under the influence of the Stoic philosophy, which was in this respect the precursor of Christianity.

When Jesus Christ appeared on the earth, the Hebrews were no longer called Israelites, but Jews; the kingdom of Israel had become Judea, and the twelve tribes of the Promised Land were reduced to the single kingdom of Judah, which was five times conquered, and had become in the end a Roman tetrarchy. After the Babylonian captivity, the law of the Jubilee and the other Mosaic institutions which protected the poor were no longer observed. Jesus Christ found the problem of human misery intact, and He sought to resolve it by voluntary poverty and the rehabilitation of labour. Voluntary poverty was exercised by giving all, or part of one's own goods to the poor, and by making them common to all the faithful by gratuitous loans and by hospitality. The rehabili-

---

[1] *Les Césars*, t. iv. 4th ed. Paris, 1868.

tation of labour is found in these words of St. Paul: "If any would not work, neither should he eat;" and by his own example, for at certain times he preached and at others he fabricated tent-cloth in order to earn his bread. •

Alms were distributed through the diaconates, which were true institutions of beneficence. The origin of the diaconate is found in the *Acts of the Apostles* (chap. vi. 1–6): "And in those days, when the number of the disciples was multiplied, there arose a murmuring of the Grecians against the Hebrews, because their widows were neglected in the daily ministration. Then the twelve called the multitude of the disciples unto them and said, It is not reason that we should leave the word of God, and serve tables. Wherefore, brethren, look ye out among you seven men of honest report, full of the Holy Ghost and wisdom, whom we may appoint over this business. But we will give ourselves continually to prayer, and to the ministry of the word." There were at Rome seven diaconates administered under the surveillance of the bishop by seven district deacons, one for each ward, and by them a head was chosen who was called the arch-deacon. The deacons were aided in the discharge of their office by acolytes, sub-deacons, and deaconesses, the number of whom was in proportion to the requirements of the service. The distributions of alms were made at the gate of the churches or in the interior, or in a special place called the *diaconium*, or lastly, at the homes of the recipients.

During the first three centuries, charity had no other treasury than the alms of the faithful, no other ministers than the bishops and deacons, no other centres than the diaconates, and no other asylums than the houses of the poor. But when the militant church had changed the cross into a crown, when the humble bishop had become an opulent prelate, when the pompous imperial donation was substituted for the modest oblation of the faithful,

and when at last the great ones of the earth had embraced
the faith of the poor, then the faith became aristocratic,
and the riches which had been transformed into poverty
became riches again; the diaconate was dissolved, and the
individual charity of the first Christians became petrified
into the hospital.[1] This happened in 325 at the Council
of Nicea, when the Church universal assembled for the
first time in all its splendour under the presidency of the
Emperor Constantine. The construction of the churches
was changed in many of their parts, and the dwelling-
house of the bishop became the episcopal palace. And
then there arose an *infirmary*, a *leper-house*, a *hospitium*
separated from the palace, under the special direction of a
clerical head.

An asylum, opened at first for strangers, came to be
destined for the Christian poor, who were aided in it like
the strangers, and no longer succoured at home. The
Council of Nicea in its 90th Article had ordered the
building in every city of a public asylum under the name
of *Xenodochium.* Designed at first only for pilgrims and
strangers, these *Xenodochia* were opened at length to all
sufferers, and when they became insufficient for their
purpose, it became necessary to create special *hospitia ;*
and thus alongside of the Xenodochia destined for
hospitality, there arose *Nosocomia* for all who suffered from
disease, *Ptochotrophia* for the poor, *Arginoria* for incur-
ables, *Brephotrophia* for foundlings, *Orphanotrophia* for
orphans, *Gerantocomia* for the aged, *Paramonaria* for
invalid workmen, &c., &c. A law of Justinian contains
the nomenclature and the regulations of these charitable
institutions.

Justinian recognised the bond which unites beneficence
with religion ; and he placed all the dispositions of the
dying under the special surveillance of the bishops and
archbishops in order that they might see to their being
executed. The Canon Law assimilated the goods of pious

---

[1] See Moreau-Christophle, *Du problème de la misère.* Paris, 1851.

institutions with the goods of the Church, so much so that some writers even came to maintain that they belonged to the Church, thus denying a separate individuality to institutions of beneficence. Hence these institutions stood for a long time under the jurisdiction of the bishops, both on their spiritual side and in the administration of their patrimony; and when any one attempted to withdraw himself from it, the councils were solicited to confirm their subjection. This, however, did not go on permanently. The State claimed its share of supervision in the time which preceded the French Revolution. We may refer for an instance to the administration of the Tanucci at Naples. After the Concordat, however, councils of hospitals were established; bishops were called to take part in them; and they intervened specially in the settling of the budgets when they were discussed. A decree of the lieutenancy of Naples of 17th February 1861, regarding the administration of pious works, abrogated every preceding disposition which excluded the free action of the civil authority, or which prescribed the obligatory interposition or interference of the bishops. The law of 3rd August 1862 assigned to the provincial committees the guardianship of pious works under the higher supervision of the Minister of the Interior. In the most absolute manner, it respects their individuality, leaving every one of these institutions to be administered according to the rules established by their founders, or by old customs.

Things have gone quite otherwise in England. In the time of the Saxons, the island was populated by freemen, proprietors, and soldiers; and almost all these were reduced by the Norman conquest to a state of servitude or nearly so. But they rose again and succeeded in getting their prestations in labour and natural things determined; and then in getting them converted into fixed burdens which were not subject to augmentation. However, when personal services were transformed into land burdens, the

Lord of the manor began to make war on the small proprietors. Having no longer a right to their services, he
had no interest in keeping up many vassals; and thus he
found it more advantageous to have to do with a single
farmer, and to limit the number of the co-participants
in the pasturage and forests. The high price of wools in
the fifteenth century contributed to increase the pasture
lands; and the breaking up of the small properties has
continued till our day by means of the *Enclosure Acts*
successively passed from 1710 to 1843. These laws
permitted the Lord of the manor to appropriate under
various pretexts the communal property up to more than
7,000,000 acres. Whereas in the Middle Ages and in the
sixteenth century the *Copy-holders* had been despoiled
because their proprietory titles were in the custody of the
feudal archives, we see to-day the small powers disappearing, not from usurpation, but by purchase. When a small
holding is exposed for sale, it is almost always acquired
by a rich capitalist, because the expense of examining into
the titles of origin is considerable. Thus the large hold-
ings became compacted, and then they fell into mortmain
from the law of primogeniture and substitutions. In the
fifteenth century, according to Chancellor Fortescue, England was cited as an example to Europe on account of
the number of its proprietors and the property of its inhabitants. In 1688, G. King estimated the number of
proprietors at 180,000, without counting 16,560 noble
proprietors. In 1786 there were still in England 250,000
proprietors; but the most recent statistics give only
30,760. This number is not to be taken literally, but
it is certain that in England there are whole provinces
in the hands of some five or six persons. "Do you
know," said John Bright, in a speech delivered at
Birmingham on the 27th August 1866, "that the half
of the soil of England is possessed by 150 individuals, and
the half of the soil of Scotland belongs to ten or twelve
persons? Are you aware that the monopoly of property

is incessantly increasing, and that it is always becoming
more exclusive ? " [1]

Before the Norman conquest, the obligation to succour
the poor was incumbent on their relatives and on the
rich. Afterwards it devolved on the Church and the
feudal lord; and when the bonds of feudalism were
relaxed, the poor found relief only from the Church.
The State intervened from time to time only with its barbarous laws against vagabonds and mendicants ; but after
the suppression of the convents by the Protestants, the
State had to take the place of the Church, and it adopted
the maxim proclaimed by the Canon Law that the poor
had a right to nourishment and shelter. The laws of
Henry VIII., Edward VI., and Elizabeth, gave legal value
to this duty, which in itself was entirely moral. The statute
of Elizabeth of 19th December 1601, divides the poor
into the able-bodied, invalids, and children, and commands
the procuring of work for the first at home, the giving of
relief to the invalid, and the teaching of a trade to the
children : all this to be done at the expense of the respective parishes. In 1834, this statute was modified to the
extent that there were formed *Unions* among the parishes
in order to maintain workhouses in which the able-bodied
poor were to be obliged to work, and the guardians were
to be elected by the taxpayers. The tax was thus
lessened ; but on account of the power assigned to the
guardians to grant domiciliary relief, it has been tending
to rise again. The economists are unanimous in their cry
that the poor-rates should be gradually abolished;[2] but this
wish cannot be listened to so long as the land is not free

[1] See the work of Laveleye
already referred to, and Fawcett *On
the British Labourers.* London, 1878.
Also Boutmy, *Developpement de la
constitution et de la société politique
en Angleterre.* Paris, 1887.
[2] See Fawcett, *Pauperism, its
Causes and its Remedies.* The
statutes referred to applied to

England and Wales, but in 1824
taxation for the poor was also introduced into Scotland, although the
social conditions were somewhat different. It was extended to Ireland
in 1838, and notwithstanding the
reforms of 1843, it proved quite insufficient to cope with the sufferings
of that unfortunate country.

from the bonds which bind it, namely, primogeniture, entails, and substitutions of every kind.. The law of primogeniture is the rule in successions of immovable goods, but the will of the testator may change it. It is common both to the nobility and to the common citizens. Substitutions now render the title uncertain, and cause heavy expense for legal inquiries in cases of purchase. By adopting the principles of the French legislation in matters of succession, testament, and contracts, property would be made divisible, and the old yeomanry would rise again without any impediment being caused to it by the new methods of cultivation.[1] The peasant proprietor is the true remedy against the proletariate; and where the lands are arable, association may harmonise the holding of small properties with cultivation on the large scale.

Between the English system of legal charity and the continental system of free charity, the choice is not doubtful. The first is the offspring of special circumstances, and with these it will cease; the second,· as embodied in our Italian Law of the 3rd August 1862, will gradually resolve the problem of poverty. Is this indeed possible? In view of facts we may at least say that mechanical invention is promising to reduce man to the simple director of material labour by making the forces of nature work for him, and that if the progress of industry has abolished slavery, it may also abolish poverty. On the other hand, instruction will make labour more efficacious, and education will promote economy. Societies for insurance will always tend to confine within narrower limits the function of hospitals and other charitable establishments; and physical misery will cease at the same time as moral misery.

[1] The best English jurists advocate codification, as may be seen by the treatise of Professor Sheldon Amos : *An English Code, its difficulties and the mode of overcoming them.* London, 1873.

CHAPTER VII.

JUSTICE.

THUS far we have indicated the rules for the attainment of the principal ends in which the good specialises itself. In so doing, we have objectively determined the attributions of the individual and of the State, reserving the consideration of them as Subjects of Right for the Second Part of our work. But what would be the use of excogitating those rules without providing in the least for their execution, unless it were only to exclaim with the poet: " The laws are there, but who put hands to them ? "

The State provides in three ways for the realisation of Right: by preventive means, by commands, and by punishment. It provides against it by the preventive institutions of morality, and especially by the police; it commands reparation of injuries and indemnities for every obligation that has not been carried out, or for culpable negligence ; and it punishes every infraction of the social order.

The first conceptions of a rule of right were indicated in the Homeric poems by the words *themis, themistes; themis* signifying an assistant of Jupiter. When a king judged a cause, his sentence was regarded as the effect of a divine inspiration. Grote says that Jupiter himself was not a legislator but a judge.

Procedure therefore arose contemporaneously with Right, and it was thus furnished with all the apparatus necessary to impress the imagination of the people. The judge formulated in a sentence the juridical rule which sprang from customary observances, and he was often assisted in his functions by a number of persons who accompanied the one who was to be judged in the quality of witnesses or *conjuratores*. It is disputed as to whether the civil or criminal tribunals arose first. But the most recent writers have proved that delicts were at first considered as wrongs, or as violations of individual rights; and that it was only gradually that the community felt itself injured as the protectress of the social order, and that it intervened at first by single acts, and then with general laws. The principle remained intact that in civil questions the initiative belongs to the individual, but that the penal action is essentially public, although in certain cases of minor importance, action at the instance of the injured or damaged party is rendered necessary to set the case in motion.[1] The consequence is that when this party has selected the civil tribunal, it is held that he has renounced the penal process.

Both the civil and penal procedures have as their object the reintegration of Right; and therefore they require to investigate facts, to examine evidence, and to pronounce a sentence of judgment. Hence the positive institution of justice has established the profession of advocates, who assist the parties in presenting their reasons, and the judges who pronounce the sentences. And as human judgment is fallible, the decisions pronounced may thus be submitted to the re-examination of higher judges, both in regard to the facts in question, and as to the legal right at issue. There the points of resemblance between the two procedures take an end.

In the civil procedure, the subject of dispute turns on a right, or the contesting of a fact which it is believed may bring damage. Hence the *actio* (from *agere in jure*) raises the question which is developed *ciendo in judicio* whoever opposes the right (*reus in judicio conventus*);

---

[1] This applies to slight wounds, injuries, defamations, offences against the moral order of families or against property, if committed by collaterals who do not live together.

and he having put in an appearance, the action is declared upon him, and the judicial dispute begins (*contestatio litis*). The defender, denying the existence of the right in the *actor*, lays down the opposition which he maintains by the *exceptio*, a word compounded of *capio*, which expresses the ancient Quiritarian right of *mancipatio*, and of *extra*, which signifies the non-existence of the right in the *actor*. The judicial process is carried on by the contraposition of the arguments of the *actor* in reply to those of the *reus* in the form of the *replicatio;* and in that of the arguments of the *reus* to those already declared by the *actor* in the form of the *duplicatio*, and so on, until the judge puts an end to the process by his sentence, assigning the right to him to whom it belongs. Then follows either the acquiescence of the parties, or an *appellatio* or *provocatio*.

The Romans had no tribunals subordinated to each other, such as would have formed what the moderns call appellate jurisdictions, or stages of jurisdiction. The process of appeal began to be practised under the Empire; and it was brought before a magistrate of a higher grade after the commission was obtained from him for doing so within a useful time (*dimissoriae litterae*). In order that this remedy might not be abused, the law at first condemned any one who had employed it without sufficient reason to a fine of the third of the value of the subject in litigation, and to four times the cost; but this rigour was gradually mitigated.

The French National Assembly by the decree of 19th July 1790, founded the *Cour de Cassation*, as a supreme court of remedy or appeal. It does not constitute a third grade of jurisdiction, and it judges not so much the suits as the sentences, the object of its institution being to secure the execution and uniform interpretation of the law in all the jurisdictions.

In speaking of contracts, we distinguished between civil and commercial contracts. In the Middle Ages society

being divided into classes, the merchants wished also to
have their own special tribunal. And as their demand
was founded on the nature of things, this special tribunal
survived the Middle Ages. "There arose two species of
jurisdictions," says Sclopis: "that of the consuls sent by
one State to another foreign State, who had the double
office of inspectors over all the acts of the national
commerce, and of judges of the merchants their fellow-
countrymen who were located in the country where they
resided; and the other, which was also generally called a
consular jurisdiction, was exercised in the country itself
by judges appointed over all causes relating to merchandise. These privileged jurisdictions were a consequence of the corporations of arts and trades which existed
from ancient times among the Italians."[1] In France, the
edict of 1653 already contained dispositions relating to
the institution, competency, and procedure of the consular
jurisdictions. The ordinance of 1663 added to them the
power of judging causes relating to insurances, maritime
exchange, and other obligations regarding commerce by
sea, which functions were afterwards assigned to the
courts of the admiralty. The decree of the 24th August
1790, created tribunals of commerce which judged of all
controversies relating to commerce both by land and by
sea. The judges of the tribunals of commerce, as the
consular judges once were, are elective both in France
and in Italy. In France, they are elected by all the
merchants with letters patent by an absolute majority,
with the intervention of three-fourths of the inscribed
electors. In Italy, the Chambers of Commerce propose
to the king certain names in the form of a list, and their
number has to be thrice the number appointed. In
appeal, commercial causes which are supposed to be
already sufficiently expiscated, follow the course of civil
causes.

The system of proof in civil causes in Italy consists:—

[1] See *Storia della legislazione italiana*, vol. i. Torino, 1857.

1. Of written documents. 2. Of oral witnesses in suits involving value to the extent of 500 francs, or in any case in which there is any beginning made with written proof, or where it has become impossible to procure it; or lastly, where a document has been lost by some grave accident. 3. Of presumptions or the consequences which the law or the magistrate draw from a known fact to an unknown fact. 4. Of the confession of parties. 5. In the supplementary oath ordained by the magistrate, or the decisory oath offered or referred to by the parties. In commercial causes, the means of proof are enlarged, the account-books of the merchants, which have been regularly kept, being admitted to serve as evidence in causes between the merchants, as well as books of public brokers, or their simple notes. But proof by testimony may be always employed when the judicial authority believes it even against what is written (Art. 44, *Comm. Cod.*). In order to give authenticity to contracts and to judicial acts, the Romans introduced the *tabelliones* and *executores*, who were in many respects similar to our modern notaries and bailiffs.

The subject of penal justice is of a different nature, as it has for its principal object not the damage or injury, but the discovery and punishment of the one who has been guilty of a wrong act. It is divided into two periods: the first consists in the investigation of the proof (*inquisitio*), and the second in the discussion of it (*disquisitio*). In the first, the process is treated according to the inquisitorial system; in the second, the judicial procedure is developed under the form of accusation. The judicial procedure cannot have place without a preparatory inquisition; but the effect of the latter is limited, as it is not able to decide anything definitively to the prejudice of the party under process on its own basis. Hence the maxim that no one can be subjected to a penal condemnation, except in virtue of a sentence emanating after a solemn trial in accusatory form. The penal system did not reach this perfect form until after a long course of ages, and until the accusatory and inquisitorial systems were fused together. The first to appear in history was the accusatory system, which lasted down to the times of the Roman Empire. The principles which it consecrated are the following :—1. Every one is free to accuse, but there is no judgment without an accusation, so that, this failing, the State cannot proceed. 2. The judge must be freely accepted, and consequently the best judge is the popular tribunal formed by lot with the right of free challenge. 3. The judge cannot make investigation of himself, but he ought to confine himself to pronounce judgment on the proofs advanced by the parties to whom is assigned the function of investigating and preparing the matter for the trial.

In such a system, the examination of the proofs ought to be made on the triple foundation of the contradiction of the parties, whose presence in court is therefore indispensable, of the oral or immediate examination of documents and testimonies on the part of the judge who has to pronounce sentence, and of the publicity of the discussion.

The germs of the inquisitorial system are found in the last determinations of the Roman Law. They were developed in the Canon Law by the institution of the *inquisitio ex officio*, which, through the medium of the Italian practitioners and the statutory laws, passed over into the lay tribunals, and became dominant in the whole of Europe, except England, up to the end of the eighteenth century. The principles by which the inquisitorial system was regulated were the following :—1. There is no need of an accuser, because the State in name of the social interest proceeds *ex officio* to the prosecution, investigation, probation, and punishment of the crime. 2. The judge is appointed by the Sovereign of the State with permanent power, and is chosen from among the jurists, as he has to apply the law to the established facts. 3. The judge ought to make examination himself and to investigate the truth without being limited to the proofs adduced by the accuser and the accused in order that he may thus know the guiltiness or innocence of the parties, so that it is given to him to go beyond the requisitions of the contending parties in order that the truth may be discovered with regard to the accused and to the guilty ; and accordingly, the judge may declare the guiltiness of a party notwithstanding the desistance of the accuser, and in like manner he may declare the innocence of the accused notwithstanding his confession. 4. The foundation on which the judgment of condemnation is raised, is the examination of the proof, but this examination has as its basis the written instruction and what is secret, without the necessity of the form of an immediate contradiction : the discussion of the accusation and the defence sufficing along with the re-examination of the witnesses heard in the process. 5. There are three institutions which serve as a check on the arbitrariness of the permanent judge : *a*, the proof is regulated by the law, which gives a legal criterion according to which proofs are to be held sufficient or insufficient ; *b*, the double stages of jurisdiction by means of the institution of appeal ; *c*, the nullity of the acts where the substantial forms of the procedure have not been followed.

Revolutionary France of 1789 had the merit of fusing these two systems in the Laws of 1791 and in the Code of Criminal Instruction of 1808, from which have sprung most of the existing legislations. The following are the principles of the so-called Mixed Systems:—1. The proceeding *ex officio* is conjoined with the form of the necessity of the accusation, the office of public prosecutor in the penal jurisdiction being usually assigned to the public minister. 2. The power of judging is entrusted at the same time to permanent judges skilled in the law, and to sworn temporary judges or juries chosen by lot from the lists of citizens who by their intelligence and morality

give a guarantee of sufficient aptitude for judging in
matters of fact. 3. The written inquisition, being secret
and without contradiction, was adopted as a necessary
preparation for the proofs, as well as the first stage of the
penal procedure; and the contradictory, oral, and public
discussion, was recognised as necessary in the case of
sentences of condemnation. 4. The system of legal proofs
was abandoned, and the criterion of free moral judgment
substituted for it; but the liberty of conviction was
limited within the circle of the proofs taken in legal
form.

For the sake of economy, and in order not to lay too
heavy a burden on private citizens, juries are empanelled
only in the case of greater accusations (and in cases of
offences by the press), and after the sentence of accusation
has been formulated. For the slighter offences procedure is
taken without the preliminary adjudication of an accusation,
and in such cases the same judges pronounce both on fact
and on law. There is, however, a remedy in the way of
appeal, except in cases of the˚slightest offences, which are
punished by a pecuniary penalty.

In all sentences of condemnation there is the supreme
remedy of the Court of Appeal, where the law or the form
of procedure has been violated. As regards the proof,
writings play but a small part in penal cases; for the
delinquents are interested in not leaving writings to found
upon, or in destroying them. Accordingly, there is only
the testimony of circumstances in criminal cases as matters
of fact (generic proof), or of men regarding the doer of
the delict (specific proof). The confession of the accused
resolves itself into a testimony against himself, and does
not form a full proof as in civil cases.

Hitherto we have supposed both parties present at the
trial in court; but it may happen that the person cited
does not appear, and then judgment goes by default, or
on the contumacy of the said party. The effects of this
are different in civil and penal cases. In a civil case, the

defendant may render himself contumacious either by not
appointing a legal procurator within the term laid down
by the law, or by the procurator he has constituted not
presenting himself at the appointed day to conduct the
cause. Judgment will then be given, and the defendant
will always be condemned, provided the demand of
the pursuer is found according to justice. Nevertheless,
in the first case, which is called contumacy of the party,
when it appears that from unavoidable circumstances the
party had not received the citation, he is granted a longer
time to give in defences on the issues of the case. This
will be intimated to him by an officer of court, and that
he may cause the sentence to be quashed by the tribunal
for reasons which will have to be expounded. In the
second case, which is called the contumacy of the procurator, it is supposed that he had no valid reasons to
oppose to the pleas in law, and he will undoubtedly be
allowed to show opposition to the sentence, but in a shorter
term and in a determinate form.[1]

The effects of contumacy, under the penal tribunal, are
different:—1. This contumacy does not give occasion to
opposition in appealable sentences, because they may be
altered by means of appeal. 2. Opposition finds place in
sentences not capable of being appealed in order to get
the cause to be re-examined under a contradictory form, but
a second contumacy makes the opposition produced void
and renders the sentence definitive. 3. Condemnation to
a criminal penalty is a condemnation *pro forma*, and it
is only civilly effective under certain conditions, but is
unproductive of effect as regards the penalty in its
material contents, and falls with the presence of the
accused, either by spontaneous presentation, or as the
effect of his arrest. 4. Sentences of absolution are valid
even when pronounced *in contumacia* or in absence.[2]

---

[1] There is no need of a legal procurator before praetors and tribunals
of commerce.

[2] See Errico Pessina, *Sinopsi del
procedimento penale.* Napoli, 1876.

Civil sentences are executed on the patrimony of the unsuccessful litigant, and penal sentences are principally executed on the person of the condemned.[1] This is so because the former aim at the reparation of the damage or loss, and the second punish the offence. This brings us to investigate the nature of a criminal act and its penalty, and what is the origin of the right to punish. In the Prolegomena we said that the internal ends of morality are the moving forces of right, and from this arises the necessity of their conservation and development. This is not attained by simple precepts, but by menace or the application of a castigation. The moral order embraces the totality of our duties towards God, towards ourselves, and towards our neighbours. But ought every violation of duty, or every reprehensible act, to be subjected to human justice? Human justice, answers Rossi, can only intervene when the duty violated concerns the social order. Now it is evident that the violation of duties towards our neighbours (including the State, which, as a moral person, represents them), is the only one which can injure the social order in one of its essential elements, namely, the protection of the rights of society as a moral body and of its members. A crime is thus defined as the violation of a duty to the detriment of society and of individuals. This definition, adds Rossi, errs by being too extensive; for the State in order to protect the free development of man can demand only the fulfilment of the duties which are co-relative to those rights for the protection of which it can employ force, that is to say, of exigible duties. Hence legal crime is properly the violation of an exigible duty committed to the prejudice of society and of individuals, and the observance of which is advantageous or useful to the political order, which may be secured by a penal sanction, and the infraction of which may be ascertained by a court

---

[1] Personal arrest in a commercial matter was a penal sanction under civil form.

of human justice. Such a definition eliminates from the penal legislation several categories of reprehensible facts, including those which may be provided for by the natural or religious sanction; those which the State can deal with by less severe measures, or measures that are less dangerous than those belonging to the penal administration of justice; and those for which the administration of civil justice provides a sufficient reparation. Besides, this definition guards against the limitation of penal justice, which results from the imperfection of our knowledge, and while it takes morality as its basis, it finds its limit and measure in utility, meaning by utility the necessities of the social order, which is a means primarily of good, and secondarily of well-being.[1]

Penal justice operates by means of punishment, which is a pain inflicted on the delinquent in proportion to the quality and quantity of the evil done by him, that is to say, according to the importance of the duty violated, and according to the special gravity of the violation of it committed, as determined by the conditions of the concrete and particular fact. The criminal by violating a duty denies a right, and the punishment reaffirms this right both in the consciousness of the criminal and in that of human society. Accordingly, punishment is a means of making right reign, and its essential requisites are that it be directed against the will which violates right or puts it in danger, that it serve both as a punishment and as a prevention in case of the criminals, and that it seek the amendment of the guilty. It has to be in proportion to the crime, although no longer with the *similitudo supplicii*, or an eye for an eye, or a tooth for a tooth, which amounted to punishing one crime by another; but it has to be carried out by depriving the guilty one of the advantages of civil liberty or of part of his fortune. Respect is thus shown to the integrity of the human person by recalling it to its proper destina-

[1] *Traité du droit penal.* Paris, 1829.

tion. As to the quantity and measure of the punishment, it ought to be proportioned to the evil of the crime, that is to say, to the offence and injury it involves. It has not to be equalised with it, otherwise this would be falling again back into the *lex talionis;* and such proportion ought to proceed in a ratio compounded of morality and utility. Such a proportion is what has been appositely called by Vico the geometric measure proper to rectoral justice, that is, a measure conformable to the merit or demerit of the persons to whom it is shown that the punishment pertains, and not the arithmetical measure which is proper to equalising or commutative justice, which renders to every one equally his due.

In order to attain this end, the punishment ought to be moral, personal, divisible, easily capable of estimation, reparable or remissible, equitable or satisfying, exemplary, reformative, and sufficient. The relationship of the punishment to the crime is thus wholly a truth of intuition which awakens an echo in the conscience. The faculty of reflection ought therefore to lend an ear to the revelations of the conscience, to compare them with each other, while eliminating the disturbance produced by the too excited passions, and then to give consideration to the social danger in order to determine what ought to be the degree of severity. Beginning from the gravest crime, it will be easy to descend gradually to the lightest crimes. It follows that death cannot enter into the catalogue of punishments, as it is neither reparable nor reformative, and as it extinguishes instead of diminishing the human personality.

Before applying the punishment, it is incumbent to consider the degree of imputability in the doer, and the objective evil. If he acted in defence or under the impulse of an irresistible force, he is exempt from any punishment, as he has a justification for what he did. If he was infected by mental disease, frenzy, lunacy, or intoxication, his responsibility vanishes; and if he yields to provocation it diminishes ; and hence arises the theory of excuses. Our positive law is not satisfied with this general estimation of imputability, but admits an estimation quite special to the individual doer under the designation of extenuating circumstances, which have the effect of lowering the punishment by certain degrees.

With regard to the objective evil, the crime may be attempted, frustrated, or consummated, and the punishment increases in proportion unless the party desists voluntarily from the criminal act. On these considerations, there is founded the theory of tentative crime and its various degrees.

Sometimes several wills are united with the object of committing a crime. This wrong association aggravates the moral evil and often also the objective evil, the first being produced not in one, but in several wills, and the second becoming more easy, more inevitable, and often of more gravity, from the concurring of many forces directed to a guilty end. Finally, the falling again into crime is an indication of a depraved mind, and threatens greater social danger ; and hence repetition and relapse into crime are more severely punished.

Such are the principles to which criminal law has attained. The question now arises as to whence criminal right takes its origin. We have already said that at first crimes were considered as private affairs, which were treated mostly as the subject of composition. But it was not long till society felt itself injured in each of its members by such deeds, and hence arose the *judicia populi* and *quaestiones perpetuae*. Punishment was established according to the crime, and it was avoided by the accused before it was pronounced if he preferred to go away into banishment; or, in other words, to renounce the benefits of the civil association. At the beginning, therefore, society established a compensation with the view of turning aside private vengeance ; and later, it used punishment in its own defence, that is to say, with the view of preventing

crimes, obliging the criminal to expatriate himself, if he
was not willing to submit to it; and finally, it looked to
his inward amelioration. The penal doctrines were developed in consequence; and there were some who derived
the right of punishing from vengeance, such as Mario
Pagano, and others from the need of social defence, as
Beccaria. Romagnosi holds that punishment has not as
its object to take away an evil that has been already committed or to re-establish morality, or to exact a useless
vengeance, which would be a second crime, but that its
aim is to repress the criminal impulse by means of
example, and that the punishment ought to be related to
it in its quality and its measured quantity. The Bavarian
Feuerbach, exaggerating the doctrine of impulse and
counter-impulse maintained by Romagnosi, supposes that
all crimes result from deliberation or calculation; and he
proportionates the punishment not by reference to the
evil deed committed, but to future and probable deeds.
Bentham maintains without ambiguity that virtue is a
good on account of the pleasures which it procures; that
vice is an evil on account of the pains which follow from
it; and that right properly so called, is the creation of
law properly so called. As to the actions which law
abstains from ordering or prohibiting, it confers the positive right to do them or not to do them, thus entitling us
to remain standing or seated, to eat or to fast, &c.; nevertheless we have the exercise of these rights from the law
which raises to a crime any interference which would
hinder us from doing them as we please. In order to
find the real origin of the right of punishing it is necessary to go a considerable way back.

Plato was the first to recognise the expiatory element
of punishment. " If justice," he says in as many words,
" is the good and the health of the soul, as injustice is its
disease and shame, chastisement is their remedy. Chastisement is not a greater evil, which is added to injustice,
and heaps up its measure; it is a good, painful it is true,

but salutary, which repairs the evil deed. If the man is happy when he lives in order, then when he is out of it, it is of importance for him to enter it again, and he enters it through chastisement. Every culpa demands an expiation: the culpa is ugly, because it is contrary to justice and order; the expiation is beautiful, because all that is just is beautiful, and to suffer for justice is also beautiful."[1]

From the dogma of redemption the Canon Law derived the conception of penitentia which Thomas Aquinas and Dante expounded in the Middle Ages, and which Selden, Leibniz, Vico, Kant, and Mamiani[2] followed in modern times. Grotius and Pellegrino Rossi adopted the principle, but subordinated it to the social necessities. Hegel and Stahl found a happier formula, that of juridical retribution, which has been adopted by various penalists, among whom may be mentioned the distinguished Pessina. The right of punishing is thus derived from justice, which descends from honestas and regulates utility.

"At the same time," says Mignet, "that this revolution was accomplished in the theories and practice of criminal justice, another revolution was being prepared which was destined to serve as its complement. Men of an elevated mind and of a merciful soul had been touched by the miserable state of degradation into which the criminal fell after having been condemned. They had conceived the generous thought of remedying it by reforming the state of the prisons. Viscount Vilain XIV. in the Low Countries (1775), the virtuous Howard in England (1785), and the Quakers in Pennsylvania, devoted themselves to this pious mission. The condemned, classed according to their age and their crimes, had been subjected to the discipline of silence, of labour, and sometimes of isolation. A beginning had been made to render the prison a place of penitence and education, and alongside of the fear of

---

[1] From the *Gorgias*, the *Republic*, and the *Laws*.

[2] Mamiani e Mancini, *Fonda-* *menti della filosofia del diritto e segnatamente del diritto di punire.* Livorno, 1875.

chastisement, which had been till then the only end of the law, there was now found repentance for the evil deed and the means of no longer falling into it again. This beautiful idea, after much time and many attempts, was thus changing into a vast system under the name of penitentiary reform. It tended to make crimes be treated as infirmities, and the culpable ones as diseased subjects whose fury might be subdued in solitude, if they had been impelled to the evil deed by the violence of their passions; and it aimed at correcting their vicious habits by the aid of labour, if they had come to them through idleness; and to enlighten their minds by means of instruction, if ignorance had led them astray. By this last improvement, the law from being vindictive had become just, and from being just it became charitable; and it completed the art of punishing by the art of healing." [1]

The penal system thus became a penitentiary system, of which Livingston in America was one of the principal legislators. He sought an intermediate way between the regime followed in the prison of Auburn, which isolated the prisoners during the night and made them labour together but in silence during the day, and the regime adopted in the prison of Philadelphia, which isolated the condemned day and night, obliging them to labour in their cells. Livingston proposed special prisons for those under trial, other prisons as houses of correction for the condemned who have not yet attained the age of eighteen years, penitentiary prisons for the condemned who were older, and lastly houses of refuge and labour for those who have been liberated. There would thus be places of custody before being judged, penal hospices where cure would be reached, and houses of convalescence to be used for passing from the regime of the moral disease (in the prison) to the regime of cure (in society). For those who have relapsed into crime, he proposes in every case perpetual imprisonment.

[1] Mignet, *Notice sur Livingstone.* Paris, 1872.

Experience having demonstrated that prolonged isolation is injurious to the body and mind of the condemned, other modifications have been sought in the Crofton regime, which has been also called the progressive system. Professor Prins describes it in the following terms: "The Crofton regime, as practised in England, includes successive stages. The first stage is the cell regime, and it lasts nine months. At the end of this time, the second period commences. The cell regime continues during the night and during meals, but work is done in common. This stage is characterised by the system of marks. Good conduct, zeal in work, and activity in the school are valued at so many good points, which by degrees may bring the prisoner on to the third stage, or to the intermediate house, of which the type is Smithfield and Lusk in Ireland. The prisoners there sleep in cells, but in the day they go by detachments of fifty men to work in the open air, and particularly under the supervision of overseers, they apply themselves to the work of clearing lands. At the end of this period they receive their ticket-of-leave as a ticket of conditional liberation. The pivot of the system is the appreciation of the conduct of the condemned by the number of marks obtained. In proportion as he receives more points, his situation is ameliorated. It is therefore a regime of encouragement which stimulates the initiative action of the condemned, and puts their future into their own hands, by allowing them to abridge their punishment by labour and good conduct."[1]

The small results obtained by the penitentiary system have attracted the attention of certain other criminalists, and this has given origin to a new school. Emile de Girardin, Odilon Barrot, and Alfred Fouillée in France, Cesare Lombroso, Enrico Ferri, Raffaele Garofalo, and Alessandro Lioy in Italy, have taken account rather of the delinquent than the crime. By means of anthropology, they believe that they have found physiological characters

[1] *Criminalité et répression*, p. 152. Bruxelles, 1886.

corresponding to the criminal inclinations. Invoking the
Darwinian doctrines of heredity and evolution, they have
defined the criminal as a *contemporary savage*. "The in-
corrigibility of the criminal," writes Alessandro Lioy, "is
one of the postulates of the new school. When the crime
is no longer the absolute effect of the will, but the result
of an abnormal organism, what wonder is there if sometimes the crime turns out to be incorrigible just as certain
diseases are incurable?"[1]

After having destroyed the criterion of imputability,
there remains to the new school only that of liability to
fear, the responsibility increasing with the power of hurting. Punishment is reduced to the elimination of the
culprit by death, imprisonment, or deportation. Garofalo
exclaims: "Examine the precedents of the criminal, his
hereditary and acquired sentiments together with the
damage done by him, and you will know to what degree
you will be able to eliminate it." It is true that the
new school divides delinquents into two classes: habitual
criminals and occasional criminals. It shows itself in-
flexible towards the former, whom it calls "born criminals,"
and it goes so far as to declare in the words of Garofalo
that nothing hinders the treatment of the insane as instinctive delinquents. It shows itself more mild towards
occasional delinquents, whom it still believes susceptible
of adaptation to the social environment. These ideas were
not foreign to the voting of the French law of 27th May
1885, on habitual criminals, and the law of 14th August
of the same year, on the means of preventing the repetition of crime.

Justice has great efficacy in promoting the attainment
of human ends. It is both an end and a means at the
same time: it is an end in so far as it pursues the equal
partition of the good; and it is a means in so far as it
secures it by force. Those authors who define right as
the totality of the conditions necessary for complete human

[1] *La nuova scuola penale,* p. 26, 2nd ed. Torino, 1886.

development, regard it only as a means. Right, as we observed above, is also a moral power which man has to attain the good, not only as good, but as useful. Special institutions ought to guarantee the material order, while retributive justice completes distributive justice.

Before passing on to the second part of our work, we pause a moment to co-ordinate the human ends which we have now severally reviewed.

History exhibits religion beside the cradle of humanity : then we see science and art separating themselves in order to form their separate domains. Industry and commerce have followed their example, and in the course of time morality and justice have also constituted themselves separately.

Religion was preponderant in almost all the States of the ancient East. The Old Testament (in 1 Samuel viii.) shows us how the civil government was substituted for the theocracy. In vain did Samuel insist on the inconveniences of the monarchy. "Nevertheless the people refused to obey the voice of Samuel; and they said, Nay ; but we will have a king over us."

In China, science prevails. A sort of Academy of Moral Sciences definitively regulates the relationships of man with the infinite. A strong central power, with its mandarins, and its occasionally admirable police, gets rid of all that could inflame the minds of the people or stir up too lively discussions. A religion of a simple construction crowns the administrative edifice, which has as its basis an elementary instruction widely diffused, and as its support the class of the literati perpetuated from among the academic graduates who compete for the public offices. Industry and commerce flourished among the Phenicians, but they were often subject or tributary to the Egyptians, Persians, or Greeks. Carthage, the great Phenician republic, carried on war with the aid of mercenaries.

The beautiful arts shone forth in Greece with the

liveliest splendour; they were almost a national institution. Nevertheless, Greece owed her independence only to the rivalry of the peoples who surrounded her. No sooner had Rome absorbed them than Greece became the prey of the conqueror.

Rome is considered as the fatherland of morality and of right. So we have the juridical maxim: " Honeste vivere, neminem laedere, suum cuique tribuere." The Roman legislation has been adopted by all peoples, and it has deserved the epithet of " written reason."

By the cradle of modern Europe, we find the Church converting the barbarians in order to initiate them into civil life. In the universal disorder, the Church acquired great power; but when, at the end of the eleventh century, she tried to subject society to the clergy, the clergy to the papacy, and Europe to a vast theocracy, her attempts proved vain. The modern world is composed of heterogeneous elements which need to be harmonised by each one being accorded its own legitimate sphere of action. We have endeavoured to determine that sphere of action in this first part of our work.

And now that we know the goal, we are able to seek out the way to attain it; and this will form the subject of the second part of this work.

SUMMARY OF THE FIRST VOLUME.

Metaphysical Speculation.

The principal difficulty which philosophy encounters lies in its point of departure and its method. Hardly had man fixed his look on the external world and upon himself than sensation and ideas captivated his attention. A moment of discomfort produced scepticism, and the need of faith led to mysticism. We find in the history of philosophy the names of other systems than Sensualism, Idealism, Scepticism, and Mysticism, such as Materialism, which is a simple modification of Sensualism, and Pantheism, which admits the unity of substance, but which it is easy to reduce to Idealism if the sole substance is conceived as Idea, or to Materialism if it is conceived as matter. The same may be said of the Positivism now in vogue, which is only a masked materialism 9–10

A considerable part of the East did not advance beyond symbolism and a species of theology. Philosophy began in China and India. China believed from the outset in spirits which symbolised the various forms of nature, and then in the heaven (*Tien*), the origin of all things. In the sixth century B.C., Confucius extracted a sort of practical philosophy from the ancient sacred books called *King*. Mencius, his disciple, formulated a sort of mystical pantheism which savours of the influence of the Indian philosophy. Lao-tseu, a rival of Confucius, sets out from a void unity, the *Tao*, from which all beings have their origin, and it seems to have numerous relations with the Pythagorean and Platonic Ideas as they were understood in the School of Alexandria. In India philosophy began with the simple interpretation of the Vedas. Pantheistic idealism predominated, but it was not unaccompanied with Sensualism, Scepticism, and Mysticism . . . 9–12

In Greece, thought rose to a great height. Sensualism was represented in the Ionic School, and Idealism in the Pythagorean and Italic School. The dialectic of the School of Elea ceases to be a logical instrument, and becomes in Plato the very law of the movement of Ideas. Aristotle explains the formation of ideas by means of two faculties, sense and intellect. After Plato and Aristotle, philosophy declined, and Epicureanism and Stoicism, which succeeded, have one point in common, namely, that they reduce philosophy to Ethics. Reason, now weary, turns to the East, and seeks repose in the mysticism of the School of Alexandria 12–18

A new light illuminated the human mind with Christianity. What was vague in the Platonic doctrine was rendered precise by St. Augustine. The result was not so successful in dealing with Aristotle. A passage of the translation by Boethius of the *Isagoge* or Introduction of Porphyry, which raises the question whether genera and species exist in themselves or only in the intelligence, and whether they exist separate from sensible objects, or make a part of these objects, served as a text for the Scholastic philosophy 18–20

Scholasticism may be defined as the alliance of the Christian dogma with the philosophy of Aristotle. It has three distinct epochs: the first from the eleventh to the thirteenth century, in which philosophy is the *ancilla theologiae;* the second from the thirteenth to the fifteenth century, in which the two sciences are most closely allied; and the third from the fifteenth to the first years of the sixteenth century, when their complete separation began. What Augustine had done for Plato, Thomas Aquinas did for Aristotle. Anselm approached Plato in his demonstration *à priori* of the existence of God by rising in the *Monologium* from imperfect goods to the sovereign good. Occam opens the conflict between religion and philosophy; Gerson and Thomas à Kempis land in a pure mysticism . 20–26

The Renaissance, under the guise of the ancient systems, put forward the boldest ideas. Telesio and Campanella attacked Aristotle. Bruno transmitted to Descartes methodic doubt and evidence as the criterion of truth; to Spinoza he gave the idea of an immanent God; to Leibniz the germ of the theory of monads and of optimism; to Schelling the famous expressions *natura naturans* and *natura naturata;* and to Hegel the conception that a secret logic presides over the order of the universe 26–30

Modern philosophy begins with Bacon and Descartes. With

Bacon are connected Hobbes, Gassendi, and Locke; the
first applies the experimental method to politics, the second
to erudition, and the third to metaphysics. From Descartes
descend Malebranche, Spinoza, and Leibniz. Vico was the
true renovator of philosophy. The human mind sees all
ideas in God, who generates *ad intra* and creates *ad extra*.
This is a new step taken by the Platonic doctrine by means
of the principle of creation, which unites the divine to
the human 31–39
The movement, initiated by Bacon and Descartes, was carried
out in the eighteenth century by the materialism of Holbach
and Lamettrie in France, and by the scepticism of Hume
in England. The Scottish School sought in vain to overcome them by the doctrine of common sense. Kant saw
acutely that on the one hand the contingent concrete cannot be thought without the generic, and that on the other
hand the subjectivity of the judgment cannot be harmonised
with the objectivity of the idea. But instead of conjoining
the generic and concrete absolute with the perception and
objectivising the judgment, he subjectivised the idea,
denied perception the power of grasping the contingent
concrete, and reduced all cognition to the generic element
alone, which, when the concrete is subtracted, could have
no other than a subjective value. Fichte held that since
we know only what is produced by our thought, only the
Ego exists, and it ought to be conceived as absolute, and in
virtue of its unlimited energy it begins to determine itself
and posits the non-Ego 39–44
The nineteenth century enters on the work of restoration.
Schelling thinks that the Ego can produce the sphere of the
practical life, but that it does not generate physical nature.
Hegel added the dialectic to the system of Schelling. The
universe is the product of the evolution of the absolute Idea.
The detractors of Hegel (once his adorers) now maintain that
he only substituted the word Idea for the word God, and the
becoming for the creation, and they regard his system as a
last echo of theology. The absolute idealism has been succeeded in Germany by a species of physiological materialism
in Moleschott and Büchner, and by a most desolating
pessimism in Schopenhauer and Hartmann . . 44–51

Italy reacted against the French sensualism and the German pantheism. Pasquale Galuppi illustrated the direct relation of sensible perception which necessarily supposes the reality of the object, and hence sensible perception is the intuition of the object, by which view he took a step beyond Reid. Antonio Rosmini distinguishes two kinds of perception, the sensitive and the intellective; and he calls body the co-subject of the mind. The idea of being, although a mere logical and universal possibility, yet contains all the ideas with the indeterminable series of the genera and species and their perfect types, and it appears in the conjunction which arises in the intellective perception between sensation and intelligible truth. Vincenzo Gioberti has shown that rational cognition cannot depend on the intuition of a possible being, but on the relation of intelligence to an infinite reality, an inseparable condition of all thought and of all existence. The theory of cognition is embraced by Gioberti in the ideal formula: *Being creates the existent,* which reflection decomposes and language expresses. In the ideal formula, we see the infinite, the intelligible finite, and not the sensible or phenomenal finite, which in the posthumous works of Gioberti is presented to us as the implicit intelligible which by degrees is explicated. Being is perceived by us only in existence by successive thought, but it is contemplated in itself as creating by immanent thought. In the double state of thought is found the double state of nature, and it is not wonderful for spirit and nature to constitute the existent, which, in so far as it is created by Being, should resemble it. Now Being is one and infinite, and the existent ought likewise to be one, but its unity being finite, it ought to include multiplicity. To Gioberti dialectic is an art, and not the absolute method, nor the perfect science. Mamiani takes a position intermediate between Rosmini and Gioberti, but he maintains it vaguely 51–61 Laromiguière and Royer Collard in France, combated sensualism and the materialism of the past century. Maine de Biran studied the voluntary and free activity of the Ego. Cousin endeavoured to wed the pantheistic idealism of Germany with the Scottish philosophy by means of a temperate

eclecticism. Auguste Comte, admitting with Kant that
we cannot know things in themselves, confines himself to
investigate the laws of phenomena, that is to say, their
relations of succession and likeness, *their positive and real
state.* According to Comte, philosophy registers and co-
ordinates the results of the six fundamental sciences:
mathematics, astronomy, physics, chemistry, biology, and
sociology, which follow and complete each other in turns,
and give us the systematic conception of the world 61–63
John Stuart Mill, Alexander Bain, and Herbert Spencer, have
introduced and developed positivism in England. Herbert
Spencer is not satisfied with the external study of facts ;
he wishes to penetrate into their cause, and he finds that
the infinite variety of phenomena depends on the metamorphosis of force, and that all movements obey the laws
of evolution, that is, equivalence, rhythm, and cohesion,
which are corollaries of the same ·principle, of the persistence of force. Matter and motion are manifestations of
force variously conditioned. In order to explain nature,
recourse is had to other hypotheses. Charles Darwin
fertilised the ideas of Lamark, who said that vital force
was excited by want and strengthened by exercise. Plants
and animals are derived from some ten primordial species
by means of the perfecting transmission and the vital
struggle. Acquired qualities are perpetuated by heredity
and by adaptation to the various conditions in which
plants and animals are called to live .   .   . 63–69
In Germany, the system of Darwin was received with open arms,
and Haeckel began forthwith to show that all organic
beings are derived from one primordial form, that is, from
the cell or the ovular vesicle formed by spontaneous
generation at the first cooling of the earth. But the
French chemist Pasteur has advanced a decisive argument
against spontaneous generation by showing that the air
contains millions of corpuscles organised like germs which
diminish as we rise in the atmosphere, and which being
eliminated, we no longer obtain the production of infusoria   69–71
Summing up this review of metaphysical speculation,. we see
that speculation reached the highest point in Greece ; that

Christianity perfected Plato and Aristotle; and that the Renaissance expounded a false Aristotle and a false Plato, interpreting the first in a materialistic sense, and making the second a pantheist. Leibniz wished to act as a reconciler, extracting from all the systems a *quaedam perennis philosophia.* He applies the principle of contradiction to investigate the possible, and that of sufficient reason to lead us to the real. Vico says more openly that the true is the fact, and that therefore God is the first truth because He is the first Maker. God makes, that is, creates *ad extra* and generates *ad intra.* Gioberti has perfected philosophy, distinguishing carefully intuition from reflection, and immanent thought from successive thought, by which he puts the objectivity of the ideas out of all doubt. He has given the best explanation of the connection between the subject and the object; and between things and ideas by his theory of the creative act foreshadowed by Vico . . 71–76

Psychology is the substratum of metaphysics. Plato considers the soul as an active force, and distinguishes in it the rational part and the animal part from the θυμός. Aristotle defines the soul as the first entelechy of a natural organised body which potentially contains life. The ancient philosophy had, however, left a lacuna, that of the free-will. Christianity put forward charity, the love of one's neighbour, and consequently duty, but right was left in the shade. The first systems of the modern period, those of Descartes and Leibniz, did not assign to the will the place due to it. The former did not distinguish exactly the faculties of the mind, and he confounded the will with the intellect. The latter, denying all reciprocal action among the monads, had recourse to the hypothesis of a pre-established harmony. Vico recognised the fact that *knowing is necessary, but willing is free.* Kant gave great prominence to the will, and reconstructed in his *Critique of the Practial Reason* what he had overthrown in his *Critique of the Pure Reason.* Maine de Biran, studying facts, put the action of the will out of doubt, and in the present day a whole school of Leibnizians in France is combating the attacks of the positivists . . 77–88

ETHICS.

Ethics came forth full armed from the head of Plato, who summed up Pythagoras, the ancient sages, and specially his master Socrates. He distinguishes the absolute good, which he identifies with God, and which we ought to seek to imitate. The good in everything is order, and the soul in order to be happy ought to be well ordered. The soul effectuates the good by means of virtue, while evil is committed through ignorance. Aristotle attributes greater value to the human individuality. In metaphysics, he had distinguished potentiality and actuality : in ethics, he explains that actuality is identical with the end, and designates as desire the aspiration nourished by every being to pass from potentiality to actuality. The end of a being can only be the good, and the perfect being will be one in which there will not be potentiality, but everything will be actuality. Man loves action, and is the complement of activity, as beauty is that of youth. Zeno combats pleasure as unstable and deceitful, and places happiness in the fulfilment of duty or in the observance of the laws of nature 89–91

Christianity considers morality as a resurrection. The soul has lost its purity by original sin, and the sacrifice of a God was necessary in order to redeem it. The fundamental precept of Christian morality is this : love God above all things, and thy neighbour as thyself. True perfection consists in the contemplative life, in prayer, and in ecstasy. Plato established a sort of natural society between man and God. Christianity proclaimed man's absolute dependence. Human liberty is not annihilated, but is sustained by divine grace, which is granted to whoever does not reject it 91–92

The Renaissance attacked the Christian morality, and Bacon denied the superiority of the contemplative life when it does not tend to perfect the active life. He desiderates the study and description of the passions and affections, and this is carried out by Descartes in a treatise which analyses them from the physiological and psychological

THE PHILOSOPHY OF RIGHT.

Christianity weakened the sentiment of right, giving as a religion the preference to morality, and exhorting men to love their persecutors. Scholasticism resuscitated the distinction of Aristotle, and Dante defined right as follows: *jus est realis et personalis ad hominem proportio, servata hominum servat societatem, corrupta corrumpit.* Grotius wished to emancipate jurisprudence from theology, and sought the principle of right in sociability, which is taken not as a material fact common to men and animals, but as a mark of reason. Pufendorf declared that by natural right ought to be understood what is ordained by right reason. Thomasius made a step in advance by distinguishing for the first time right from morals. Leibniz proceeded to confound everything. Wolf stops with a vague idea of perfection. Kant takes up the distinction between morality and right, and makes the last a condition for the explication of human liberty. There is involved in it the power of coercion, seeing that the faculty of removing the obstacles to our liberty forms an integrant part of our liberty. Fichte commented on Kant, and wrote noble pages on liberty. Schelling turned to the objective point of view, showing how the divine action which is fatal and unconscious in nature, becomes free and conscious in the spiritual world, where it is manifested as will. In the view of Hegel, right is liberty realised, the universe attaining consciousness in man. Krause keeps himself free of the formulae of Hegel, and approaches Schelling. Ahrens applied the system of Krause to right. Like his master, he believes individuality to be an eternal divine determination without a proper existence of its own. In the first editions of his *Cours de Droit Naturel* Ahrens separated right in a way from morals, but in the last editions he combined them together without confounding them. Trendelenburg, in his treatise on *Natural Right on the Basis of Ethics,* marks the return to Platonism corrected by Christianity 113-121

France exercised a certain influence on the ethics of Germany. Rousseau had proclaimed the freewill to be the essence of man. This principle is the transition to the doctrine of Kant, of which it is the foundation, as is shown by Hegel . 124

PART FIRST.

OBJECTS OF RIGHT.

CHAPTER I.—RELIGION.

Chapter II.—Science.

Science separated itself slowly from religion. The severance began in the East, and was completed in Greece. The Greeks sought the laws of nature no longer in theogonies but in observation. But while it was permitted to interpret tradition allegorically, a direct attack upon religion was not tolerated, as was shown by the danger run by Anaxagoras, and the death encountered by Socrates. The government left education to private enterprise, and it is only in the time of the Roman empire that we find subsidised schools 199–203

Christianity was a kind of reaction against knowledge. But after having spoken to the heart, it felt the need of entering into alliance with the Greek philosophy and appropriating those useful inventions which render the exercise of virtue less severe. On the irruption of the barbarians, the clergy saved what they could of the ancient sciences and letters, copying manuscripts and teaching the seven liberal arts, namely, grammar, rhetoric, and dialectic (*trivium*) ; and arithmetic, geometry, astronomy, and music (*quadrivium*). 203

Material necessities drove the Arabs to study the scientific works of the Greeks; but medicine, physics, and astronomy were so bound up with philosophy, which at first embraced them all, that the study of it was rendered indispensable. The Arabic science and philosophy were but a poor translation of the Greek science and philosophy. To the Arabs we owe the mariner's compass and the system of numeration, which they are said to have borrowed from the Chinese and the Hindus 203–204

The Universities contributed very greatly to the resurrection of knowledge. The school of Salerno shone brightly in the eleventh century, but its origin is lost in the night of time. In 1196, the celebrated Irnerius was called from Ravenna, where he was a judge, to Bologna, to teach the Roman Law. In the course of the twelfth century, there was added to the curriculum the canon law, medicine, theology, and philosophy. Fourteen colleges gathered the students of different nations, some founded by the popes, and others by foreign princes or magnanimous donors. At their side arose colleges and corporations to examine the students and to confer upon them the degree of doctor in theology in name of the pope, and that of doctor in jurisprudence in name of the emperor, by the authority of whom these doctorates were instituted. Literary studies were afterwards added. This served as a type to the other universities of Italy and Europe. England still preserves it in the twenty colleges united around the University of Oxford, and in the seventeen colleges of the University of Cambridge 204–205

The exact and natural sciences do not owe their progress to the universities, which were wholly absorbed in jurisprudence and theology. Roger Bacon was driven from Oxford because he laid little account on scholasticism and on ratiocination in general, for its conclusions were regarded by him as only hypotheses when not confirmed by experience. The Renaissance completed the revolution begun by Roger Bacon. Galileo taught that the laws of nature are the simplest of all. By mathematical calculation and experience, Galileo discovered the law of gravity and that of the pendulum, the hydrostatic balance, and the telescope, with which he saw the satellites of Jupiter, the phases of Venus and Mars, the spots on the sun, and the mountains of the moon. Francis Bacon of Verulam reduced to axioms the method followed by Galileo, and himself made discoveries. Descartes with his analytical geometry, and Fermat with the first elements of the infinitesimal calculus, which was perfected by Leibniz, paved the way for Newton, who gave a sketch of the sidereal movements, and it required the common efforts of great mathematicians and great astronomers for the sketch to become a picture. Astronomy brought along with it the development of physics, which was begun by Galileo and carried on by Volta, Oersted, Ampère, and Melloni. The eighteenth century was not to remain behind the seventeenth century; it created chemistry by the work of Lavoisier; and it made physiology more perfect through Bichat, who gave a new direction to medicine, with a more exact knowledge of the organism. The work of Bichat was hardly sketched when

Chapter III.—Art.

The beautiful appears when the Idea presents itself to us commingled with external reality, from which it is separated by the mind without being carried up to its abstract generality. When the Idea surpasses the form, we have the sublime; when it is in a certain equilibrium with it we have the beautiful. In the arts, the sublime appears first, because it is nearer the Idea. Art begins as interpreter of the religious ideas, expressing by symbols the relations of the invisible principle with the objects of nature. In oriental art there is displayed fervid imagination, a vague and confused thought. In the East, architecture is the art *par excellence;* and sculpture is still but a vast hieroglyph which represents the attributes of the divinity. With the Greeks, sculpture and painting ceased to be simple accessories of architecture, and they introduced a new element, the art of grouping personages, which we call composition. The Greeks further created style and taste; that is to say, they perfected the expression of created things without taking account of the hieratic types, and they acquired that practical familiarity with the good and beautiful which leads to a reasoned choice. The Romans, occupied with politics and administration, sought utility in the beautiful arts. In architecture, they preferred the arch to the entablature or architrave; they constructed magnificent bridges, aqueducts, and cloacas, and invented buildings of a special kind like the baths and amphitheatres . . 227–231

In the Greco-Roman art, the lines are straight and sometimes monotonous in their simplicity; they do not rise to any considerable height from the soil, but constitute an architecture that is horizontal and characterised by length. On the other hand, in Persia the ancient Assyrian architecture made progress; its lines showed a predilection for curves, and they darted up towards the heavens, forming a species of architecture that was perpendicular, and characterised by height. Certain distinguished authors have maintained that the Byzantine art was derived from the Persian. The architecture which is improperly called Gothic was produced by the style, called Romanesque, as Arabic architecture was produced by the Byzantine style. The two styles were akin. The ogive style had remained a long time in the East in a sporadic state, and the great builders of the twelfth century did not go there to obtain it .

In sculpture, Greece remained unsurpassed, having reproduced the human form in greater perfection. The Greeks had made use of painting in order to give greater relief to the architectural forms, but it was not long till they used it to imitate nature and to reproduce also human facts. Christianity occasioned a decline of both sculpture and painting. But by degrees, the traditions of ancient art revived ; and the Italians excelled the Greeks in painting. The Flemish and Dutch School showed great mastery in the reproduction of accessories, and of some of the common objects of life. The other nations were guided by the examples of Italy and the Low Countries .

The arts of speech followed the same development. The East began epical and lyrical poetry ; and Greece perfected them, adding the drama and the various kinds of prose : narrative, descriptive, oratorical, and didactic. The Romans showed themselves at first opposed to the arts, but when they conquered Greece, they were morally taken captive. Christianity radically changed the conception of life, sanctifying suffering, poverty, and ugliness, and enlarging the basis of society. But Christianity and ancient art were wedded by the Renaissance, and produced marvellous masterpieces. After the French Revolution, the social basis was again enlarged. Comfort, a thing unknown to antiquity, made our habits prosaic ; scepticism rendered inspiration more difficult ; and the governments by founding museums, schools of the fine arts, and periodical exhibitions, proceeded to aid the arts of design, while the arts of speech were furthered by the industry of the printer. Music, which had served in antiquity as a simple accompaniment of poetry, rose to be an independent art in the seventeenth century with the invention of the lyrical drama, which was due to the Italians. Most of the continental governments now subsidise the lyrical theatres . . . .

CHAPTER IV.—INDUSTRY.

The daily support of man is produced by labour, the spontaneous fruits of the earth being scarce on the whole. Labour supposes property as ownership (1) of the personal faculties, and (2) of the matter to which they are applied. Property, like society, is natural to man as a being endowed with liberty. Property includes the right to labour, to form capital, to exchange, to make donations, and to transmit to others 246–249

In the beginning all men have implicitly the right to use external things for the rational ends of life; but as such things are not directly presented in sufficiency for all, society has established rules according to which the individual can acquire, preserve, or lose the immediate power over them. The State, which represents society, has always a supreme dominion over property. It claims a part of it in the form of taxes, and it establishes the organic connection between the generations, determining the modes of transmission and succession . . 249–251

So long as primitive man lived by the chase, fishing, and wild fruits, he did not think of appropriating the land, and he considered as his own only those objects which were captured or fashioned by his hand. Under the pastoral regime, the notion of property in land began to crop up; but it was limited to the space which the herds of each tribe were wont to traverse. When the populations became settled, the lands were occupied in common, and divided among the different associated families; their produce only was distributed according to households. The agrarian community and the city constituted by the union of families, were bound] together by intimate relationships. In its development, property followed the status of the persons 251–253

Both collective and individual ownership of property have had scientific defenders. Plato was for the first, Aristotle for the second. Christianity mitigated the rigour of individual ownership by recommending alms . . . 254–262

In modern times, Sir Thomas More and Campanella have reproduced the ideas of Plato slightly modified. Morelly, Rousseau, and other writers of the eighteenth century, also declared themselves averse to individual ownership. In the nineteenth century, Proudhon revived the thesis of Rousseau, along with socialists and communists. Grotius was able to rise above what was taught by the Roman jurisconsults with regard to property. Locke was the first to derive property from labour, which doctrine was adopted by the economists. Some authors, like Montesquieu and Bentham, have made the right of ownership in property depend on the law 263–271

From the point of view of quantity, ownership is exclusive or joint (*condominium*), according as one physical or moral person possesses the rights of property over the whole thing or over an ideal part of it, such as a fifth or sixth of the whole. From the point of view of quality, ownership may be full and entire, or incomplete and divided. Ownership may suffer dismemberments by necessary or conventional servitudes, and it may have increments by means of accession, immovable, or movable, and industrial. Special 'rules of law are established for ownership in property, whether industrial, artistic, or literary, or in mines and forests 272–273

What are the relations between industry, science, and art? If in the past, religion assigned a very subordinate position to industry, it nevertheless admitted it within the social organisation in India and Egypt. The *collegia opificum* of the Romans were sorts of confraternities like those of the Middle Ages, when industry put itself under the patronage of a saint. Science has been often occupied with the interests of industry, which would return to its rudimentary state without the aid of mechanics, physics, and chemistry. To industry, art lends taste, that indescribable charm which makes the commonest objects of life so dear. The modern States are striving to open up outlets for industry, and to aid its progress by means of more technical and professional instruction . . 274

CHAPTER V.—COMMERCE.

The word "commerce" has two different significations: in the wide sense, it indicates every human relation; in the strict sense, it indicates the exchange of products and services. The Romans seem to have used it in the first signification, comprising in the *jus commercii et connubii*, which were gradually conceded to the plebeians, almost the whole of civil right. In the primitive times, only the heads of families could be bound by obligations, but they took place very rarely, and with such formalities that the least inobservance of them issued in the nullity of the obligation. The most ancient form of contracting among the Romans was the *nexum*, which the scholars defined: *omne quod geritur per aes et libram.* At first the *nexum* served to give solemnity to the alienation of goods, and then it was applied to other contracts which were considered as incomplete sales. The nexum gave origin to four forms of Contracts: verbal, written, real, and consensual. To these four classes of contracts only was given an obligatory form; and in the first three, certain indispensable formalities had to be observed, the consent of the contracting parties sufficing only for some of them. Besides contracts, there were Pacts which did not produce a civil action. But many of these gradually obtained this from the praetor or by the imperial constitutions, or because they were immediately joined to *bonâ fide* contracts 274-278

Domat and Pothier freed this part of the Roman Law from the rubbish of the past, and introduced into it what was necessary of consuetudinary right. The compilers of the French Code only reduced their treatises to articles. According to the French Code, contracts are obligatory by the sole consent of the parties without there being necessary any delivery of the thing, or the fulfilment of the fact on the part of the contractors or of any extrinsic formalities. Kant, in his *Metaphysical Principles of Right*, classifies contracts according as they have for their object a unilateral acquisition, a bilateral acquisition, or only a guarantee. This classification is practically retained by Hegel, Ahrens, and Gans, but Gans observes that it does not include the contract of society. Trendelenburg tried a simpler classification. Relatively to their content, he says, contracts have principally in view either a donation or a simple exchange, or an agreement of several wills in reference to a common affair. In contrast to these, there is a species of contract which aims at resolving the claims which have already arisen in business (the transaction). In the matter of contracts, positive law hardly leaves anything to be gleaned by the philosophy of right 278–281

In the strict sense, the word commerce indicates the relations arising from the exchange of present or future values, which constitutes commercial law properly so called. Such exchange forms the special occupation of certain persons who buy in order to sell. The positive laws, following the dictates of reason, have modified by a reference to such persons the rules of certain contracts, such as sale, location, mandate, pledge, society, and they have admitted certain specialities, as the letter of exchange, borrowing and lending in maritime exchange, and maritime insurance. The contract of society or partnership suffers greater modifications, such as collective partnerships, anonymous society, co-operative associations, &c. 281–286

All the other branches of human activity promote commerce. From the most remote times religion aided it. Science discovered new ways, new regions, and new products. Steam navigation, railways, and the electric telegraph have turned the whole earth into a single market-place. Art did not promote commerce, but was promoted by it ; industry was, so to speak, the mother of art, giving value to raw materials, and creating others by means of chemical combinations. The State in ancient times did not lay great account on commerce. In modern times, it has sought to protect it by imposing custom tariffs, but now it generally limits itself to removing the obstacles which could not be overcome by private enterprise . 286–289

Chapter VI.—Morality.

The State cannot leave to the pleasure of the individual the fulfilment of the whole moral law. History shows us public power arising out of the family. At Sparta, private life hardly existed, all the hours of the citizens being regulated. At Athens, liberty was entire, but the Areopagus jealously scrutinised the conduct of every candidate for public offices. In the year 444 B.C., two magistrates were appointed at Rome to whom the material and moral supervision or censorship of the republic was entrusted. Towards the end of the Roman Empire, and during the whole of the Middle Ages, the Church claimed the censorship of manners, and the ecclesiastical prescriptions also obtained civil effect. After the French Revolution the State became secular, and hence the greater importance of the police as the inheritor of the ancient censorship and of the ecclesiastical supervision 290–291

Public Beneficence is the corrective of individual ownership in property. Not that the State is under obligation to relieve the poor, but it ought to intervene in great national misfortunes, such as inundations and the destruction of whole cities by fire, and it ought to give a good direction to the founding of works of piety. Thiers, in a report presented to the French Assembly of 24th January 1850, enumerates the institutions of beneficence that ought to be promoted 291–293

Antiquity was not entirely lacking in benevolent institutions. The institutions of the patronate and hospitality, the *leges agrariae*, the *leges annonariae*, the *largitiones, epulae, sportula*, and the *tessera frumentaria*, were directed towards relieving the people from distress. Nor were there wanting societies for mutual help both at Athens and Rome. Some of the dispositions of the Digest enjoined on the cities the duty of consecrating the surplus of the revenues for the relief of children and of the aged indigent . 293–298

Christianity enlarged the sphere of beneficence. Jesus Christ inculcated voluntary poverty and labour, and St. Paul gave an example of it. Among the first Christians alms were distributed by the Diaconates, which were real offices of beneficence. During the first three centuries, charity had no other treasury than the alms of the faithful, and no other ministers than the bishops and deacons. When the pompous imperial dotation was substituted for the modest oblations of the faithful, the construction of the churches was changed in many of their parts; the dwelling of the bishop became the episcopal palace, and the poor had a separate building called an infirmary, a leper asylum, or hospice, with a priest specially appointed to it. Justinian recognised the bond which unites beneficence with religion, and put all the bequests of the dying under the special supervision of the bishops and archbishops. The Canon Law assimilated the property of charitable institutions to that of the Church. In the time which preceded the French Revolution, the State claimed its right of interference. The Italian law regarding works of beneficence of 3rd August 1862, while respecting their individuality in the most absolute manner, assigned the guardianship of them to Provincial Committees under the higher supervision of the Minister of the Interior . . 298–301

Where property is badly divided, and the transmission of it is fettered, beneficence assumes the form of legal charity. England is an example of this. Before the Norman Conquest, the obligation to succour the poor was incumbent on parents and on the rich; afterwards it fell upon the Church and the feudal lord, and when the bonds of property became loosened, the poor found no longer any relief except from the Church. After the suppression of the convents, the State had to substitute itself for the Church, and it adopted the maxim of the Canon Law, that the poor had a right to support and shelter. The Statute of Elizabeth of 19th December 1601 divided the poor into classes, and prescribed that work should be furnished to the able-bodied at home, that relief should be given to invalids, and that a trade should be taught to the children, all at the expense of their respective parishes. In 1834, this Statute was reformed, to the effect that Unions were formed among the parishes, and workhouses were kept up where the able-bodied poor were constrained to

If the progress of industry has abolished slavery, will it suffice
to abolish want? It is necessary to distinguish poverty
from want. Poverty is one of the consequences of the
natural inequality of men, and cannot disappear. Misery
is excess of poverty, and it may be avoided when instruction will make labour efficacious, and education will promote thrift. Provident institutions and insurance will
then restrict more and more the function of hospitals and
other benevolent establishments, and physical and moral

CHAPTER VII.—JUSTICE.

The general significance of the term Right is the direction of
an action towards a determinate end; and hence Vico
places the regulative principle in the infinite reason of
God as substantially identical with the truth and the order
of things. This does not clash with the view that Right
has to serve as the means for the attainment of the other
ends above enumerated. Right is an end when it pursues
the equal distribution of the good; it is a means when it
secures it by force. The State provides in three ways for
the realisation of right: by preventing, commanding, and
punishing. It prevents by its institutions of morality,
and especially by the police; it commands restitution for
injuries and compensation for every obligation which has
not been maintained or which has been occasioned by
culpable negligence; and it punishes all infraction of the
Procedure was born contemporaneously with Right and Justice,
to which it lent all the apparatus necessary to impress the
imagination of the peoples. It is disputed whether civil
or penal tribunals first arose; the most recent writers
have proved that crimes were first considered as wrongs
or as violations of individual rights, and that the community then gradually felt itself injured as the guardian
of the social order, and intervened, first by single acts,
and then with general laws. Both the civil and penal

tribunals have as their end the reintegration of right, and
therefore they require to investigate facts, to weigh evidence, and to pronounce sentence. And as human judgment is fallible, the decisions ought to be subjected to the
re-examination of higher judges, both on the side of facts
and that of right. These points exhaust the resemblances
between them 305–306
The origin of a civil process arises from the contestation of a
right, or the resistance of a fact which it is believed may
bring damage. The pursuer or plaintiff begins by setting
forth the question, and calling into court whoever opposes
the right, by which the action is put before the judicial
authority. The defender, denying the existence of the
right in the pursuer, lays down his objection, which he
maintains by an exception. The process continues by the
contraposition of the arguments of the pursuer and the
defender, until the judge puts an end to the suit by his
sentence, assigning the right to whom it belongs. This
is followed either by the acquiescence of the parties, or
an appeal. The appeal came into use under the Roman
empire ; it was carried before a higher magistrate after
his permission had been obtained in a useful time. The
national French Assembly, as a supreme remedy, founded
the Court of Appeal (*Cour de Cassation*), which does not
constitute a third grade of jurisdiction, and judges the
sentences rather than the parties, the end of its institution
being to secure the execution and uniform interpretation
of the law 306–307
The importance which industry and commerce acquired in the
republics of the Middle Ages gave origin to the consular
competency with its procedure and jurisdiction, as that of
consuls sent abroad and exercised over their countrymen
residing there, and also to that other jurisdiction exercised
at home by tribunals appointed for all suits relating to
merchandise. As this distinction was consonant to the
nature of things, it survived the Middle Ages. The
judges of the tribunal of commerce both in Italy and
France are elective, as the consular judges once were.
Before the tribunals of commerce, procedure is more
rapid ; but commercial causes in appeal, being supposed

to be already duly expiscated, follow the course of the
civil tribunals 307–309
In the penal tribunals the subject matter is different, as the
principal object in view is not the damage sustained,
but the discovery and punishment of the culprit. The
process is divided into two parts, the first consisting in
the investigation of the proof, and the second in the discussion of it. In the first, the process is treated according
to the inquisitorial system ; in the second, the judgment
is developed under the form of an accusation. It was
the merit of the French Revolution to fuse the two systems
in the laws of 1781, and in the Code of Criminal Instruction of 1808, from which most of the existing legislations
have taken form. In the most ancient times, the judge
was assisted in his functions by a number of persons,
who attended the process of judgment in the quality of
witnesses or *conjuratores*. These *conjuratores* gradually
became the judges of fact under the name of jurymen,
the function of expounding the question of law and
applying the punishment being left to the magistrate.
In the case of lighter offences, the same judges pronounce
both in matters of fact and law. In such cases, there is
the remedy of an appeal, except in the lightest offences,
which are punished by a pecuniary penalty. In all sentences of condemnation, there is the supreme remedy of
appeal on the special ground of violation of law or procedure 309–313
Civil sentences are executed on the patrimony, and penal
sentences principally on the person; the former look at
the making up of the damage, and the latter also at the
punishment of the offence. A crime is the violation of
an exigible duty to the damage of society and of individuals, the duty being one of which the observance is
useful to the political order, and the infraction of which
can be certified by human justice. Punishment is a pain
inflicted on the delinquent in proportion to the quality
and quantity of the evil, *i.e.*, according to the importance
of the duty violated, and the special gravity of the violation committed, which is determined by the conditions of
the concrete and particular fact. A crime in violating a

duty negates a right, which the punishment reaffirms both in the consciousness of the culprit and in that of human society. As to the quantity and measure of the punishment, it ought to be proportioned to the evil of the crime, that is, to the offence and damage in a ratio compounded of its moral and utilitarian elements. Accordingly punishment ought to be moral, personal, divisible, easily valuable, reparable, and remissible, equal and satisfying, exemplary, reformative and sufficient. Before applying the punishment, it is incumbent to look at the imputability of the agent in order to estimate his responsibility, and to the objective evil, or to the fact as to whether the crime was attempted, frustrated, or consummated. Penal right is the sanction of every kind of right; it springs from justice, which arises from the *honestum*, and regulates utility 314–321

On the other hand, there is a new penal school which does not look at the evil in itself, but merely at the delinquent, with regard to whom it is necessary to take measures of precaution, eliminating him from society by death or deportation on account of grave crimes, and putting him into a condition where it becomes impossible to do harm, by imprisonment or criminal discipline, on account of light crimes. Accordingly this school substitutes for the criterion of imputability that of liability to fear . . 321–323

.

www.ingramcontent.com/pod-product-compliance
Lightning Source LLC
Chambersburg PA
CBHW030858270326
41929CB00008B/469